Sword and Pen

Other books by Manfred Weidhorn:

Dreams in Seventeenth-Century English Literature

Richard Lovelace

Sword and Pen

*A Survey of the Writings of
Sir Winston Churchill*

Manfred Weidhorn

UNIVERSITY OF NEW MEXICO PRESS

Albuquerque

Grateful acknowledgment is made to Charles Scribner's Sons for permission to quote from Sir Winston Churchill's *The World Crisis,* 6 volumes (1923–31) and *Marlborough. His Life and Times,* 4 volumes (1933–38); to Houghton Mifflin Company for permission to quote from Sir Winston Churchill's *The Second World War,* 6 volumes (1948–53). Quotations in Chapter 6 reprinted by permission of Dodd, Mead and Company, Inc. from *A History of the English-Speaking Peoples,* Volumes 1–4, by Sir Winston Churchill. Copyright © 1956–58 by The Right Honourable Winston Leonard Spencer Churchill.

Photos copyright Radio Times Hulton Picture Library

TO PHYLLIS

Acknowledgments

My dear friend, Professor Stanley Friedman of Queens College, City University of New York, read the entire manuscript of this book and made numerous stylistic suggestions, many of which I have adopted. His thoroughness went far beyond the call of friendship, and I am deeply grateful to him for his erudition and conscientiousness.

Yeshiva University granted me a sabbatical leave of absence during the fall semester of 1970. This enabled me to undertake important research in England and to make great strides towards the completion of my project. I am grateful to the board of trustees and the president, Dr. Samuel Belkin, of Yeshiva University, and to the dean of Yeshiva College, Dr. Isaac Bacon.

Contents

Hase de alargar la mano primero a las hazañas y después a las plumas; de la hoja a las hojas, que hay gracia de escritores, y es eterna.
(You should first reach out for great achievements and, afterwards, for the pen; turn from the sword to the word, because writers grant favors, and they are undying.)

—Baltasar Gracián, 1647

My pen is mightier than any sword.

—Winston S. Churchill, 1898

Introduction

In 1898, the publication of an unobtrusive little volume about a minor military episode in a remote corner of the British Empire, in which the author, a young lieutenant, had participated, marked the casual public beginning of a uniquely long career encompassing book writing, war making, and politics. Within two years—as he later observed of himself—Winston Churchill could "boast to have written as many books as Moses"; "I have not stopped writing them since," he went on, "except when interrupted by war." At career's end, indeed, after sixty-two years of composition, he had produced thirty-three titles in fifty-one volumes, in addition to more than five hundred articles and hundreds of uncollected speeches and state papers. The total of over eight million words makes him one of the most voluminous of all writers.

The thirty-three works consist of eighteen collections of speeches (a number perhaps unequalled by any other political figure), one of newspaper articles on foreign policy, four of war dispatches transformed into histories, two of essays and character portraits, one novel, one travel book, two biographies, one autobiography, two world war memoirs, and one history of a people. Preeminent in scope among these are six massive works: three devoted to earlier historical periods—one political biography, one military biography, one national history—and three sets of war memoirs, two of them written from the vantage point of high public offices during global conflicts.

Churchill certainly knew the creative delights of composition, the artist's compulsion to communicate. The man who could speak of "achieving a memorandum," remarks Reed Whittemore, was among those who think by writing. A master of the written word, Churchill believed it a matter of self-discipline to commit his views to paper; a born orator and writer who soon turned even the dispatches he sent as a young officer-journalist into art, he poured everything into the only means of expression—English prose —which, because of a limited education, he at first possessed. At a very early age he became one of the greatest (and highest paid in the world) of a new breed of war correspondents. He advanced quickly in politics because of his way with words and soon found fame as a military historian and political biographer. He was probably the last major politician to write all his speeches and books himself, and pride in craftsmanship as much as desire for renown and money caused him to take the unusual step of publishing his speeches in book form before his thirtieth year. In his middle years such men as Shaw and Lloyd George thought that he would be remembered rather as one who set his stamp on the English language than as a statesman; in his climactic years his eloquence rallied the free world in the face of mortal perils; and in his old age his *Second World War* and *History of the English-Speaking Peoples* were outsold only by the Bible. His responsiveness to the sheer resonance of words shaped a dual career devoted to turning words into action and then action back into words. He was hardly joking in old age when, in reply to a question about the qualifications necessary for an aspiring young politician, he cited a knack for foretelling events—and the "ability afterwards to explain why it didn't happen."[1]

As he moved from the army to Parliament, the young Churchill even showed signs of turning to literature as an end in itself. His well-received first volume generated a flood of requests from editors for articles and more books, and he toyed with the idea of writing short stories, biographies (of Marlborough, Randolph Churchill, or Garibaldi), or a history of the American Civil War. Confident that he could do many literary things well, he declared —unwittingly echoing Keats—"I may live to write something that will take its place in permanent literature." But politics supervened, and, eventually torn among journalism, historiography, and politics, he embraced all three and made them one in a life of action and self-expression.[2]

Though Carlyle believed that a man cannot both act his romance and write it, though a Shaw character complained of having "trouble enough living without writing it all down afterward," and though he himself said, "a man's life must be nailed to a cross either of Thought or Action," Churchill managed to combine the two commitments. It has often been remarked that he first made history and then reflected on it in a deliberate cycle.

He also did the reverse: to write *Marlborough* and then lead Britain at war in emulation, not imitation, of his ancestor, were manifestations of a single creative impulse. He wrote history in order to mold it and sometimes seemed to make it in order to write it; several wags have remarked that wars were waged so that he could write about them or that he became prime minister mainly for the purpose of perpetrating more memoirs.[3]

The only prime minister to have been an experienced memoirist and historian before his years of greatness, Churchill ranks with the very few men—Thucydides, Caesar, Clarendon[4]—who have been ambidextrous in this way, who have achieved political and literary prominence, combined dynamism of word and deed, enacted the roles of both Pericles and Plutarch. No major statesman in the world so richly documented his own career in peace and war for so long a period with such wit and style, made such a contribution to history *and* literature, and built his own huge monument in words as stirring and unique as the actions they describe. Certainly, in the British tradition of modern politicians dabbling in letters—Disraeli, Gladstone, and Morley—Churchill is preeminent, is even the only one to make, according to R. R. James, "a genuine, original and valuable contribution to the literature of his country." Aneurin Bevan considers him the greatest artist ever to enter politics, while H. S. Commager gives Churchill the perhaps ambiguous praise of being in Britain "that statesman who became the greatest historian and that historian who became the greatest statesman."[5]

The alternation of political activity and quiescence in his life enabled Churchill periodically to devote himself primarily to his writing. The writing was thus dependent on adverse fortune in politics. His political setbacks and resultant "unemployment" gave us, in 1915–17 and the early 1920s, *The World Crisis;* in the 1930s, *Marlborough* and a draft of the *History;* in the late 1940s, *The Second World War;* in the late 1950s, the revision of the *History.* (As he said after World War II, "You know I write books nowadays" and would continue to do so if "my life and the life of the [Labor] Government are suitably prolonged.") His return to prominence, notably in the 1920s and the late 1930s, was perhaps due as much to his writing as to his political activity. During each of three major periods of composition, moreover, he turned from writing personal memoirs of recent events to detached history—from the frontier war books to *Randolph Churchill;* from *The World Crisis* to *Marlborough* and the *History;* from *The Second World War* to the revision and conclusion of the *History.* Consisting of three types of works, his six major books are, in order, a chronicle of a war, a biography, a war memoir, a biography, a history, a war memoir.

Yet, though the statesman and the writer lived symbiotically —rich stores of knowledge gained in either field nurturing the other—the writing proved ancillary to the politics. The aged Churchill would not resign the peacetime prime ministry merely to finish the *History;* he considered the book an anticlimactic standby in case he became unemployed in Whitehall, as *The Second World War* had been in the wake of the "effectively disguised blessing" of his 1945 defeat. He did not regard himself as primarily a great stylist or historian, and his literary achievements were but vital adjuncts to his first love, politics.[6] Though he attributed his advancement under Asquith to the stylistic proficiency of his own memos, he was aware that his two vocations of politics and writing could interfere with each other; he thought Curzon had been undone by his "characteristic weakness" of thinking too much about stating his case and "too little about getting things done." Churchill wrote only when he could not do.

*   *   *   *

Churchill's unique career and the distinctive quality of his books were made possible by a series of heroic feats resulting from a combination of genius, industry, and unusual luck. Fusing authorship and action was one Churchillian feat; another, equally rare, was to mesh, both in politics and writing, his military and political interests. Yet a third was Churchill's careful tailoring of his career, with the help of his precociousness and intensity, as if it were a work of art. He was, moreover, able to impress his greatness on everyone, himself above all. A last talent—and one of the strengths of his writings—was his instinctive, mysterious ability to turn up in the right place at the right time.

Early observers were impressed by his display of proficiency in five positions—as officer, journalist, author, lecturer, politician. Indeed, during his long and complex career, he proceeded to move through no fewer than seven phases, each of which was crowded and important enough to have absorbed a lifetime's energies for a less talented man: jingo officer and war correspondent in the 1890s; radical parliamentarian and biographer in the 1900s; civilian chief successively of each military department, before, during, and after a world war in the 1910s; Conservative finance minister and memoirist in the 1920s; man of letters, historian, reactionary, and prophet in the 1930s; coalition supreme wartime leader in the 1940s; peacetime leader of the opposition, progressive Conservative prime minister, and memoirist in the late 1940s and the 1950s.

At one time or another, he headed every major government department, except the Foreign Office (which he often influenced from without), and he was in government under Liberal, Conservative, or coalition auspices. At the beginning of each world war, he was close to the prime minister. In a political life spanning three generations, he grappled (with varying success) with every major political, social, economic, and military problem in twentieth-century Britain. The prominent political and military men of all nations whom Churchill met and knew constitute a roster of the great from the 1890s to the verge of the 1960s; nearly a century of politics was in his blood and was affected by his presence. There is hardly an important event of that period with which Churchill did not have personal contact in one capacity or another and about which he did not write. He lived for crisis—to prophesy it, to participate in it, and then to chronicle it. "I certainly must be," he mused in 1932, "very tough or very lucky, or both."[7]

Reading Churchill is therefore like having privileged access to twentieth-century history. For his books reflect or record in detail almost every period of his long, exciting life, except the unsuccessful 1920s at the exchequer. *A Roving Commission* not only summarizes the material covered by his four early volumes on the frontier wars but fills the gaps and thus provides a continuous narrative of the first three decades of his life. *The World Crisis* picks up the story a few years later, and *The Second World War* begins where *The World Crisis* ends, in 1922; the result is a gigantic tale, a perhaps unprecedented personalized commentary on world events. It covers sixty years in eighteen volumes written by an adventurer-chronicler who was often at the center of things, with special concentration on the Thirty Years War against Germany, which Churchill was the only man to live through in high offices and to write about comprehensively and eloquently. (The war years are central, while the years of domestic reform, treasury work, or opposition to postwar socialism are shadowy in his memoirs, but even his opinions in the 1901–11 and 1945–58 periods can be found in the collections of speeches of the time; only the 1920s remained prudently buried, in exchequer archives, in Hansard, and in private papers.) The *History,* in turn, places this continuity within the larger continuity of British history; these works add up to a vast epic tale of Britain and a vision of a dying world.[8]

No one else, declares Commager, covered so many varied lands, so many and such different wars, from so many vantage points —from cavalryman to lord of the admiralty to supreme commander—and no one understood so well the roles of tactics, global strategy, politics, public opinion, and diplomacy. At the same time, paradoxically, few historical writers have been so limited in range. Before he became the great war leader, Churchill's eminence had been partly established by a trio of major works—*Randolph Churchill, The World Crisis,* and *Marlborough*—which were actually vast apologies for the men who mattered most to him, the three Churchills. In fact, every book—except for the fictional *Savrola* and, in part, the *History*—is explicitly about a Churchill and even in a sense autobiographical. The early ones present history through the eyes of a young lieutenant; the later ones, through a world statesman's eyes; and the heroes of the two biographies of his middle period, Marlborough and Randolph Churchill, are alter egos. The author is present, whether as soldier, statesman, or commentator, in all the works. As Commager notes, "never was there more personal history" or a man so fascinated with himself. Even the *History* endows the English-speaking peoples with Churchillian qualities. Well might Churchill come to see British history as a family affair, and he probably would not have written at all had it not been for this personal dimension of his books. Hence Balfour's witticism about one of them—that Churchill had written an autobiography and called it *The World Crisis*—should be applied to virtually all of them, as should Whittemore's apt description of *The Second World War* as impersonal autobiography and personal history. If Whittemore wondered whether any literary man's work can with greater difficulty be divorced from his life, Churchill himself, in writing of Alfonso XIII, raised the question which confronts his readers: "Are we dealing with the annals of a nation or with the biography of an individual?"[9]

The answer often eludes us because, in the course of such a long career, writing became many things to Churchill. At first it was a shortcut for an officer on the road to fame, then a vocation and livelihood and therefore a means of egress from the army. Later, writing helped his political career by staving off melancholy and keeping Churchill's name in the public eye even when he was not active in politics. It also allowed him to justify or whitewash his (or his alter ego's) actions in office and his frequently unconventional opinions and prophecies out of office. It was a form of philosophizing, of counseling his colleagues and would-be statesmen, and of criticizing military experts; a delineation, by means of immersion in a tradition which was a living reality to him, of his rather antique vision of politics, history, and Britain; a celebration of the impact of the individual on history and a depiction of the pattern (struggle, rise, triumph, reign, fall) he discerned in the lives of prominent men; a portrayal of the characteristics of his age (even if, as in the *Marlborough,* indirectly, through contrasts). By means of his writing Churchill expressed his pride in nation, family, and self; relived his exciting experiences; advertised his adventures. Writing was also a hobby, like painting, bricklaying, and public speaking. Books were a series of impassioned missives addressed to posterity, to that mysterious entity Churchill worshiped under the commonplace name of "History," missives in which he deliberately shaped himself as a historical personage, as the man he imagined or wanted himself to be. Finally, writing satisfied his need to express himself; it was an outlet for his vast creative energies, a form of action or an elemental pleasure as exciting as—supreme compliment from him!—planning a battle.

Because he kept his eye trained on his audience, as well as on history and his own place in it, what began as "*I* was there" in the early books on the frontier wars became in the world war memoirs "I did so-and-so for the best of reasons." While someone like Lloyd George could be casual about his own role in the drama of history, Churchill, fascinated by the interplay of the self and events, needed to reenact the past continually. Writing history was ultimately, Plumb concludes, more than just a hobby or money earner but "the heart of his faith," "mainspring of his politics," and "secret of his mastery."[10]

Especially challenging among the functions of the writing is that of recapturing the past. Churchill is said to have remarked during World War II that day-by-day diaries can only make one look foolish and indecisive, that he would prefer to write his impressions *after* the war so that he could "correct or bury" his mistakes.[11] This comment seems to contradict one of his basic methods, as described in the prefaces of all his major works, namely that of providing the original documents as much as possible in lieu of an omniscient narrative, in order to present the authentic feelings of the time rather than the wisdom of hindsight. Yet Churchill did not keep any day-to-day diaries, and it seems moreover clear that, his written prefatory protestations notwithstanding, he could not let the original documents stand by themselves but needed a narrator to direct and design. Instead of authentic, objective reproduction of the past, he really produced interpretation, apologia, and, inevitably, distortion.

That his "autobiographical" writings are somewhat fictionalized is indicated by the fact that his letters to his mother reveal as early as 1895–97 his Liberal proclivities and his tendency to regard army experiences as but a means to a political career. *A Roving Commission* (1930) portrays a zealous soldier who only belatedly, with the success of his books, turned elsewhere and a politician who found the Liberal within himself later (1903–4). Certainly little in the first books, with their celebration of soldierly values, sneers at Liberal politicians, detailed study of military matters, and silence on domestic politics, would contradict the myth introduced by the later autobiography. All his works are in fact imaginative projections, not mirror images, are limited as well as strengthened by their author's *engagé*, politicized personality. For, perhaps because of his other career as politician, Churchill was a compulsive and compelling writer who, consumed by thoughts of what might have been, distorted history to suit the imperious needs of his voracious ego, private myths, and romantic dreams. He journeyed thus through a half-century of global turmoil, from crisis to crisis, bringing to each his military-diplomatic-political virtuosity, his activism, and always leaving in his wake a book recording his own tale, his prophecies, and his commentary on the "facts" observed from a high vantage point.

*   *   *   *

Although much of Churchill's written work is autobiographical, the goal of this survey is not biography but psychography—a tracing of the workings of his mind, of the interaction of his ideas with each other and with experience. The world of his books, the geography of his mind, can be considered as something adjacent to the world of his deeds and reflective of it, but ultimately with an equilibrium of its own. This man who often seemed erratic in politics, as many have remarked, is rational and balanced in print, and my subject is not Churchill's actions but what, recollecting them in tranquillity, he thought—or wanted people to think— he did or tried to do; not primarily the truth of any assertion of his but its relationship to others he makes in the given work and throughout his career. Undertaking a sympathetic, albeit critical, interpretation, I seek to define his philosophy of politics and diplomacy, military strategy and tactics, war and peace, appeasement and compromise; his vision of history, notably of modern Europe; his sense of Britain's role on the world scene; his reconciliation of the ideas of empire and progress, tradition and technological change; his judgments on parliamentary democracy and the new totalitarianisms spawned by the modern social, political, and economic crises; his conservatism confronting the challenge of radical movements and the more moderate proponents of the welfare state; his evaluation of many important historical personages. What were his views of his own career, on the roles of chance, talent, impulse, reason, fortitude, obduracy, flexibility in his successes and failures? What was his sense of providence or personal destiny; what of his ideal of heroism; his moral values? How did he celebrate the men who influenced him; how did he acknowledge, or explain away, his own debacles? What were the sources of his acute prophecies and of his periodic tiresome posturing as would-be prophet?

Does this vast corpus of writings have a shape—are the individual books related to each other or do they reflect only the needs and interests of the moment? Are there any unifying threads running through so many years of self-expression, and, if so, are these ideas developed from work to work or merely repeated? Whether or not they conflict with the facts or with other men's opinions, do Churchill's ideas have a consistency of their own?

Concerning myself with ideas rather than the minutiae of literary art, with things intellectual rather than aesthetic, I concentrate, in short, on that area where, as Otis Pease, Leo Braudy, David Levin, and Russell Nye have reminded us, history and literature overlap in their common effort to shed light on the human experience by means of language and the creative imagination. I begin with the impression commonly gleaned from an initial reading of his books, that Churchill is always an interesting writer, and I will attempt to ascertain whether—irrespective of Nobel Prize for literature on the one hand and neglect by literary critics on the other—he is also a great writer and an original thinker.

A Chronology of the Activities and Writings of Sir Winston Churchill

THE FIRST PHASE: THE 1890s
Subaltern-Journalist at Imperial Frontier Wars

ACTIVITIES

1895	Commissioned in the army; at age 21 visits the Spanish army fighting insurgents in Cuba
1896-97	Serves as a lieutenant in India and sees action on the Northwest Frontier
1898	Joins Kitchener's army in the Sudan War
1899	Resigns from the army; defeated as Conservative candidate for Oldham
	Correspondent (and later officer) in South Africa; captured by and escapes from the Boers
1900	Returned as MP (Conservative) for Oldham; lectures in Britain and North America

WRITINGS

1895	Dispatches from Cuba
1897-99	Dispatches from India, the Sudan, South Africa
1898	*The Story of the Malakand Field Force*
1899	*The River War* (2 volumes)
1900	*London to Ladysmith via Pretoria*
1900	*Ian Hamilton's March*
1900	*Savrola*

THE SECOND PHASE: THE 1900s
Filiopietistic Biographer and Parliamentary Radical

ACTIVITIES

1901	Enters Parliament and begins criticizing his own party
1904	Changes to Liberal Party (over the free trade issue)
1906-8	Undersecretary for the colonies; role in South African conciliation
1908-10	President of the Board of Trade; supports Lloyd George "radical" program, establishes Labor Exchange
1910-11	Home secretary (Tonypandy and Sidney Street incidents)

WRITINGS

(A) 1906   *Lord Randolph Churchill* (2 volumes)
(B) Early Speeches and Travel
   1903   *Mr. Brodrick's Army*
   1906   *For Free Trade*
   1908   *My African Journey*
   1909   *Liberalism and the Social Problem*
   1910   *The People's Rights*

THE THIRD PHASE: THE 1910s and 1920s
Minister in War and Peace; Memoirist

ACTIVITIES

1911	Appointed first lord of the admiralty; modernizes the navy during a 4-year tenure
1914	Important role in July mobilization and in Antwerp defense
1915	Gallipoli debacle; resigns and eventually becomes battalion commander on the French front (until 1916)
1917-18	Minister of munitions in Lloyd George's ministry
1919-20	Minister of war and air; organizes demobilization and, reluctantly, withdrawal from Soviet Russia
1921-22	Colonial secretary; important role in Irish and Middle East settlements and in Graeco-Turkish crisis
1922-24	Out of government and Parliament
1924-29	Return to Parliament, government, and Conservative Party as chancellor of the exchequer

WRITINGS

1923-31   *The World Crisis* (6 volumes)

THE FOURTH PHASE: THE 1930s
Belletrist, Reactionary, and Prophet in the Wilderness

ACTIVITIES

1929-39	Churchill out of government
1931	Resigns from Baldwin's "shadow cabinet"
1930-35	Assails dominion status for India
1936	Stands alone in abdication crisis
1933-39	Warns of German rearming and ambitions

WRITINGS

(A) Belles Lettres
   1930   *A Roving Commission: My Early Life*
   1932   *Thoughts and Adventures (Amid These Storms)*
   1937   *Great Contemporaries*
   1929-39 Newspaper and magazine articles
(B) 1933-38 *Marlborough* (4 volumes)

(C) Foreign Policy Speeches and Articles
   1931 *India*
   1938 *While England Slept (Arms and the Covenant)*
   1939 *Step by Step*

THE FIFTH PHASE: THE 1940s
Wartime Supreme Commander

ACTIVITIES

   1939 In September becomes again first lord of the admiralty
   1940 On May 10 becomes prime minister, forms a national coalition government with himself as minister of defense, and later becomes leader of the Conservative Party
   1942 Turns back two attempts to censure him
   1945 Victorious in war but defeated in general election, he becomes leader of the opposition

WRITINGS

   (A) Speeches
      1941 *Blood, Sweat, and Tears (Into Battle)*
      1942 *The Unrelenting Struggle*
      1943 *The End of the Beginning*
      1944 *Onwards to Victory*
      1945 *The Dawn of Liberation*
      1946 *Victory*
      1946 *Secret Session Speeches*
   (B) 1948-53 *The Second World War* (6 volumes)

THE SIXTH PHASE: THE LATE 1940s and the 1950s
Leader of the Opposition, Moderate Conservative Prime Minister, Chronicler Summing Up

ACTIVITIES

   1946 Important speeches at Fulton, Missouri, and at Zurich
   1951 Becomes prime minister again
   1953 Knighted; awarded Nobel Prize for Literature
   1955 Resigns prime ministership
   1964 Retires from Parliament
   1965 Dies on January 25, age 90

WRITINGS

   (A) Speeches
      1949 *The Sinews of Peace*
      1950 *Europe Unite*
      1952 *In the Balance*
      1954 *Stemming the Tide*
      1961 *The Unwritten Alliance*
   (B) 1956-58 *A History of the English-Speaking Peoples* (4 volumes)

1

The First Phase:
The 1890s

Subaltern-Journalist
at Imperial Frontier Wars

What other subaltern of twenty-two would have gone through so many phases?—G. W. Steevens, 1898

The hero of five wars, the author of six books, and the future Prime Minister of Britain—Churchill's American lecture manager, 1900

Enter the Chronicler, Persona, and Critic

During his first burst of creativity Winston Churchill produced five books in six volumes within less than three years. G. B. Shaw aptly said that Churchill's "real" career was not as a politician but as "a soldier and an author"; the two latter vocations in fact began concurrently. In 1895, fresh out of the Royal Military College at Sandhurst, he journeyed as far as Cuba to observe the only war of the day. His plan was to round out his training with direct experience of warfare and, simultaneously, to report to the world on what he saw. Two weeks after his twenty-first birthday, the first installment of his initial professional writing assignment, "The Insurrection in Cuba: Letters from the Front," was published, thanks to family connections. The opening dispatch, in the *Daily Graphic* of 13 December 1895, started with a semireflective, characteristically self-conscious sentence: "Most people have probably noticed that the initial difficulties of any undertaking are in many cases the most insuperable." He therefore plunged at once into the middle of his subject and, unwittingly, into a sixty-year writing career.

Two years later, while he was on his first military assignment abroad, as a subaltern in India, he began his only extended work of fiction.[1] *Savrola,* a slight work about a Liberal revolution, did not appear until 1899, in serial form, and its "not unfriendly reception" prompted him, as in the case of all the early works (except the Cuban dispatches), to publish it in book form. The next work he began, which would be his first published book, the nonfiction *Malakand Field Force,* was about military operations rather than love or politics. It grew out of his initiatory experiences as a participant in war making, when he served as a correspondent with British forces operating against border tribesmen in India. The favorable reception of his dispatches encouraged him to transform them—in a mere five weeks—into a "more substantial work."

In a sense, Churchill the author was born, like Athena, fully mature. We find already in his early works many of the ideas and structural devices, as well as the sophistication of style, humor, and imagery, that were to mark his writing through the decades. His conversion of the dispatches, for instance, into a consecutive narrative incorporating those original passages which seemed "appropriate," like the appendix of official dispatches, was to become in most of his works a systematic compilation in text and appendix of original documents for the sake of authenticity. Nor is Churchill merely a journalist-historian. He is also an adventurer who enters the story nearly halfway through, and his entry changes the work from impersonal history to personal recollections. Or, as he later put it, having "watched the drama from the auditorium," the reader is invited to "step on the stage and take an actor's interest in the final scenes."[2] The subjects being history and Churchill in history, the result is that peculiar blend of journalism and memoir which was to characterize his world war books and which anticipates Norman Mailer's oscillation between historical and novelistic techniques in *The Armies of the Night* seventy years later. Incidents are recorded because they occur to Churchill, whose career and experiences are, he thinks, the most interesting in the world and will remain at, or be imposed on, the center of his many books.

His next military-journalistic adventure took him to Africa and Kitchener's reconquest of the Sudan. Here again dispatches and interviews, this time buttressed by considerable reading in government and scholarly publications, become the basis for a nonfiction narrative, *The River War,* which, Churchill insists, is the definitive account of the conflict. It is certainly closer to the later historical works than is the journalism of the *Malakand.* The book comprises four sections, nearly equal in size; the first, on the geographical and historical background, the second, on the initial phases of the war, and the fourth, rounding out the war, are constructed by the omniscient narrator from books, articles, and interviews. But the third section, describing the climactic advance on Omdurman, is almost a self-contained story of the author's personal experiences and observations. Hence the change again from detached narrative to a chatty, detailed account based on his own dispatches.[3]

If the *Malakand* represents a turn from fiction to expository writing, *The River War* betrays a certain nostalgia for the genre the author had abandoned. The book begins with a summary applicable to Shakespearean tragedy: "A tale of blood and war, . . . of wild extravagance and cruel waste, . . . of wisdom and incompetence."[4] As the British army moves into the boiling Sudan and builds the Desert Railway in the face of the declaration by engineering and military experts that it was "impossible," "absurd," "lunatic," the story takes on the qualities of an epic expedition. Meanwhile, in the foe's capital, the khalifa harangues his 20,000 followers. Since no indication is given of how Churchill could have obtained a verbatim version, we would take this to be the historian's license established by Thucydides, until the sequel gives us a possible source. When the crowd "saw his sword flashing in the sunlight, [they] with one accord imitated him, waving their swords and spears, raising a mighty shout of fury and defiance."[5] This detail, like the one of "100,000 armed men" marching "to the music of the war-drums and the [war horns] before the famous Black Flag" or the foreshadowing of the ultimate victory of the force of good over evil, bears a striking resemblance to Milton's *Paradise Lost,* book 1, lines 540–670. Kitchener's army is the angelic host representing the forces of light—and whiteness—against a dark

Satanic majesty dwelling deep in the burning sands of an African hell. Thus, though Churchill eschews explicit mention of the "white man's burden," evinces hostility to missionaries, and betrays periodic skepticism about the commonplace distinction between the civilized and the savage, naked British imperialist aggrandizement is nevertheless subtly assimilated to, and hence purified by, Christian myth.

Perhaps Churchill, a journalist becoming a historian, thought he had not sufficiently purged himself of the "literary" tools of the novelist. Certainly his next two volumes, both on the Boer War, *London to Ladysmith via Pretoria* and *Ian Hamilton's March,* are bare of such devices. Perhaps also his growing interest in home politics, in lucrative lecture tours, and in other literary projects made him rush these books into print. Even with revisions and additions, they seem still to consist of separate pieces of journalism. They are two of his duller works, even though they treat of his imprisonment and escape, the relief of besieged Ladysmith, and the march to Pretoria.

*   *   *   *

Though the narrator of all these nonfiction books may be self-mocking, the curiosity, confidence, and zeal that sent Churchill to distant battlefields manifest themselves in his intrepid donning of the mantle of critic, which he was to wear proudly all his life. His readiness to question experts and professionals caused him much trouble and made him many enemies, but it surely contributed to his greatness. He was not entirely self-serving when he remarked that, since specialists often devoted their lives to a subject without achieving success, he would take a general view, or when he cited Kinglake's remark that minute scrutiny distorts and only the rapid glance sees things in true proportion.[6]

He avowedly tries, with open mind and the benefit of varied adventures, to sift the mass of evidence. Nor can he be accused of failing to suggest remedies, for he "hereby exhorts" the government to certain steps, which, he fears, they will not take. He attacks historians (as a nascent historian), the press (as a journalist who would never cease to quarrel with it), politicians (especially Liberals, whose ranks he would soon join), and the chaplaincy (he briefly had thought of joining the church),[7] but he gives by far the most searching review to the military. Having gravitated to this vocation since the days when he played with toy soldiers, Churchill radiates all the confidence—or vanity and self-delusion—of the novice with a quick mind, a brash personality, and a sharp pen.

These dispatches and books are, in fact, frontline commentaries on military manuals and practices. Though aware that criticism is cheap, Churchill thinks nothing of lecturing erring graybeards on the basic military principles he has but recently learned himself. His youthful iconoclasm enables him to look at conventions with fresh eyes, and he examines the entire military establishment, from the War Office down to the lower officers and the soldiers. Thus the extensive and bitter critique in *The World Crisis* of the generals of World War I grows out of a longstanding hostility and skepticism, the global war merely seeming to confirm what he had discovered and asserted long before. A measure of his early success as a critic is that the *Malakand,* which at first so nettled some officers that it was referred to as "A Subaltern's Hints to Generals," within the year came to be officially recommended to officers preparing for promotion.[8]

The young Churchill's freshness of outlook, for example, reveals itself in his assertion that even though the Spanish troops had the discipline of the Romans, European strategy was irrelevant to the Cuban guerilla war, and that, until the Spaniards realized this fact, reinforcements would be useless. (This, his first of a long series of prophecies, would haunt the western powers often in the twentieth century.) Anticipating his analysis of Marlborough's operations and the theme in his world war memoirs of "crouched" rather than "sprawled" armies and of concentrated navies, Churchill advised the new Spanish general to combine movements into "one concerted scheme" and to "concentrate" the 50,000 men now "frittered away" in protecting villages, killing a few rebels or seizing a hill of no importance.[9]

In the Boer War, a few years later, he was quick to discern the importance of the "new and little-understood" firepower of a modern army. Long-range rifle fire ruled out sword charges, orderly retirement, and simultaneous attacks from several directions. Churchill wanted to exploit this firepower further. Percussion shells or shrapnel should be used; each cavalry regiment should have two machine guns, even though those weapons were foolishly scorned by artillery officers; the revolver should replace the sword for cavalrymen.[10] Churchill was probably not the first champion of the pistol and the machine gun; what is noteworthy and characteristic, however, is the alacrity with which he discards military conventions and sentiments—however much he may treasure tradition in British life and policy—and recognizes the important innovations.[11] In the young man, we see already the champion of the "Wizard War"—the race to apply science to warfare—in the two global conflicts.

The Adventure of War, the Game of Life, the Flush of Youth

Churchill's extended military critique springs from his keen passion for war. This perennial interest of his is due in part to his love of a life other than the normal, the civilian, the conventional. Churchill attributes an aesthetic, even moral, superiority to army ways. Men in civilization sacrifice "joy" to "luxury," whereas in the field "life itself, life at its best and healthiest, awaits the caprice of the bullet."[12] The absence of comforts on the front leads the soldier-narrator to the stoic view that the only necessities are "a little plain food and a philosophic temperament," for, despite severe hardships, the many compensations of combat "invest life with keener interests and rarer pleasures."[13] The importance of the present erases "minor" anxieties about past or future and creates "precious memories." On the eve of battle, the veil of the future becomes palpable. Which men will die? The wise man wants no answer. An adventure, by definition, is a voyage into the unknown. The very matters that render army life repulsive to stay-at-homes make it dignified and exciting to the understanding few. "There are men"—like Churchill, notably as war leader in 1940—"who derive as stern an exaltation from the proximity of disaster and ruin, as others from success, and who are more dauntless in defeat, than most people are in victory."[14]

Thus the ardent, reckless, youthful Lieutenant Tiro arouses in the envious politician, Savrola, the hope that the latter may "open this strange book of war, and by the vivid light of personal danger read the lessons."[15] When that test comes, Savrola finds that in the presence of death life becomes most precious. Running through a line of rifle fire, he waves his hat at the barricade and, asked why he risked his life in order to taunt the foe, replies melodramatically that the gesture was directed at Fate. Combat, according to Bryan Magee's reading of this novel, contains the secret of life because man, then living at the top of his bent, reveals his inner self and thus makes his only true self-discovery and self-realization; each character in *Savrola* has faith in a creed or code which crumbles in the face of death, except for Savrola and Molara, whom pride and self-dramatization sustain.[16]

Once death is faced and properly domesticated or made the catalyst of an enhancement of life, combat takes on the character-istics of a sport. The arrival of the Twenty-first Lancers at the front reminds Churchill of his childhood games, of his taking the carefully packed toy soldiers out of the box and setting them up in rows. War becomes a joy in itself. Of one tribesman's ensconcing himself behind a boulder and for a week firing at all "objects of interest," Churchill says, only half ironically, "What could be more attractive?"; on the other side, soldiers returning from a skirmish are vastly pleased because "nothing . . . is so exhilarat-ing as to be shot at without result."[17] And for excitement, what is comparable—even among "the pleasures of the chase, of art, of intellect, or love"[18]—to the sight of moving masses of men, artillery, and ships, the shapeliness of a dawn offensive, the clash of two forces? Churchill becomes a hedonist of war, opening all his senses to it. In Cuba, a fine dinner in a moonlit shack, mingled with the silhouettes of soldiers on guard and the noises of the camp, produced an "impression hard to forget and impossible to convey." Even at the end of his long life, he insisted that the education of a young man can only benefit from a period of military training, especially if the "bonds of discipline are genial" and the "background of service great."[19]

If death has no sting, life itself comes to be seen as a greater pastime of which war is a part or phase. The joie de vivre intimated by the association of war with adventure is reflected in a commonplace metaphor—life as a game or theater piece—which pervades the early books and the later autobiography, *A Roving Commission*. The letters of the young Churchill are no less filled with the image and suggest that here was a central element in his *Weltanschauung.*[20] In a world without God or immutable values, a world of geologic time and cooling planets, in which individual and species are swallowed by some inscrutable evolutionary process, life yet contains pleasures and beauties for the sensitive person. It is a game in which we participate with mock earnestness while realizing that nothing counts, a game we play for our amusement as much as for our advantage, or a drama in which we play some temporary role allotted to us, a drama with little meaning and yet interesting to behold. The eagerness to put on a "good show" on behalf of uncertain and transient values, which are all that one has in this dark vale, results in the Renaissance aristocratic stance of *sprezzatura,* of paradoxical detachment amid involvement. Confronting annihilation, the rare great man, conscious of his role before the world and history, wishes to "leave life's stage with dignity." Death being nothing more fearful than a last inning or scene, and manner of exit rather than longevity being crucial, war becomes the ultimate game or drama.[21] So the jaunty, aristocratic young Churchill dashed off to whatever wars this impoverished world could offer—in Cuba, India, East and South Africa.

This outlook is close to that sometimes celebrated by Joseph Conrad, and Churchill indeed seems in these early works to be a character out of Conrad, albeit without the tragic dimension. (Conrad's early fiction, it should be noted, like Churchill's early nonfiction, treats of the civilized-savage theme in exotic regions on the fringes of the empire.) Although *Savrola* was published just as Conrad was beginning his writing career, the true analogue to his work is not Churchill's lame novel but the *Malakand.* In some ways, it covers the same area of experience as Conrad's *Youth,* whose refrain is, "Oh, the glamor of youth!" Youthful and amusing as well is the letter to the Boer secretary of war left by Churchill upon breaking prison. Closing with regret at being unable to bid him a more "ceremonious" farewell in person, it expresses the debonair swagger of the young adventurer—soon to have a twenty-five pound reward placed on his life—and recalls the cheerful narrative tone of the early works and *A Roving Commission.* To bring levity and ceremony to bear at such a solemn moment is either to have a monumental confidence in one's chosenness or to treat life as a jolly lark and a good show. Churchill's attitude here is that of the true adventurer, and his bringing a sense of play and adventure into politics was a secret of his greatness.

Churchill moves through these books devouring experience, radiating curiosity, seeking extreme states of being, marveling at his luck, and sensing glimmers of that special fate he would feel possessing him in *The Second World War*.[22] The great advantage he delights in is his "roving commission," his freedom to "rove at random or caprice"[23] in his quest for adventure and perhaps for a vocation, a destiny. This became the major theme of his early years when he looked back on them. He had had many strange experiences, from which much could be learned. To describe them he reached prematurely and with characteristic ingenuousness for superlative, occasionally fanciful statements. "What followed reads like a romance"; a landscape with many castles "suggested Grimm's fairy tales, . . . some strange domain of fancy, the resort of giants or ogres."[24]

Now, as he would a half-century later, he hastens to the frontline vantage point, to the key battles which turned the tide in the last of the picturesque wars. Despite his claim to be zealously trying to avoid dangers, "my fortunes in this land are to be a succession of adventures and escapes, any one of which would suffice for a personal experience of the campaign," and he innocently wonders why he "must be so often thrust to the brink and then withdrawn."[25] The universe becomes his living room; adventures vibrate sympathetically; time is riddled with patterns. As a fugitive in the South African veld, he looks at the stars: "Orion shone brightly. Scarcely a year ago he had guided me when lost in the desert to the banks of the Nile." Here is the quintessential young Churchill: "The fascination of the adventure grew."[26]

No less was granted him in the world of men. In each campaign, he circulated among the big brass at headquarters as well as on the front. He parades the fact that he knows prominent persons and moves easily in the highest circles. In composing *The River War*, his thoroughness took him as far afield as a Cairo prison for an interview with the notorious slavetrader, Zubair, who barely appears in the periphery of the story; this is an early instance of Churchill's interest in personal contacts with the makers of history. Even in sleep he dreams of breakfasting with a suddenly deferential Boer president! He confides in us—in a sentence conjuring up the personal diplomacy of *The Second World War*—that few great men are "destitute" of charm. Like the ingenuous Samuel Pepys making his way in the world and delighting in himself, he says of his various meetings with prominent officers, as he would say of the much more earthshaking Teheran Conference nearly a half-century later, "Never before had I sat in such brave company nor stood so close to a great event."[27] This romanticism would remain with him all his life and would receive climactic fulfillment in World War II, when the burdens and freedoms of office would be his supreme game and adventure, when he would often visit the battlefield, fuse love of travel, food, talk, and the company of great men with a personal diplomacy he believed was the fulcrum of world events.

*   *   *   *

Young Churchill does not, however, lose himself in romance and fantasy. He concedes that, despite all the pleasures of war and fame, six months of active service will make anyone delight in the "comfortable monotonies of peace" and home.[28] War, like champagne, can be savored best by sipping. He is aware of its dark side. The twists of fate are swift and surprising; peace comes through exhaustion on both sides; the battleground is filled with images of horror, which Churchill does not hide from us. The soldier's lot consists usually of routine, ennui, discomfort, hard work, fatigue, danger, slow promotion, and subordination to fools. The military career in fact differs from all others in that the soldier is much more dependent on chance than on prudence and wisdom. He can rise only by risking his life often. "All his fortunes, . . . his position . . . in the world, his accumulated capital . . . must be staked afresh each time." An erring statesman may retrieve his fortunes, but for a soldier "the indiscriminating bullet settles everything."[29] Though the wounded may be cheered by thoughts of how narrowly they escaped death, a worse fate probably awaits them: discharge from service, an insufficient pension, a "broken life," a "pauper's grave"; and for the enemy wounded, without antiseptics and anaesthetics, the suffering must be beyond words.

This sense of the horrors of war grows with each volume. In *The River War,* Churchill concedes that, often viewed from a distance which falsely suggests magnificence, war is actually shabby. Inquiring into the condition of the wounded, he provides the type of grim, realistic portrayal of the consequences of combat common in literature since Tolstoy. Hence Churchill hopes that men will control "their tastes for the barbarous, though exhilarating, sport of war."[30] So he has learned a lesson. War is after all not only a game or adventure. He reluctantly takes leave of his youthful romantic dream: "Ah, horrible war, amazing medley of the glorious and the squalid, the pitiful and the sublime, if modern men of light and leading saw your face closer, simple folk would see it hardly ever."[31] The loss of innocence is due in part to his growing up and in part to the changing nature of combat itself. As he will in later works, he finds "modern" warfare disappointing as a spectacle. Instead of the colorful pageantry of Omdurman, the scene consists now of combatants scattered over a great expanse of ground, concealed wherever possible, clad in neutral tints. Having the bad fortune to come of age just when the romance of war died out, Churchill is unwittingly prophetic in his remark that soon the supply of barbaric potentates to conquer on exotic, relatively safe expeditions will run out. He is right in seeing the end of such frontier wars but wrong—and Victorian—in thinking they will be replaced by prosperity. For he makes the worst prophecy of his career in calling Britain mistaken in the supposition that her armies will fight again in Europe.

The dedication of the *Malakand* speaks of the Indian operation as the "most valuable and fascinating experience" of his life—ironic when we consider how his initial foray would be dwarfed many times over in a half-century of active life and how these words could be the motto of each of his subsequent memoirs, as his power, his scope of action, and the range of his experience progressed geometrically. But another secret of his success was his voracious appetite for military and, later, political adventure, his curiosity, his zest in scrutinizing and enjoying everything that came his way—and in making sure that much did. All his experiences were enjoyable because he knew how to extract their significance or to seek out only significant experience. The persona in these books has soured not on adventure but on the army as the road to it and war as a species of it.[32] Perhaps Churchill was influenced by what he had seen of politics and diplomacy.

The Politics of Firmness, Militancy, and Empire

Although so far mainly interested in military matters, the young Churchill was already delivering himself of worldly political pronouncements. Notably revealing is his analysis of revolutionary movements. Despite sneers at Liberal policies, he draws the liberal conclusion (as he would on the Irish problem in *Randolph Churchill*) that the blame for the River War, which many assigned to the Mahdi, is shared by "the unjust rulers who oppressed the land," by incapable commanders and vacillating ministers.[33] All rebellions need two spurs: a knowledge of better things, which the Dervishes obtained from General Gordon, and a "spirit of combination," which the Mahdi provided. Basically a secular soul, Churchill insists that social and racial issues, not religious enthusiasm, beget revolts; the important point was that the Sudan was being ruined and plundered by Egypt. At the same time, men are not bestirred by material causes alone; their actions need "at least the appearance of moral right" so that they have something "sublime to fight for," even though the war has a practical basis. They also need a leader, and, as usual in the East, the leader is a "fanatic" who rouses men by means of patriotism and religion. He is nevertheless himself vulnerable; like Napoleon and, later, Hitler, "the Mahdi depended on success for existence. . . . Retreat meant ruin."[34] Churchill, as always, respects success and momentum.

Where popular support is dormant or passive, it can sometimes be aroused by such drastic actions as, in Cuba, the rebels' willful destruction of the sugar crop in order to paralyze the island's economy and turn the people against the Spaniards. Churchill adjudges this an effective but dreadful resort not excused by past bad government and oppression. For, just as he can give the Indian tribesmen, the Mahdi, and the Boers their due without rejecting British imperial policy, so does he in Cuba, taking note of the overtaxation and the administrative corruption which made revolt against Spain inevitable, manage to arrive at an ambiguous conclusion: "I sympathize with the rebellion—not with the rebels." Unable therefore to take sides, Churchill would have Europe demand of Spain a redress of grievances, though not so long as the rebels are in arms. As the war drags on, Churchill raises the pragmatic-liberal question of whether success would redeem the cost: "Is it worth ruining Spain for Cuba?" This query (similar to ones heard in America in the late 1960s) springs from his fear that the consequences of the war might create a revolutionary situation reminiscent of that in the France of the 1780s.[35]

In the frontier wars, Churchill witnessed native rebellions against an empire. In *Savrola,* however, begun before he had seen any such uprisings, he delineated, within a mythical republic, a revolution with ideological foundations. A dictator yields to popular pressures for an election and thereby isolates the extremists. The latter, exploiting the rigging of the elections and the deaths of some protesting laborers, look beyond Savrola's envisioned reforms to radical change. They attempt to capture the liberal revolution which began when a Savrola opposing a law and order maintained by bayonets came reluctantly to see that only force will do the job. The book thus dramatizes the classic pattern obtaining from 1789 to 1917 of a bourgeois-liberal revolution struggling with a radicalism to which it is allied or to which it has given birth. Reaction, in short, forces liberalism to align itself with radicalism and to resort reluctantly to violence, in which radicalism is more proficient and as a result of which anything can happen.[36] Although Savrola temporarily loses control of the situation, liberalism finally triumphs. The "chronicler" finds few great events to recount other than the opening of colleges, railways, and canals, as "peace and prosperity" return to Laurania.

And yet Churchill finds certain aspects of liberalism contemptible. If life is a game and war an adventure, mere good intentions are not appropriate values. Even in his very first articles, he proposed to analyze the Cuban situation not with sentiment but with common sense and "cool calculation of profit and loss."[37] Whether resulting from his disillusionment with war or irrationally coexisting with his romantic view of it, a characteristically Churchillian toughness makes its appearance in these first books. It was to become one of the leading themes of his career and writings in the form of the paradox that peace can be obtained by militancy, not by pacifism.

He scorns Britain's "vain and unwise" clinging to a policy of peace in India and her delaying the use of force in South Africa as part of "an expensive tribute to the argument, 'Do not seek peace with a sword.'"[38] Had Britain entered the South African War peremptorily, the "wonderful loyalty" of the Dutch might have shown itself, but, after months of "hesitation," the entire colony was on the verge of rebellion. In India, the Liberal government's reluctance to seize a frontier town was interpreted by the hostile tribes as an encouraging sign of weakness. To Churchill this was indeed a "moral" if not "physical" weakness, and he pronounces starkly the conceit which pervades his books and on which his career would by turns flounder and flourish: "War has been aggravated by the Peace Party; and thus these humanitarian gentlemen are personally . . . responsible for the great loss of life."[39] In short, the very depravity of man, which some would invoke as an argument for turning the other cheek rather than going to war and loosing worse evils, Churchill implicitly uses as a reason for toughness, for the paradox of peace through might; only militancy can control the old Adam.

The imperial policy of gradual advance, intrigues, subsidies, and small expeditions is valid only if it is rigorously pursued. Government must not foolishly expect the political officers to obtain authority "strictly according to regulations" or deny General Gordon the help of the resourceful slavetrader Zubair. Such a moral posture, Churchill asserts, merely obliges the government to provide alternatives and, later, "to rescue the garrisons." *Savrola* dramatizes his pragmatic willingness to use whatever help is available. The hero justifies employment of the slimy turncoat Miguel: "You must take men as you find them; few are disinterested. . . . He is of use." Politics is, moreover, complicated by—or is even at bottom a network of—human considerations: though a viper, Miguel "saved my life, and asked me to save his in return. What could I do?"[40] Nothing is more indicative of Churchill's unideological, antiidealistic stance, or of his dissent from general opinion, than his assertion that, "fanatic" or not, the Mahdi was among the greatest Arab heroes, on the grounds that we have no way of distinguishing a genuine prophet from a spurious one, "except by the measure of his success." And Churchill measures "success" solely by the degree of power. Clearly here speaks the man who would, in *The Second World War,* justify working with, or using as tools, men like Stalin, Tito, Badoglio, Darlan, Doenitz—men who held power.

The wish to mollify liberal public opinion prompted officials to camouflage the harsh realities of military force. Churchill ridicules the government for asserting that "great care" was taken to destroy only the houses of "guilty parties" in India and only fortified villages, when in fact all border villages are fortified and all border tribesmen are soldiers in rebellion. The "war is war" approach informs his remarks on the morality of the "ghastly" dumdum bullet. Not only does it perform the job of killing more effectively and with no greater pain than the ordinary kind, but, whereas European soldiers sit down when wounded, the tribesmen cease fighting only when "hopelessly disabled." Hence the instinct of self-preservation justifies the dumdum. Churchill was to defend with similar arguments the use of gas in World War I and of area bombing and the atomic bomb in World War II. Once a war is justified, virtually everything (except treachery) is fair, and surrender by one's own men is excused only "by clear proof that there was no prospect of gaining the slightest military advantage by going on fighting"; otherwise, it merits "sentence of death."[41]

The defense of the dumdum seems reasonable enough until we note that in order to quiet the reader, and perhaps his own conscience, Churchill goes to the extreme of suggesting that physical pain has been taken out of war. During the shock period of fifteen minutes, he claims, the wounded feel nothing, and by the time the shock has passed, they are usually under sedation at the dressing station. As a description of modern warfare, this is monumentally fatuous, especially since he often laments elsewhere that many wounded are left unattended for days. Churchill indeed conceded privately that in print one does not even allude to the horrors of the dumdum,[42] and the defense of that bullet, reiterated in *The River War,* is abruptly dropped in the Boer War books, apparently because this time the foe resorted to it. Suddenly we hear of Boer "guilt," of an "expansive bullet of a particularly cruel pattern,"[43] and of the spite of the Boers for wanting to lacerate the foe.

But whatever the weaponry, men should not flinch at conflict. A chapter of "Military Observations" closes with a matter-of-fact acceptance of war as a normal human experience which one should not decry and moralize on but should understand better and render scientific. The imperial frontier wars are valuable in giving British soldiers combat experience, and war in general, he asserts in an article, is a "good instructor." Blamed by Europeans for the ensuing wars, the Mahdi is exonerated by Churchill for having animated his countrymen and freed his land of foreigners. To the philosopher, the consequent destruction of trade, property, and life has a certain value in contributing to the development of men's souls, and the Mahdi is a great man.[44] Savrola concedes reluctantly that "might is a form of fitness, . . . a low form, but still physical force contains the elements of human progress," and technology will enable an effete Europe to preserve moral ascendancy against the "valiant savages."[45]

For in this wicked world, right must sustain itself with force or threat of force; in the Fashoda case, only British determination to fight made the unreasonable French yield. Similarly, though Churchill is able to suppose that the British may seem savage to the Dervishes and though he moralizes (in a remark anticipating his special theme of magnanimity in victory) that "all men improve under a generous treatment,"[46] he sees no alternative in the Sudan. Civilization, everywhere eager to reason and compromise rather than use violence, must be stern. Islam is so powerful and proselytistic that if Christianity were not protected by the science it once had opposed in vain, European civilization might suffer the fate of Rome. This is preeminently the Churchillian credo—pragmatic, realistic, patriotic—and the linchpin of his career, at its worst and best. Not only is he unruffled by the alliance of the religion of the Prince of Peace with war and scientific weaponry, but his hysterical description of Islamic expansionism centuries after the fact and at a time when militancy and proselytizing were primarily the traits of Christian-scientific civilization is an obvious instance of the projection of one's guilt on others.

Churchill's toughness opposes not only the sentimental but also the misguidedly parsimonious. He defends a questionable artillery barrage by declaring that "all war is waste, and cartridges are the cheapest item in the bill" if they do the job of harassing the foe.[47] With the political-military priorities of heavy expenditure, risk taking, and persistent offensive action, Churchill, now, as he will in the two world wars, sees that machines and ships must remain the servants of man: "So long as the loss of guns is considered a national disaster instead of only an ordinary incident of war,

Cavalry officers will regard them rather as sources of anxiety than as powerful weapons."[48] When proposing that the lighter web belts to be used in place of leather ones, he dismisses the objection that web wears out by arguing that belts are cheaper than soldiers. On the other hand, the worst extravagance in war is an "economy of soldiers," because of which Omdurman is yet another case of a victor failing to exploit his triumph.

If strategy takes precedence over human lives, so does the British military code. Churchill admits that according to strict military considerations the besieged Ladysmith garrison should have been left to its fate, but rescue must be attempted, even at the cost of thousands of lives and of failure, "on the grounds of honor, if not on those of policy."[49] So in later years would he insist that in war military strategy is one with, or must yield to, political strategy; "not to occupy a place is one thing: to abandon it after it has been occupied another."[50] The military code, national honor, or political-diplomatic ramifications turn out to be the sentimentality of the tough, pragmatic man; for them, "some things have to be done, no matter what the cost may be."[51]

The politics of firmness and the critique of British Liberal policy, like his grasp of the new weaponry, lead to Churchill's characteristic prophetic stance. A prophet is a critic who devotes most of his attention not to the present evils he decries but to their future consequences, a man many of whose sentences begin with "if." Churchill's major prophecies are and will be of two sorts: those in the military field, where his openness to new developments in technology goes with a distrust of conventions, received wisdom, and experts; and those in the political field, where his faith that peace consorts with militancy and strength upholds him in his lifelong quarrel with idealists, pacifists, little Englanders, sentimental Liberals.

In military matters, Churchill's emphasis on the importance of the new firepower and his contempt for the traditional lance and sword were to be vindicated by subsequent wars. Noting how dependent the Malakand expedition is on mule trains and how the tribesmen are becoming better marksmen, Churchill warns that the tribesmen will bring British operations to a standstill once they see the significance of firing at the mules. Hence "whatever is to be done on the frontier should be done now before the process of arming is more complete."[52] This last sentence could easily come from one of his speeches of forty years later on Germany. Also amazingly like the Churchill of the 1910s and 1930s are his remarks to a Boer: "The country did not wish for war with the Boers. Personally I have always done so. I saw that you had six rifles to every burgher in the Republic. I knew what that meant. . . . Armed and ambitious as you were, the war had to come sooner or later. I have always said 'sooner.' Therefore I rejoiced when you sent your ultimatum and roused the whole nation."[53] And in one of his first South African dispatches, he concludes correctly from local conditions and the Boer character that, in spite of general optimism, the war will be bloody and long.

But the most farsighted of his pronouncements, eerily adumbrating his indomitability in 1940, must have seemed histrionic in the days of imperial splendor. If evil days were to come and "the last army which a collapsing Empire could interpose between London and the invader were dissolving in rout and ruin," Churchill hopes that "even in these modern days" some men "would not care to accustom themselves to a new order of things and tamely survive the disaster."[54] Decidedly the man and his message were already on the scene, but they would have to wait four decades before history provided the rendezvous with destiny.

The Imperial Theme and the Lion Rampant

Frontier wars—clashes between a European state and nonwhite tribal people on the fringes of its overseas empire—were common in the nineteenth century. They were seen as conflicts between "polite," progressive European civilization and non-European savagery, fanaticism, and backwardness. It is hardly surprising to find Churchill, coming from the ruling class and apparently beginning a military career, filled with many of the assumptions which we now dismiss as Victorian and some of which he himself was soon to question. The smug rhetoric of Christian, white, European, scientific, imperial, British superiority is nowhere more apparent than in his discussion of the enemy tribes, who, without any such endowments, seem to lack dignity. Though he does not indicate whether he considers their ignorance to be invincible, some of his phrases—"inferior race," "low-grade races of Africa" —would today be regarded as racist.

The key to this rhetoric is, of course, that by emphasizing technological progress, by taking divergence from European mores as signs of lapses from grace, and by ignoring western man's butcheries and vices, the conquering westerner could speak readily of "savages" and of his own duty to civilize them. The horrors of twentieth-century life, more even than the growth of humanitarian sentiments or cultural relativism, have made such self-deception about "barbarism" and white superiority impossible. A psychologist would define such name-calling as "projection," as when Churchill insists that great "barbaric kingdoms living side by side but differing in race and religion"[55] cannot long remain at peace—as though that differed in any way from great "polite" republics of similar religion in Europe. Just as silly is his remark that "Orientals appreciate results [and are] eager only to be on the winning side."[56] Such a phenomenon, he implies, is unknown in Europe; were this the later Churchill, one would suspect irony, but one cannot here. A few pages earlier, he had casually aligned himself with the winning side in history by adjudging "success" to be the only trait distinguishing a genuine from a spurious prophet!

Churchill is hardly aware of these abounding smugnesses, self-contradictions, and ironies. The religion of "blood and war," Islam, confronts that of peace, and he rejoices that the latter is "better armed" and that, as a result, "credulity and fanaticism" are being destroyed by "rationalism and machine guns."[57] When, after frequent application of the words "savage" and "barbarian" to Africans, he speaks of the difficulty of improving the Egyptian army, because "the Egyptian is not a fighting animal,"[58] one infers that truculence ceases to be "savage" when it is organized and efficient, as in Europe. He goes so far as to use the canard of the "inscrutable Oriental": "No Europeans can gauge the motives or assume the point of view of Asiatics"; "civilization hardly knows whether to laugh or weep" at their mentality.[59] Of course we now know all of this to be, like the "white man's burden" thesis, mainly imperialist rationalization. The Asiatic was "inscrutable" not because he was exempt from human nature but because he was more tradition directed than "progressive" or scientific and because conquerors rarely have the moral intelligence and the sympathy to see things from the vantage point of subject peoples. To a naïve westerner all customs not European and all actions not according with western plans seem barbarous. Thus, when noting that in India British attempts to eradicate cobras by offering rewards for cobra skins merely stimulated cobra farming, Churchill laments, "The most rational expedients operate in a manner exactly contrary to European anticipation." Yet surely this is an example, not of oriental inscrutability and ineducability, but of the workings of the market economy Churchill is usually so fond of.

In contrast to the mysterious East stands Europe, in whose progress and mission, in whose nationalism, religion, and science Churchill has an only occasionally wavering faith. He believes that "the larger associations" of men—the "national idea" or centralized government (but not military dictatorship)—are good. Moreover, though the imperial drive is more healthy than wise, it is innate and, if used in the right way, a sign of competitive vigor in the polity. Christianity, however it may be perverted, moderates the passions and prevents fanaticism; and to the god of science, Churchill would gladly sacrifice the "beautiful" Temple of Philae for a large Aswan dam which could store much life-giving water. Science having made possible in the Sudan "the most signal triumph ever gained . . . over barbarians,"[60] he composes a chapter of "Military Reflections," lest the "science of human destruction fall behind the general progress of the age. The moral of a tale" concerned with slaughter must "tend to improve the methods of killing."[61]

Such statements, without a hint of irony, sit awkwardly alongside other expressions which indicate that Churchill had his doubts about modern tendencies. Indeed, in *The River War,* he sometimes undermines the Victorian antithesis of civilization and barbarism; the words "polite" and "civilized" commonly used of western countries, like the "barbarian" and "savage" of the African, may appear in ironic contexts. Moreover, if Europe is not, in his opinion, as good as claimed, the natives are not as bad either. Periodically, Churchill is able to overcome his prejudices sufficiently to see that some of the oriental "fanatical" traits resemble admirable western ones. The warlike Mamunds exhibited "courage, tactical skill, and marksmanship"; the Pathans stood by their word and fought "against countrymen and co-religionists." Churchill's consequent ambivalence expresses itself in oxymora—"the statecraft of the savage," "a fine specimen of proud brutality"—and in uncertainty as to whether the natives are "less sensitive or more valiant" than westerners or whether some of the khalifa's acts were not "far more rational than the anti-Semitism from which even the most polite nations have not purged themselves."[62] And Churchill's liberal, compassionate, imaginative comparison of the Mahdi to Gordon was in its day a daring stroke.[63]

Imperialism itself, the premises of which he would accept throughout his life, comes under critical scrutiny. Speculators, missionaries, and soldiers, he observes, often exploit the subject peoples for their own interests. Furthermore, because many Britons cannot accept military operations for "political objects," they first convince themselves that the enemy must be saved from his utter vileness and then they tolerate barbarous behavior in the conquering army; the British soldiers, led by the rhetoric about "avenging Gordon" into regarding the Dervishes as "vermin," would rather kill than take prisoners. The notion of Dervish inferiority was, in any case, as unjust as it was dangerous, Churchill pointed out; the Dervishes were not "abandoned savages" but "valiant warriors" whose state was "tolerable" to them and whose leader was esteemed, while the victors' maltreatment of the Dervish wounded was rendered more hideous by lying. The official statement that they received " 'every delicacy and attention' is so utterly devoid of truth that it transcends the limits of mendacity and passes into the realm of the ridiculous."[64] A few days later, the British troops, off to another part of the world, were "pacifying the Cretans, and hanging those who objected to the pacification."[65]

The natives, more interested in liberty than progress, resist with a noble, valorous fury the "philanthropic invaders." That they are therefore called "fanatic" by white men may be a further injustice, for that is but a charged word by which those supposing themselves virtuous and superior "airily" dismiss "rebellions of natives goaded to fury by brutal oppression. . . . Why should we regard as madness in the savage what would be sublime in civilized men?"[66] Nor should the "fanatical" leaders of revolt, who come like biblical judges to their distressed people in an hour of need, so easily be deemed "impostors." Occasionally, Churchill evinces outright sympathetic understanding of the other's viewpoint: "Perhaps to these savages, with their vile customs and brutal ideas, we appeared as barbarous aggressors."[67] Indeed, the chivalric conquerors destroyed the tomb of the Mahdi, exhumed and mutilated the body of one who was, after all, a patriotic and noble soul; and if in England, the martyrlike death of Gordon gave the idea of revenge the consecration of religion, "what community is altogether free from fanaticism? The spirit of the Crusaders stirred beneath the surface of scientific civilization."[68]

Remarks like these show the degree to which Churchill's critical mind could free itself from the preconceptions of his age and anticipate the critique of the idea of progress in all the books he wrote after World War I. At one point, Churchill even touches on a major philosophic problem and questions a cardinal premise of book, war, and era: "If the reader inquire to what end the negroes should labor that they may improve; why they should not remain contented, if degraded; and wherefore they should be made to toil to better things up so painful a road, I confess I cannot answer him." But these intellectual heights, to be surveyed by twentieth-century thinkers, are too much for Churchill, and he lapses back into a Victorian anodyne: "If, however, he prove there is no such obligation, he will have made out a very good case for universal suicide."[69] Had he pursued this question further, he might not have become the Churchill we know; but that he even raised the question in the first place reveals an inquisitiveness that helped make him the Churchill we treasure.

*   *   *   *

Once the imperial civilizing mission is, despite all objections, validated, there arises the question of who is best fitted to undertake it. Britain's role is justified for Churchill by her presence at the frontier, and, given the bellicose reaction of the tribes, further expansion was inevitable.[70] While laying claim to political neutrality, Churchill, having grown up during the zenith of the empire, concludes after "cautious inquiry" that frontier wars are part of the British heritage. The victories of 1897 established Britain's faith in her own higher destiny, with its contribution to the happiness, learning, and liberty of mankind. That no other empire has been so successful can be explained by her religious toleration, by the uniqueness of the Briton, and by the rise of heroic leaders in times of trouble. Thus, at the very beginning of his career, Churchill sounds the motif of the special role of Britain (which later events will expand into "English-speaking peoples"); here also, in inchoate form, is Churchill's theme of the British oscillation between early sloth and late vigor, between peacetime "delay and disaster" and wartime "perseverance" and victory.

But on South Africa Churchill entertains no sentimental nonsense about a civilizing mission or the spreading of Christianity. The world is simply a garden for the white man's, especially the Briton's, overpopulated cities (though Churchill ignores the question of why with the same advantages spacious Canada, Australia, and New Zealand could not serve this purpose). Unfortunately this frontier land was being held not by dark-skinned primitive barbarians or savage Moslems but by advanced white Christian European stock. The British press called the Boers "barbarians and savages"—familiar words—but Churchill, who saw them from up close, knew better. Crafty and cool, dignified and honorable, with quiet valor and superb marksmanship, these "honest ignorant peasants with wits sharpened by military training" meant to fight to the bitter end.[71]

Yet the imperialist, never at a loss for a moral rationale, defends the war against the noble Boer by citing British benevolence toward the black native. The root of the trouble is that the Boer associates Britain with "violent social revolution. Black is to be proclaimed the same as white. The servant is to be raised against the master."[72] Churchill dwells on this point because it nicely places the expansionist empire in the paradoxical and cozy position of being the defender of human rights and liberal principles against a repressive regime. Britain is vindicated by "the loyalty of the natives" to her.

Indeed, Churchill's smugness about Britain periodically enters, in statements which ill accord with his realism about war and politics, the realm of the sentimental, the ridiculous, and the morally indecent. When the Boers claim, not without cause, that the war is being fought because British capitalists desire the gold mines, Churchill insists that the lives of British soldiers are "much more precious" than mere gold. He never, remarks D. A. N. Jones, sees an economic motive in any war he (or Britain) is in, only duty and nobility.[73] Such rhetoric remains with him to the end but seems more appropriate to the heroic stand of 1940 than to some of the morally dubious battles here.

Churchill is so hypnotized by the British mission that, as in the case of the civilized-savage antithesis, various incongruities and ironies escape him. He had at least been able to see through some of the Victorian clichés about progress and savages, but his patriotism is shockproof.[74] Thus an Arab prisoner in the Sudan, asked by Kitchener, "Why have you come into my country to burn and kill?" replies, "I have to obey my orders, and so have you." Praising the dignity of the answer, Churchill ignores the temerity of Kitchener's words, "my country." He notes that, of three men involved in rescuing the body of a fallen officer, a captain and a lieutenant were awarded the Victoria Cross, while a corporal received only the Distinguished Service Medal, "I know not on what grounds of discrimination."[75] Can Churchill here be an uncomprehending witness of the viciousness of a class and caste system? It would seem so, for elsewhere he tells us solemnly that officers should have better rations than their soldiers because they are used to superior fare. Again, glad that both Sikhs and Afridis are in the British army, he wants the Victoria Cross opened to all British subjects, for "in sport, in courage, and in the sight of heaven, all men meet on equal terms"; yet, with the other side of his mouth, he asserts that the day cannot come when "British and native officers will serve together in ordinary seniority, and on the same footing."[76]

Churchill's discussion of the causes of the River War exhibits considerable complacency. In the first place, the miserable condition of the Dervishes aroused British humanitarianism. This pity, reinforced by national pride in the regeneration of Egypt and the momentum of modern imperialism, worked harmoniously with the military desire to redeem honor lost (by prior evacuation of the Sudan) and to extend the imperial frontiers. The military pressure "may not be very broad," he ingenuously adds, "but it is a very powerful influence—for it is ceaselessly applied." The death of Gordon had come to seem a Christian martyrdom and turned the idea of revenge into one of consecration—a "holy war," as a

Moslem might put it—and "fused the military, the fanatical, and the philanthropic spirits." Thus "the sentimental, the intellectual, and the political" considerations overcame the anxieties of the taxpayer about expenses.[77]

Churchill's naïveté comes into play again in the discussion of the postwar agreement between Britain and Egypt. The Sudan could not be left to the mercies of Egypt, but, in the light of Egypt's participation in the reconquest, Britain could not keep the land either. She therefore discovered a "diplomatic 'fourth dimension' " of joint ownership which would bring "Peace and Plenty" to the Sudan. The modern reader is not distracted by this pretty slogan from noting the interesting refinement of imperialism, whereby Egypt, itself a pawn, is like a child rendered content by being given the illusion of also playing the imperialist game, while everything, including Egypt, remains under British control. Thus Britain uses mainly Egyptian troops and money for the advance but keeps control of both the conquered land and its partner in the conquest. This is imperialism by proxy and at a uniquely small cost to the citizenry at home.

As for the loss of life on both sides, though deplorable, it can be justified if the war can be. This "great, though perhaps academic, question" haunts the closing chapter: "Was the war justified by wisdom and by right?"[78] In answering it, Churchill abruptly acknowledges the existence of nominal and real causes of war. The nominal reason was to avenge Gordon, but "it is time to have done with such talk."[79] He concedes, for the first time, that Gordon "was killed in fair war," and vindictiveness is, in any case, undignified in a "great people." Nor was the Sudan reconquered in order to "chastise" the wicked Dervishes, who were not so very savage after all. The real reasons, as he now sees them, were to sweep out a society annoying to "civilized nations"; to strengthen British grasp of Egypt, which like that of India, is a "source of strength"; to give Britain a vast territory coveted by every great state and, in the Nile, a powerful weapon. What happened was "for the good of the world, of England, and of Egypt."[80]

One hardly knows what to make of this. Has Churchill presented one set of reasons for the war at the beginning of the story and, by the time he reaches the end, changed his mind? Or does he give at the beginning of the book the expressed or nominal reasons which moved people before the war and now the true reasons which inspired the government and which have become clear only in the aftermath? In any case, the confidence with which he speaks of the "annoyance" to civilization (almost a contradiction in terms) and of the benefits accruing to everyone—an early expression of his "harmony of interests" theme—can at best be described as bland. This little war is a classic case of imperialist pious rhetoric and ruthless expansion, studied with a microscope that reveals, whether or not the author is aware of it, every last pockmark.

It was the last such war Britain was to fight, coming significantly in the very last years of a century filled with frontier wars; within the year she would discover in South Africa that some potential victims defend themselves. Thus Churchill received his military and, incidentally, political initiation in the dusk of Victorian imperialism, before being launched, along with the world, into a very different century.

First Harvest

Whatever the ultimate value of these first works, they will always remain fascinating as source books of Churchillian ideas and phrases at the beginning of a sixty-year career. Equally interesting are the connections of these works with Churchill's future life.[81] Not only does *Savrola*, for instance, contain the germ of the Dardanelles battle, but the predicament of Savrola at the end of the novel bears an interesting resemblance to that of Marlborough and, years later, Churchill himself: He "had won them freedom," and now the people deserted him. During the struggle he had been indispensable, but in the moment of triumph, they would rather "go on alone." We likewise read with fascination the vivid account of Savrola as orator, in the light of the author's future greatness. Since, as *A Roving Commission* informs us, Churchill had not yet shown any marked speaking ability, we seem to have in this triple tribute to the arts of oratory, composition, and politics the author's revery of what he would like to become, a revery which, as it rarely does in life, came true.

Where, then, do these works stand? Manifestly, *Savrola*, Churchill's first book, is also his worst. He had wandered into a discipline for which he had insufficient talent and maturity. The novel abounds in lapses of every sort, only some of which may be attributed to the sensibility of the age. Sentimentality of thought and manner prevails, and melodramatic coincidences proliferate. The novel appeared in the age of James and Conrad[82] and indeed shares some of its subject matter with the soon to be written *Nostromo*, but it is not even remotely comparable in quality. A parallel suggests itself also with a novel that would appear three decades later, Hemingway's *A Farewell to Arms*, for here also a man in love turns away from a nation falling apart, from a cause losing its meaning, from a word like "honor" which sounds hollow. Churchill, unlike Hemingway, avoids the existentialist depths and tacks on a happy ending; his stilted Victorian emotionalism is wholly unlike the American's impassive but moving style. Whereas Hemingway's book, moreover, makes use of personal experience and reflects his values, Churchill's does neither, and that perhaps explains the lameness of the product. He never said farewell to politics and seems not to have placed the love of a woman above it at any time, at least not in any dramatic, overt way.

Compton Mackenzie suggests that the book is a daydream of a life of action by an ambitious young man, a daydream which an inactive man would have rewritten repeatedly throughout his life. Bryan Magee adds that, since Churchill's character remained unchanged, *Savrola* is a "gold mine of insights into the buried assumptions carried by Churchill into adult life"; Peter de Mendelssohn, finding in it a veiled portrayal of the author's family situation, regards it also as retrospective, as self-therapeutic and self-liberating. The book is likewise a testament to Churchill's early sophistication in military and political matters, interests which remained constant for six decades. It is, says H. S. Commager, about power, about the ruthlessness of war, the fickleness of the mob, the brevity of fame, and, above all, about a man in some ways sounding and acting like young Churchill. All of his works are preoccupied with the military and the political, and the two central figures—a soldier trying to be a statesman and a statesman finding he has to be a soldier—are to come to life in Churchill and to be the subjects of his books.[83]

The composition of *Savrola* suggests that Churchill in 1897 wavered, as he later said General Ian Hamilton did, between the vocations of writing and the military. He entered upon neither. It is as though, by telling a tale about a man turning from military and political affairs to a love affair, he purged himself of such "escapist" temptations and at the same time rid himself of the desire to be a novelist. Despite the failure of this book, one cannot but wonder what sort of writer he would have become had he gone into imaginative literature. It is hard to visualize a great novelist here (although *Marlborough* will read like a great novel) but no harder than to see the future indomitable war leader in the man who wrote this book, with its sense of people as unmanageable, politics as hopeless, life as absurd. And yet perhaps his greatness came because of, rather than despite, this disenchanted attitude.

The *Malakand* exhibits a Churchill who is a curious amalgam of correspondent, student of war, and writer with poetic and philosophic inclinations; a further amalgam of man of action, observer of men of action, and amused observer of the self as observer, writer, and interlocutor with the reader.[84] The young adventurer-soldier-journalist is also an intellectual or artist of sorts, a talented young man who hardly knows which of the many roads open to him he should follow. He has come to the battle area as correspondent in order to see warfare, and he leaves, pursuing both the military and journalistic vocations while stumbling upon a third—that of historian. This book, devoted to what truly interested him, written in a vivid descriptive style replete with humor, poetic imagery, and reflectiveness (in lieu of character portrayal), is of far greater literary quality than *Savrola*. One of the most charming of his works, the *Malakand* shows Churchill finding his medium.[85]

The road of literature would not take him through fiction writing but through journalism and especially historical memoirs heightened by imagination and style. Just as Montaigne discovered that he, like every one of us, is a microcosm of the race precisely by virtue of his uniqueness, Churchill found that, though each soldier has a tale to tell, his own tale was representative because he had the good sense, the will, and the luck to be everywhere, or at least at the right places at the right time; he also had the inquisitiveness and the writing itch to record it and the style and wit to make it memorable. He had discovered that the proper study of mankind, at least in its political and military endeavors, was himself; that, as he would say in *The Second World War,* facts—when carefully selected and arranged—are "better than dreams" and the author-adventurer himself a better representative of some ideal being, a more appropriate central intelligence or alter ego, than was a projection or dream-figure like Savrola. He had in the process virtually invented a new literary genre of personalized journalism-history, a genre which, thanks to his rich life, he would take far. Though the man still had much to experience, the writer had little left to discover.

In *The River War,* Churchill further capitalizes on his achievement, by adding the dimensions of history and scholarship. The result is another success, a definitive history of a war, even if the length and historical pretensions involve a regrettable loss of charm and philosophical reflectiveness.[86] The *Malakand* is one of Churchill's most literary works, in its striving after "poetic" effects, its many epigraphs, allusions, and quotations, and its references to historical events, but in *The River War* Churchill's reading is not so much paraded as incorporated into the structure and symbolic landscape of the work, as in the use of the Miltonic effects.

Whereas the *Malakand* lacked any clear characters or dialogue, Churchill created in *The River War* several portraits of individuals. And in the Boer War books he introduced a variety of voices —periodic, lively brief dialogues, monologues, even a sort of brief stream of consciousness passage. Too many of the literary, reflective, and historical dimensions found in the two previous works have, however, been purged, making the Boer War books perhaps his weakest nonfiction. Neither of the two major military operations has the epic quality of *The River War.* The four-hundred-mile march in forty-five days of a force of eleven thousand which captures eight towns is curiously without interest or drama. The story is drowned in petty detail, and no human character comes through; officers, soldiers, Boers appear en masse. Abstract descriptions of military maneuvers intertwine with the author's own often casual and trivial movements. For once, Churchill has failed to give his material shape, make it come alive, and impart a vision.[87] When, at the close, he watches with emotion the departure of the troops he has been with, his final words make no impact. This has not been a joint venture. We have no such feeling of melancholy and awe as is generated by the dissolution of a band of men who shared a special adventure with us, as in, say, Xenophon's *Anabasis* or, notably, Conrad's *Nigger of the Narcissus.*

So ends this burst of literary fecundity in the last years of the nineteenth century, this first phase of Churchill's career and writings. De Mendelssohn calls it the period of seeking adventure and absorbing his heritage, of observing what had to be done and what should be recorded. Churchill had compressed an extraordinary amount of adventure into a brief span and, studying war from the command viewpoint as well as fighting it as a junior officer, had crystallized many of his military and political ideas. Some of his plans and dreams were realized as few men's are: establishing a reputation, making friends in high places, proving he could earn his living by his pen, learning to think for himself. He had found three of his major forms of self-expression: fighting wars, writing books, making speeches. With a series of works of popular, somewhat overdrawn, imperialist journalism, he had established himself as a fine storyteller who excelled in description, military narrative, commentary, and in the projection of a personality. Like Tolstoy, he participated in and wrote about minor wars in unconscious preparation for the future composition of massive books on major wars. Now mature, he was ready for bigger things. He sailed home from America at the end of his lecture tour to enter upon a new century, a new reign, and a new career—as politician.[88]

The main theme of these five first books is, ultimately, the nonacademic education of the young Churchill. He has disabused himself of most of the adolescent fantasies about the romance of war and some of the adult Victorian fantasies about the destiny of Europe. He has come to see that the true expression of manhood or adventure is politics rather than physical combat and that the former is needed to forestall the latter. He has at least acquainted himself with the anomalies and ironies of western civilization. He has concurrently developed a sense of the British imperial mission and of the need for this latest Churchill to find his place, and make his mark, within that tradition. But his original dreams have been only transmuted, not discarded. The heat of experience has burned away the reveries of battlefield glory and left a residue of expertise and common sense to be applied to the art of avoiding war or, failing that, of prosecuting it well at the highest levels. Raised in the Victorian era, he moves away from it even while taking a good part of it with him willy-nilly because it is deeply embedded in him. Some Victorian presuppositions he dismisses, some he questions or modifies, and others, despite the shock of experience, he will carry with him for years.

He must now, in his writings no less than in active life, explore and master the new field of politics, which he has known so far only from a distance and from books. Thus had he mastered the military discipline by means of this self-imposed training, which consisted of observing, reporting, and retelling in an analytic, critical, and reflective narrative. The pen was proving to be more than a transition from the casque to the cushion. It helped him gather, sort out, and comprehend his experiences, develop his intellectual life, assay the world around him, discover and express his identity.

One grand Victorian illusion was left him, however, one to which he would cling despite the many storms ahead. Though he had learned from his adventures to distrust the experts, criticize the military and political establishments, purge himself of his reveries of war, and occasionally question the civilized-savage antithesis and the belief in progress, these first books end with vistas of Britannia triumphant, of peace and prosperity, of the restoration of order, law, and progress. But the twentieth century had arrived.

2

The Second Phase:
The 1900s

Filiopietistic Biographer
and Parliamentary Radical

In political philosophy Churchill was at once a radical and a traditionalist
—John Colville, 1968

From the beginning, Churchill was a statesman rather than a politician—A. J.
P. Taylor, 1969

Lord Randolph Churchill:

The Return of the Prodigal Son

After an initial unsuccessful contest in 1899, Churchill was
elected to Parliament in 1900 as Conservative member for
Oldham. The change from a military to a political career was soon
reflected in his other vocation of writing. In July 1902, the family
trustees, impressed by the mastery of style in his published books,
gave him, at his own request, his father's papers, and the erstwhile
war correspondent and chronicler of battles turned to constructing
a massive political biography. It took him three and a half years to
finish this work, amid "some political distractions."[1]

"Distractions" is ironical, for Churchill's activities as a writer
usually harmonized with his military or political concerns. Thus,
in recording that someone during a debate advised Lord Randolph

to move to the other side of the House, Churchill notes cryptically that such "advice is often given and sometimes accepted"[2]—an allusion to his own change from the Conservatives to the Liberals in 1904, during the very composition of this book. Since the biography traces the leftward movement of Randolph, at the time of the author's similar tendencies, we see here a mutual reinforcement. The politician interprets the subject of his book by the light of his own career even as that career is being influenced by the subject.

The thirty-year-old Churchill, his entry into the world of affairs having been eased by his father's name, must proceed on his own. The book is therefore not only an homage to the father never fully known or confronted on equal terms and a revelation to the world of the greatness of the prematurely dead statesman (as well as a means of making money and achieving political and literary fame), but also a discovery of and dedication to the father's values, a study of a political program handed down from one generation to the next within the same family. Churchill was attracted to politics because of his father's career; now he undertakes to investigate, test, and comprehend the new discipline by reviewing and assessing that same career. Bearing the same relation to his own political venture as do the frontier war books to his military one, this biography is in part his equivalent of a university thesis, a display of self-imposed intellectual training. But whereas the frontier war books, growing out of his immediate experiences and journalism, are creations of and for the hour, *Randolph Churchill,* while expressing the new needs of the hour and touching on the author's current initial political forays, is a product of study, a calm, extended venture into the past no less than a charting of the future. And when the biographer writes that Randolph was close to taking the road which "might have ended in Liberalism,"[3] the book clearly becomes a piece of self-justification as well as self-discovery. For, finding himself, like his father, in the wrong party,[4] he must persuade himself that he has been true to his father's ideals, that his father, who never confronted that ultimate political decision, would have approved his change of party or would even have done the same.

Churchill's earlier change from the army to politics is also reflected here. In a book devoid—for the first and only time—of battles and military strategy, Churchill's imagination cleaves still to the art of war, and, reversing the Homeric technique, he weaves war matter into the narrative texture by means of his imagery. In a beautiful extended metaphor, for instance, he compares the record of the Home Rule debates, which seems in 1905 remote and unimportant, to the peaceful site of an old battlefield, every inch of which was once bitterly contested. The hero, moreover, is visualized in soldierly terms. Since political battles now seem to Churchill as consequential as military ones, his father is depicted as a born commander able to separate the vital from the merely important, to exploit the foe's weak points, to choose his ground well, to act peremptorily. As Leader of the House, he was "the general in the field at the head of the army. The other [his chief in the Lords, Prime Minister Salisbury] waited at home, trying to make what he could of the despatches."[5] Having run after the strange god of warfare, the prodigal son has returned home to enter upon the suddenly meaningful vocation of politics, in which his father was an adept and hero.

Despite its vulgarity and shoddiness, modern democratic politics turns out to be a form of domesticated warfare. Churchill is eager to reveal the true dignity of the life which absorbed his father and which he now himself embraces. Granted that election oratory is dreary and that the personalities and arguments of the moment lack taste and truth, yet there is "a real battle for real and precious objects," and that, according to the man who has abandoned his illusions (or rhetoric) about the charms of war and the effeteness of the stay-at-home, is as it should be. Better "popular disputation" and the "laboured progress of the common people in a workaday world than the poetic tragedies and violence of chivalric ages."[6] Heroism, perceptiveness, and leadership can take varied nonmartial forms; one riot during an election campaign or Randolph's savage attacks on Gladstone are, for Churchill, comparable to a "Homeric combat."

If, in his early books, Churchill was awed by the hazards of war, he now discovers other realms to be no less subject to the fickle goddess Fortune. He observes periodically that life, notably British political life, takes surprising turns. In 1877, for instance, the leadership of the Irish party in Parliament belonged securely to Isaac Butt, a brilliant attorney of great prestige and charm, whereas C. S. Parnell was an unknown landlord with a forbidding and inarticulate manner; yet within two years Butt was cast off and broken. Again, who among the "triumphant Liberal array" of 1880 would have predicted that that Parliament would mark the worst period in Liberal history and that in a few years the Conservatives would enter upon long years of power? Or that closure of debate, introduced by Gladstone in 1882 against the will of the Tories, would prove to be a weapon which gave the latter two decades of predominance? Who could have predicted the schism between Radicals and Whigs, the defeat of Gladstone by means of the Irish, the Tory alliance with the newly enfranchised working-class millions, the deleterious effect of the new journalism, the decline of independence among MPs and constituencies and the concurrent growth of the power of ministers in a march "backward along the beaten track": "Who would have listened to such paradox with patience?"[7]

Such surprises cluster around the hero as well. When Randolph Churchill went to the Treasury, the *Times,* "it is amusing to read by the light of afterdays," warned him against "fiscal temptations," and the Liberal press prophesied his repudiation of the economizing he had advocated while in opposition. A further irony was that his subsequent resignation helped bring about the very retrenchment and foreign policy changes that, as minister, he had demanded in vain. In 1889, Randolph suggested two measures— local government and land purchase—which at a cost of £ 100 million would pacify Ireland; more Radical than Tory, such measures were in fact implemented by the Conservative government.

The largest and most surprising reversal is that of Randolph's career itself; a thousand pages are required to elucidate it. In a dazzling rise, young Randolph became popular and powerful in Britain, famous throughout Europe. But ruin just as suddenly overtook him, and the premature end of the protagonist leads to the melancholy thought that much is outside man's control, beyond human design. The future biographer of Marlborough and author of a *History* bristling with the paradoxes and ironies of fate declares, "Men may for a time prosper continually, whatever they do, and then for a time fail continually, whatever they do."[8] The skepticism directed earlier at military experts now addresses itself to political man's power to comprehend, predict, and master his destiny. Because of all the myths about design and plotting, Churchill asserts, few will believe how much is determined by "the caprice of the hour." The future seems always to mock the statesman's leadership and foresight; the letters between Randolph and Salisbury reveal the "utter uncertainty and confusion" in the political world and show how what even sagacious men consider trivial often proves important and vice versa.

Churchill's stated aim is in fact to rehabilitate the reputation of a complex, controversial, misunderstood man left in an ambiguous position. Just as he would undertake during his own political eclipse to celebrate the ancestor-warrior who had not been acknowledged by either party, so does he here, at the very time that he picks up in the House the "tattered flag" of his father, try to vindicate one whose impact on the Tories needs to be "explained, asserted, and confirmed."[9] What ideals informed this strange, brief career? Its general turbulence Churchill attributes to Randolph's ingrained iconoclasm, his independent mind, as well as to his difficulties with "society." Specifically, Randolph's political heterodoxy began and developed with the Irish question and was shaped by his experiences in Ireland as a young man.

Sympathizing with nationalist movements abroad, Randolph eventually came to object to British imperialist expansion and continental involvement. This wish for national passivity was based on a desire for economies in military expenditures, which in turn sprang from his primary commitment to reform at home. His self-sacrifice on the altar of military reduction was meant to dramatize the domestic needs of the country. In 1883, Randolph had first spelled out his program: a social revolution which would efface "wild longings for organic change" by undertaking radical measures under nonradical auspices, such as setting up boards of health and compulsory national insurance, ameliorating the dwellings of the poor, constructing parks, museums, libraries, public toilets. Using arguments which sounded strange coming from a Tory, Randolph lauded the services rendered by philosophical radicals of an earlier generation and indeed appealed for votes on the ground that the Liberal Party in power had turned its back on its own ideals of "Peace, Retrenchment, and Reform." He was no Radical—at least not yet—and when his unsuccessful fight for domestic reform brought him close to Liberalism, the cause of union interposed itself as a barrier to a final break. He is depicted rather as a disciple of the "progressive Toryism" dreamed of by Disraeli.

Basing his views on the credo that low-priced necessities and political stability are interdependent, Randolph defined "Tory Democracy" as a government that is "democratic, aristocratic, Parliamentary, monarchical," and that says, "Trust the people"—even as he had urged, "Trust the Irish."[10] Churchill admits, in another early expression of the "harmony of interests" theme of the *Marlborough*, that moral principle was intertwined with political prudence. As as a result of the extended suffrage, the Tories, needing the trust of the working class, had to shift their power base from the landowners to the city dwellers and to grapple with the mounting complexity of modern life. Victories in the cities in the 1885 election vindicated Randolph's prognosis and encouraged him to greater radicalism. To that end, he later wanted, as Chancellor of the Exchequer, to transfer the tax burden "from comforts to luxuries and from necessaries to pleasures."[11] Such an attitude estranged him from his colleagues, who deemed him a socialist, and, indeed, Churchill finds that Randolph was attracted to the "collectivist view" at the end of his life.

While unable to point to a single concrete achievement by Randolph, Churchill contends that his contribution was noteworthy. He did not pass any great laws; he held three important government posts only briefly; he was certainly not free from error and contradiction, and his unchanging character wrought success in 1880–85 and ruin thereafter. The marvel therefore is not, Churchill reminds us, the brevity of his domination of Tory politics but rather the extent of it. Most of the proposals of his important 1886 Dartford speech became law, and the Irish policy he delineated in 1889 was carried out during the next two decades. Churchill presents a prescient Randolph declaring at the time of his "inflicting on the old gang" the "final blow" of his resignation: "I have mortally wounded myself. But the work is practically done; the Tory Party will be turned into a Liberal Party and . . . produce a governing force."[12] In the preface to the 1951 edition of this book, Churchill declares Randolph to be the one Victorian who survives best, whose vision accords with that of the contemporary world, because he gave the Tories rather than the Liberals the task of fighting collectivism by gaining the allegiance of the workers. Modern historians, while arguing over the meaning and substance of "Tory Democracy," tend to accept this evaluation.[13]

*   *   *   *

Churchill portrays Randolph as a lonely pilgrim. Gladstone held no magic for him, and Disraeli ceased to inspire him; he was contemptuous of Northcote's capacities as Leader and disquieted by Salisbury's resistance to democratic legislation. Fighting his own government as often as he did the opposition, speaking of the party leaders as "the old gang," he often went his "own way, not caring much whether anyone followed."[14] He seemed as much of an intruder and riddle as Disraeli had been.

Facing him was Salisbury, a "master of tactics" who is portrayed as a political Fabius Cunctator or a Tolstoyan Kutuzov, cunningly retreating before a temporarily irresistible force while patiently waiting for that force to burn itself out. There emerges a telling if understated portrait of the archetypal prosaic party man and trimmer, the establishment, orthodox figure who knows the language of this world and thereby wins out over the visionary, the lover, or the poet; Salisbury is one of the mundane Pontius Pilates, Octaviuses, Bolingbrokes arrayed against the Christs, Mark Antonys, Richard IIs—and Lord Randolphs. Philip Guedella indeed suggests that the theme of the book is "the defeat of brilliant youth by unimaginative age,"[15] a theme, we may add, first sounded in the *Malakand* and now dramatized exhaustively. In his father's life Churchill has found a metaphor for his own lover's quarrel with the establishment.

For Churchill did not merely render homage to his father but set out deliberately—after his military *Wanderjahre*—to emulate him. We are not surprised, therefore, that numerous similarities exist between the two careers and personalities or that many words Churchill uses about his father apply to himself as well. Some of the parallels did not become manifest until long after this work (or the autobiographical *A Roving Commission*) was published, but many were only too evident to contemporaries. Although critics have wondered whether some likenesses in temperament, taste, and opinion are not due to Churchill's compulsive need to find himself in his father and his father in himself,[16] the young man indisputably picked up the torch of the prematurely dead father and attempted to fulfill the latter's mission. The composition of this book helped show the way to him and to the world. We can see, for instance, that the sympathetic analysis in *The River War* of the Mahdi's rebellion was probably derived from the father's political philosophy, or, if original, was corroborated by what Churchill now discovered of his father's outlook.

For Randolph, noting local grievances and British folly in India as well as in Ireland, early argued that corrupt governments bring revolutions upon themselves and that the way to forestall the latter is to amend the former. Churchill's examination of the background to the Boer and especially the Irish troubles goes further than his writings on the Mahdi and on South Africa in laying responsibility at the door of the British. In South Africa, the British ignored the Boers' desire for independence until the whole population of the Transvaal arose in arms, and "what the government had denied to justice, they conceded to force." Because negotiations were made from weakness, "all the disadvantages of every conceivable policy . . . were combined."[17] Territory was abandoned without reconciliation being achieved, and the Boers, having made themselves free by their own power, owed Britain no gratitude. It was too late to make a virtue of necessity. Here is the "Either/Or; Too Little, Too Late" motif which will become central in *The World Crisis.*

The Liberal analysis is applied as well to Ireland. As long as the patient, reasonable, law-abiding Isaac Butt led the Irish, the British "listened to his argument with great good-humor, and voted against him when he had quite finished. . . . Never were courtesy and reason more poorly served," because the Irish, according to Churchill's characteristically pessimistic psychology, "received that form of respect which, being devoid of the element of fear, is closely akin to contempt."[18] Thus was the way prepared for the advent of the vigorous, ruthless Parnell. Revolution is, however, ignited not only by a leader or by an educated class animated with nationalism but also—as *The River War* likewise taught—by the masses' sense of deprivation and social evil. The first signs of turbulence may therefore be dangerous if not properly understood, since only "timely concessions and substantial gifts" can stave off trouble. Instead, facing the Land League boycotts and living from week to week, Britain suspended habeas corpus. Churchill calls this remedy "desperate, unwarranted, and ill-chosen," as the outrages were exaggerated and, since they prevented worse crimes, the least of the dangers.

Whether this shrewd analysis is regarded as betraying "softness" on the part of a member of the establishment or "hardness" on the part of a radical ready to justify the Irish resort to stringent measures, Churchill is not guilty of a double standard. If the Irish had good cause, so did the Orangemen. Randolph's appeal to Ulster to resist home rule with force is defended by Churchill on the grounds that men "in earnest" will back their words by any means. Randolph invoked the authority of various famous Liberals in behalf of violent resistance, and Churchill, anticipating an important theme in the *History,* laconically cites Gladstone's defense in 1884 of Chamberlain's threat to march 100,000 men from Birmingham to London in support of the Franchise Bill: "If no instructions had ever been addressed in political crises to the people of this country except to remember to hate violence and love order and exercise patience, the liberties of this country would never have been attained."[19] Although Churchill is consistent, he is oblivious to the fact that such situations, in which either side feels justified in using force, frequently lead to wars. His detached criticism of the British policy in Ireland in the 1880s, moreover, bears little resemblance to the febrile advice he gave the accommodating British government in the 1930s on the handling of the Gandhi movement in India.

The Ambiguous Hero

As in the case of *The River War* (and of only *Marlborough* thereafter), Churchill lays claim to exhaustiveness of scholarly research and definitiveness of result—a massive book which assembles all the evidence, much of it previously unpublished. But for obvious reasons he refrains from probing the subject's private life, and this omission, together with the concentration on the politics of the 1880s, results in an uncertain portrait of Randolph.

Churchill assures us that a key event occurred in 1876: by engaging in his brother's quarrels, Randolph irritated a "great personage" and was for eight years ostracized by the world of fashion. This event "altered, darkened, and strengthened his whole life and character," creating in him a contempt for "Society," rank, and authority, and an inclination to "champion democratic causes." An event of such putative importance for his career is thus laconically handled in half a page, and the tensions of eight years are left unexamined.[20]

Perhaps the most serious complaint to be made about the biographer has to do with his portrayal of his father—like that of himself in the future war memoirs—as a courageous, solitary idealist ready to sacrifice career and reputation, a man consistent amid changing tides of opinion and opportunity. Rarely does Churchill find anything important to criticize in Randolph's career. In the chapter describing Randolph's seizing control of the party machinery, Churchill adopts an uncharacteristically innocent approach. He steers away from the suggestion that Randolph's goal was power: "How far in his secret heart he was determined to go cannot be known."[21] Later, asserting that Randolph had not coveted Northcote's position, Churchill suggests that Northcote had merely decided to retire and that there is less design than caprice in English politics. He depicts Randolph as fighting for his opinions, "not consciously for his own interests. These had followed in the track of the fighting. His advancement had been the result, and not the reason, of his exertions. . . . He *was* the leader at that moment—natural, inevitable."[22] The narrator appears to be saying of Randolph, like Falstaff of the rebels, that "rebellion lay in his way, and he found it." The idea that what some would regard as selfishness was really a harmony of personal, party, and national interests will become the main theme of *Marlborough.*

Churchill continually insists on Randolph's "personal sincerity" on the leading questions. Yet, at one point, we are told that Randolph objected to protection in principle, because low prices are necessary for a democratic constitution, and a few pages later we hear that he was against it on the wholly practical ground that it would not work as a tariff or as a party move. In an 1885 letter, Randolph speaks of using an Irish education bill to pry the

Catholic bishops away from the Parnellites by giving them control of Irish education. This does not sound like Anglican sincerity, political innocence, Tory integrity, or even love of the Irish people. No less calculating seems Randolph's remark that if Gladstone adopted home rule, "the Orange card would be the one to play."[23] An implied harmony of interests is being used to camouflage fickleness or deviousness.

These inconsistencies hardly reinforce Churchill's contention on the resignation crisis that, had Randolph had any duplicitous designs, he would surely have taken precautions and made an effort to rally his friends. The central act of Randolph's political career therefore remains in a dubious light. He insisted on staking his official existence on obtaining what was admittedly a relatively minor reduction in the military budget. Churchill means this to prove his father's unselfishness, but it can just as easily prove his folly: a proud, overstrained man working himself into a corner over trivia and without preparation. Churchill entertains the important question of whether discretion would not have dictated compromise here; had Randolph put away his "pledges and pride," he could have revived them later, for the tide was running in his direction. But, unwilling to allow an administration which mainly he "had called into being" drift to possible war—such is Churchill's construction of the significance of the apparently petty issue—he preferred to make a stand at the outset on behalf of "a pacific and progressive domestic policy."[24] Yet, Churchill's explanation notwithstanding, personal pride and impersonal principle mingled uneasily, and we seem to have here not heroism, but the petulance of a fanatic whose idealism is submerged in his narcissism. Though Churchill insists that "there were no schemes" and that Randolph looked upon his action as the "most exalted" of his life, the evidence can be made to suggest either that Randolph did not expect his resignation to be accepted or that he even hoped to bring down the government and obtain supreme power by means of the resignation.[25]

After his resignation, Randolph had the choice of making a direct assault on the Conservative government or of confining himself to the problem of the military budget. The first alternative was one of courage and consistency, whereas the second would look like an admission of error on the larger issue of national trends. He chose the second, Churchill says, because he declined to make a break with his party over the union question. But another reason is not stressed by Churchill: the desire to gain further power in the party, Salisbury and Smith having intimated that after the estimates Randolph would be able to return to high office. Thus what may have been a sacrifice of principle for the sake of personal ambition is dressed up as noble. Though Churchill is fair enough to print in the appendix Jennings's memoir on his break with Randolph, we are not reassured as to Randolph's virtues when even one of his few remaining political allies accuses him with words like, "the deliberate and treacherous manner in which I have been thrown over, and the utter want of consideration . . . [have] sickened me of political life."[26]

Recent research has shown that the son's need to justify overcame the historian's objectivity and led Churchill to polish his father's grammar, bowdlerize his utterances, and suppress important facts. By all accounts, Randolph seems to have been a neurotic, physically ill, self-destructive man who thrived on reckless and unscrupulous partisanship, a man who, despite ideological pretensions, was without short-range goals other than a desire for power which betrayed him into numerous inconsistencies.[27] Little of this emerges in Churchill's polished, idealized filial portrait, which is meant to be the story of not just another politician but a visionary, of not a mere party squabble but a philosophical struggle of great importance for the twentieth century. For Churchill bases Randolph's claim to greatness on his rare understanding of contemporary tendencies; in the political history of the time, Randolph's predominance of a few years was an interlude without immediate results, but the brevity of his success is not so important as his character and his long-range ideological impact. These presumably endow the tale with the qualities of Greek tragedy.

Yet even if we accept Churchill's thesis—that Randolph was saintly, not Machiavellian or hysterical—what the son does not see is that Randolph's tragic flaw was the inability to compromise typical of the idealist who makes a major issue of everything. His life—his quick rise and fall—was made by ultimatums (or resignations): to his father and future father-in-law over his marriage; to his party leaders over gaining control of the party machinery, and later, over easing out Northcote; to his queen, over her making her son commander-in-chief in India; to foreigners, over claims to Burma. Though all these succeeded, the ultimatum over expenditures, made against too many forces, broke him. Such imperious absolutism is beautiful in the prophet and saint but of limited value in the politician, and the intrusion of this apparently nonpolitical personality into the political arena is the real tragic motif of the book, a motif of which Churchill was unaware. (The book shares this theme with Shakespeare's *Coriolanus;* the parallel is unwittingly underscored by the scene in which even Randolph's formidable and respected mother urges him to soften his stand vis-à-vis Salisbury and the party, in vain.) Churchill is so absorbed by politics, so persuaded of his father's benign political shrewdness, so busy with the chronicling of issues year by year that the broad pattern is missed. What might have been Greek tragedy turns out to be partly unclear and partly unconvincing hagiography.

When the young Churchill, with five sizable, impressive books to his credit, comments somewhat patronizingly on the literary value of Randolph's one book, we suddenly realize that, despite all the adulation, the father and model must have begun to seem somewhat limited in literary, military, and even political endowments to the fast-rising and richly experienced son. Randolph's values and strategies proved, therefore, to have only a partial relevance, and Churchill perhaps did not yet fully see how much more he had already learned about some aspects of politics than his father and how much further he would be able to go.[28] If *Randolph Churchill* is a pathetic tale, *Marlborough* and, in a way, the books on Churchill's own career will be epics with semihappy endings. All three men began with a meteoric rise followed by a fall and a figurative exile. But just as Randolph was about to undertake a return, he was struck down by disease; Winston Churchill, granted longevity and cleaving to his military knowledge as well as to political and diplomatic experience, followed in his ancestor's footsteps and fulfilled in his own career his father's aborted comeback. At thirty, however, Churchill is still shaping himself, and the closing pages of *Randolph Churchill,* dwelling on how events might have taken a different turn if Randolph had lived on and wondering what stand he would have taken on various issues, seem poignantly personal, a son's admiring, questioning glance soliciting guidance in life's vexations from a father whom "I knew so little personally." Churchill wrote this book, then, not merely to tell the world of his father but, as he would write *Marlborough*, to find himself and his future amid the traditions of family, party, nation.

Despite the uncertain vision of the work, the young biographer exhibits in it his great intelligence and mastery of style. Where the early books manifested a grasp of military matters, this one is signally rich in insights into domestic affairs. The young man only a few years in Parliament makes many striking observations on the quotidian political process. His sagacity results no less from quick mastery of his new vocation than from immersion in his father's ideas and era or from close study of history. The book is indeed, along with *Marlborough*, his most sustained study in politics. It is also one of his most "radical" works, with its calm study of Irish nationalism and its sympathetic portrait of the Tory Democrat veering at the close towards something resembling "Tory socialism." Though Tory Democracy may have remained a guideline for Churchill, the focus in his subsequent major works will return to war making, albeit on the international scale.

Contemporaries hailed *Randolph Churchill* as a "literary masterpiece," but its reputation has changed. Critics like Maurice Ashley and J. H. Plumb feel that Churchill, already operating implicitly with the idea that the individual shapes history and with the hypothesis (to be stated later) that history is merely "old politics," writes in pre–Lytton Strachey fashion and portrays only the visible part of the historical iceberg. Plumb notes that Churchill grasps the keys to Randolph's success—the curious rallying of the working class to the Tories, and Randolph's genius in entering upon a dialogue with the new electorate and affecting thereby the Tory leadership and action—but does not ask the question a professionally trained historian would ask: What lay behind this paradox of the proletariat responding to the aristocratic sense of the past? Plumb holds that, without conceptual powers or knowledge of social processes, Churchill would have us believe that the workers came round solely because of one man's efforts and the rightness of his ideas, that, in short, the individual shaped the course of events. In the same way, Churchill seems to simplify his father's complex character by attributing his radicalism to the quarrel with the

Prince of Wales.[29] Because of its deficiencies in sociology and psychology, its innocence of Marx and Freud, the work is not, for Plumb, one of the great political biographies of the age. He finds rather that it is a highly readable, if biased, account of a clash of personalities; an act of piety and justification rather than a detached historical assessment; a work that would now be unread if it had been written by someone else; yet, once these limitations are acknowledged, in many ways the most satisfying of Churchill's books.

Peter de Mendelssohn, noting that between the ages of twenty-four and thirty Churchill published six well-wrought books and during the next two decades only four lesser ones—collections really—remarks on the irony that *Randolph Churchill,* this "most successful literary achievement," both assured the author's literary career and for a long time ended it. Now came active years in high office, in peace and war, prepared for by the ten years of military and political experience, of reading, reflection, and writing. Thus ends, in A. L. Rowse's words, the "long and arduous but immensely varied and enriching apprenticeship."[30] The experiences which were to follow would turn the sometimes facile observer-critic and filiopietistic biographer into a major participant-historian. By allowing politics to displace literature, Churchill prepared the way for a later return to the literary scene with wider scope and with new tales cast into forms he had already developed.

Early Speeches and Travel:

The Tattered Flag

In his short autobiography, *A Roving Commission,* Churchill writes of his youthful envy of those sons of famous British statesman, like Gladstone and Chamberlain, who became comrades in arms to their fathers in parliamentary combats. Fate deprived him of that special pleasure but only to reserve for him an even more dramatic one. Not long after his entry into politics, the House considered a bill to expand greatly the peacetime army. Alone in opposing his own Conservative government, on 13 May 1901 Churchill made his first great oration. In arguing against militarism and for economy, the ex-officer appealed to the very principles on behalf of which his father had resigned and ruined himself. He was proud, he poignantly declared to the House, "to lift again the tattered flag I found lying on a stricken field,"[31] and he proceeded to try to vindicate his father by quoting highly relevant passages from Randolph's fifteen-year-old speeches. Thus the son began his long political journey at a most appropriate juncture.

His maiden speech in the House had been on the Boer War, in which he had recently participated, but his first parliamentary fight was over military expenditure. Six major speeches on the subject were brought out in 1903 as *Mr. Brodrick's Army*. By this time victorious on that issue, he turned during the next two years, as he had predicted everyone would, to the nascent debate on protection. *For Free Trade* is a pamphlet of nine speeches, delivered mainly between June 1903 and March 1905, during the great controversy over economic policy that ended with the "unprecedented" defeat of the Conservatives. In combating "Mr. Chamberlain's food taxes or Mr. Balfour's tariff wars," Churchill reasons closely on economic matters, as he was rarely to do again (except for 1925–29), and yet manages to be interesting.

This grandson of a duke having in the meantime fulfilled a long-standing wish by crossing the floor to become a "radical" or modern Liberal, questions of tariffs and economics then blossomed into the larger social issue which preoccupied Churchill for four crowded years. *Liberalism and the Social Problem* addresses itself to three important topics of the Parliament of 1906: the speeches of 1906–8 deal mainly with the settlement in South Africa and the vindication of free trade; those of 1908–9 project various social reforms and attack the Conservatives, the rich vested interests, and the land speculators; the last group of speeches defends Lloyd George's radical "People's Budget" of 1909 and assails the House of Lords in the constitutional crisis between the two houses which the budget caused.

The People's Rights came out on the heels of *Liberalism* in the last days of 1909 as a political tract for the upcoming "fateful" election, as a compendium of Churchill's ideas on the major Liberal causes. These four volumes therefore reflect the changing national debate, as each issue gradated into a broader one: the Tory desire to enlarge the army necessitated new funds, which some hoped to raise by tariffs; the consequent defense of free trade led to the question of the welfare of the people; the blocking of the ensuing social legislation by the Lords generated a fight over the powers of the upper house. Randolph would have found little to quarrel with in his son's stand on each question; the tattered flag was being carried far along.

If the first two volumes of speeches contain interesting, lucid, clearly structured, sometimes brilliant orations on somewhat dated topics, *Liberalism* is a broad-ranging survey of modern social problems; the issues it discusses are still being fought out today. Its imagery, fervor, rhetoric, variety, compassion, and wit and its careful delineation of the course between the Scylla of Tory reaction and Charybdis of socialism make it a classic exposition of the pragmatic political basis for the Liberal or progressive Conservative outlook. *The People's Rights* follows in the same vein but, instead of a gradually unfolding argumentation, offers succinct paragraphs and sections on individual topics in which bold opening statements are followed by the evidence and by rebuttals of adverse arguments. Its first section, a slashing attack, full of sarcasm and irony, on the presumption of the Lords, is written with Swiftian verve.

The large biography and the volumes of speeches are not the only examples of Churchill's meliorism. To be sure, *My African Journey,* one of his shortest books, seems at first glance to be nothing more than the record of a 1907 trip through some recently acquired British possessions, and no other book of Churchill's arouses so many literary associations. With the journey ended, the dangers passed, and the tale told, the narrator, like the legendary or allegorical voyagers to far-off places, must present mankind with an inspirational message, but Churchill's is not of a religious or moral kind: "Concentrate upon Uganda!" is his advice. Suddenly we are jolted out of the world of travel literature, allegory, or mystic experience, of the exotic and the unexplored, into the familiar civilized world—of politics and diplomacy, imperialism and progress. The brief moral vacation from the official self is over. The message is one which Robinson Crusoe rather than Dante, Christian, or Gulliver might have brought back.

We have actually never been too far from that workaday world. The traveler in Churchill coexists with the politician; the seeker of experience must grind at least some of what he reaps into rational, pragmatic ideas; above all, the white man traversing the dark continent keeps his slide rule handy and ruminates on progress. That firm belief in the superiority of western technology makes Churchill eager to transform the lush world into a modern industrial one; he does not seem to realize that much of what his poetic side responded to would thereby be effaced. In spite of his reverence for tradition and romance, Churchill worshiped modern technology and "the steady progress of development" throughout his life; conditions would be improved by means of machines, not by the old pieties. And while finding socialism irrelevant to Europe, Churchill would not mind trying it out in an African kingdom! No wonder that his conservative contemporaries discerned in some of his ideas "radicalism of the reddest type."

The frontier wars had taken Churchill to distant, romantic places, but the war correspondent rarely found the time to take much note of the exotic. Now, for a change, the lushness of locale and the author's irrepressible curiosity and thirst for sensuous experience are central; though the old adventurism is here, it has become pacific. Churchill will return to Africa on vacation trips and in wartime command crises, but only to North Africa and only briefly. The exotic regions and Britain's civilizing mission will never again occupy the foreground in his books, henceforth to be devoted to British history, European diplomacy, and, above all, the world wars that were to bedevil our century.

*   *   *   *

Thus in the second phase of Churchill's career he implements the exposition of Randolph's politics by his own zealous involvement in social legislation and administrative reforms during a dramatic period in British history. Many have called these political activities an enduring achievement of the first half of his life and a massive contribution to the national heritage. Churchill has helped lay the foundations of the welfare state. What the father but dreamed of, the son first limned with the pen and then helped realize by political action. After going his own way in the 1890s, Churchill has in the 1900s come to terms with his father's spirit.

Having examined the military establishment with a fresh, iconoclastic eye in his first books, having looked beyond convention, routine, and professional expertise to the emergent military realities of the twentieth century, Churchill now submits the political establishment to the same searching scrutiny and testing. In *Randolph Churchill,* he studies the historical background and outlines his father's philosophy; these four volumes, fleshing out and updating his father's vision, constitute a considered statement of his own gradually developed thinking on virtually every aspect of the political scene. In the process, he helps shatter the nineteenth-century political consensus and renovate the meaning of such critical words as "liberal," "welfare," "justice," "government." He is not alone in this effort, of course, for behind him stand his father, Disraeli, Bismarck, even, remotely, Marx, and beside him stand Lloyd George, the Webbs, and others. But whether in Parliament, on the hustings, or on the printed page, Churchill is a formidable, eloquent warrior who expresses himself, no matter whose the idea, in a manner all his own.

After five years as a soldier of fortune, the orator, lawmaker, administrator, minister, diplomat, and coleader of the "radical" new Liberals has found his métier and fulfilled, even surpassed, his father's own political dreams. As Ronald Hyam remarks, from the equivocal personality of Churchill the soldier-journalist-politician, a statesman sprang instantaneously to life, fully developed, mature, and "not easily deterred by apparent limitations to government action."[32] By 1909 he was already the third most important member of the government; no one could say how far he might have gone in a peacetime administration. In 1911, amid gathering war clouds, he was appointed first lord of the admiralty, the minister in charge of the greatest navy in the world. It was a return to the military way of life, albeit to an area of it entirely novel to him. Hitherto, because of his father's isolationism and his radical colleagues' pacifism, he had disliked talk of war and argued against increases in military spending. Now his radical phase abruptly ended. There is something poignant about the way in which this patrician's sympathetic response to poverty and misery left him forever; it was swept aside by his first love, war making, which in turn had in later years to fight with foreign affairs for primacy in his interests. During brief interludes of return to domestic affairs, in the middle 1920s, early 1930s, and early 1950s, the visionary gleam was fled, the paternal legacy dissipated. "War," he had pithily said, "is fatal to Liberalism."[33]

3

The Third Phase:
The 1910s and 1920s

Minister in War and Peace;
Memoirist

Mr. Churchill's war book records a life's disappointment—Peter Wright, 1925

Churchill and the First World War

The long third phase of Churchill's writing career covers the composition and the publication in installments of a single long book, *The World Crisis*. His writing once again reflects a drastic change in values. Recent interests—peacetime parliamentary politics, his father's program, benign British imperial administration, domestic reform—seem to belong to another world. Some themes of his now-remote first phase—British imperial expansion by arms, rebellious subjects in exotic places, the barbarism-civilization antithesis—are likewise defunct. Others reappear here transmuted: the persona who had been an ingratiating soldier of fortune on distant front lines is now a warrior-administrator as busy defending himself and his paperwork against domestic critics as he is planning strategy against foreign enemies. War is no longer a colorful adventure or game but a grim, protracted attrition race.

Yet other themes, gracefully touched on before, turn into veritable obsessions. For example, the ignorance and folly of the modern military experts, who are as usual remote from current battlefield experience, now cost millions of lives; on the necessity of firmness, of doing one thing or its opposite and doing it wholeheartedly, rides nothing less than the outcome of a global war and the future of the world. The forcing of the Dardanelles, a revery in *Savrola* and *Randolph Churchill*, haunts *The World Crisis* from beginning to end, sometimes as an alluring dream of what might have been and often as the traumatic nightmare of what was. This work also implicitly deals with a question periodically hurled at Churchill by professionals: What do *you*—young man and amateur—know about war making? His reply is to champion new or unorthodox ways of fighting: the tank, the attack plane, the convoy system, the amphibious flank-turning movement.

When hostilities began, Churchill, controlling at the age of forty the British navy, the nation's strongest weapon, may well have dreamed of playing a decisive role, especially if things went right in his department. Certainly he felt himself able to be a more effective war leader than "any other living Englishman." Yet, at the close of the period covered by *The World Crisis*, four years after the end of the war, Churchill found himself, in the wake of nearly two decades in high office, without a seat, a party, a leader, or a following. He was once again for a brief time the man of one vocation, alone with his pen, as he had been in 1899, 1904, and 1916. He had, indeed, a lot to explain.

*   *   *   *

As he was halfway through the composition of *The World Crisis*, Churchill happened upon Defoe's *Memoirs of a Cavalier* and was reassured to discover that he had unconsciously followed the example of a master of narrative—stringing the chronicle of great events "upon the thread of the personal experiences of an individual."[1] Churchill's book, therefore, has the somewhat peculiar form established in his early works (the *Malakand* and *The River War*), as the narrative oscillates between a comprehensive view of the "stepping stones of fate," whether in the field, council, or laboratory, and certain of the minutiae of Churchill's life. Providing an outline of Churchill's varied career against the background of international affairs, the book is not an autobiography. Neither is it a record of the war only, for it covers in detail the years 1911–22, when Churchill, in positions of power, was connected with world events. Not pretending to be a historian who, as in the case of *The River War* and *Randolph Churchill,* writes a definitive version, he presents himself rather as a participant (in "subordinate though responsible stations") with his own special contribution to the study of history, and his own doctrines of strategy inform the analysis of events.

His changing political fortunes enabled Churchill to see the war from varied vantage points during crucial periods. He no longer had to thrust himself into the center of the action as he had in the first books; events did that for him. He became, in the verdict of history, an "indispensable" head of the admiralty during three prewar years, when Britain's major weapon was developed and prepared for war, and during the first phases of hostilities, when it promptly established its mastery of the sea and participated in the Dardanelles expedition. Thereafter, while the navy lapsed into a relatively inactive role, Churchill had firsthand contact, as a colonel, with the trench-war deadlock on the western front. In the last part of the war, he ran the Munitions Office, whose large outpouring of new weaponry gave the generals the tools with which to break the stalemate. Then, in the War Office, he could deal with the problems of demobilization and of intervention in Russia which became uppermost at war's end, and in the Colonial Office he confronted the overseas consequences of the peace settlements, as well as the perennial Irish question. Clearly he was justified in writing, "I am telling my own tale."[2]

His tale barely hints, however, at the existence of a sizable body of opinion that regarded Churchill as less than a versatile hero. The narrator appears oblivious of the manner in which his ambition, lack of judgment, obstinacy, dilettantism, instability and audacity irritated many contemporaries. He managed, after all, to offend the Tories, at first by his defection, radicalism, and pacifism, then by his Ulster stand; the Liberals and Socialists by his post-1911 militancy and postwar antibolshevism; the military brass hats by his meddling and his "Eastern" strategy; the press and his colleagues by his extramural activities.

A tactic Churchill uses to enhance his own position (used again in *The Second World War*) is unobtrusively to let stand laudatory passages directed to him in memos dealing with questions of the moment. These add up to an impressive chorus of compliments from prominent persons. General French found his letters "a great help and strength"; Admiral Beatty warned Churchill about the U-boat menace "because you are the one and only man who can save the situation. I would not write thus if I did not know that you with your quick grasp of detail and imagination would make something of it."[3] Amidst his quarrel with the author, Fisher thanked Churchill: "Your splendid stand on my behalf I can never forget when you took your political life in your hands."[4] As everyone turned against Churchill over Gallipoli, the taciturn old Admiral Wilson refused to serve under any new first lord, and Kitchener said to Churchill, "Well, there is one thing at any rate they cannot take from you. The Fleet was ready."[5] Haig's remark that the artillery situation did not become satisfactory until 1918 implicitly points to Churchill's work as munitions minister, while Michael Collins's valedictory message speaks for his peacetime diplomatic talents: "Tell Winston we could never have done anything without him."[6] Not only is Churchill conscious of others' eyes upon himself; his own are there too. To French and to Fisher, he wrote, "We are on the stage of history."[7]

Churchill's ultimate defense against derogatory criticism is his claim, often implicit, that, because of grasp of information, range of vision, quickness of mind, he saw, far more than most of his colleagues, beyond the immediate issues to the long-range developments—that he was, in short, a prophet. This stance came easily to him, both early and late in his career. Along with his record of achievement at Admiralty, Munitions, War, and Colonial offices and his Either/Or analysis, it constitutes a major theme of a work whose refrain (as would be that of *The Second World War*) is, "These conclusions were soon to be sustained by the march of events" or, "This proved true."[8]

His prophecies in military matters are indeed impressive. As the prewar French strategists planned an offensive into Alsace to rupture the impending German invasion via Belgium, Churchill wrote a paper in 1911 which "named the *twentieth* day of mobilization as the date by which 'the French armies will have been driven from the line of the Meuse . . .' and the *fortieth* day as that by which 'Germany should be extended at full strain internally and on her war fronts,' and that 'opportunities for the decisive trial of strength may then occur.' . . . Both these forecasts were almost literally verified three years later by the event."9 Balfour called it "a triumph of prophecy," and historians agree that this "astonishingly accurate" prediction by a thirty-seven-year-old home secretary lecturing his naval and military colleagues is a classic military document and one of the most prescient he ever penned.10

He predicted as early as December 1914 that neither side would be able to penetrate the other's lines in the West, that the side which risked most to do so would put itself at a disadvantage, and that "several hundred thousand men" would be spent "to satisfy the military mind on the point."11 In August 1915, when the British yielded to French pressure to initiate a new offensive, he projected 300,000 casualties, which was in fact the cost of the Loos-Champagne operation. During the Somme offensive, the cabinet being assured that German losses exceeded Allied, Churchill, though then out of the government, applied his experience to all the information he could gather and estimated a terrible toll. "The experts," he concludes, "were frequently wrong. The politicians were frequently right." Historians have confirmed most of his claims, some even going so far as to say that he was the only one in Asquith's cabinet who had the ability to anticipate events, clear ideas of what to do in war, and the will to act on his ideas.12

While at the admiralty, indeed, he used his authority to try to fulfill some of his prophecies himself. Crucial here is his October 1911 memo on the need for scientific preparedness in the navy as a new factor in affairs. Although he himself invented nothing, he presents himself as a midwife to many novel constructions; with an appreciation, absent then in most of the politicians and generals, of the role of science in modern warfare, he devoted himself to closing the gap between inventors, who had only to be informed of military needs, and soldiers, who had little idea of what technology could provide. He boasts that the admiralty was on the track of most of the major inventions of the war—often despite the military experts and in advance of every other nation. Thus does he scatter throughout *The World Crisis* evidence of his proficiency and his credentials for criticizing the men who conducted the war.

The Failure of the Military "Brass Hats"

Churchill's return to the subject of war in fact marks a renewal of his old quarrel with the military professionals, whom he accuses of conservatism and blindness. The major new strategic factor was the increased firepower—in rifles, artillery, the novel machine guns—which enabled the defense to stop superior armies and to exact a toll of three enemy casualties for every man lost. Churchill (and some of the British generals) had learned this in the Boer War; the French and German generals, schooled in offense, were unaware of it. The French should have allowed the Germans to attack and dissipate their strength by exposure to firepower on French soil. Instead, Joffre took the offensive and soon was in full retreat, even as the attacking Austrians were in Russia.

In the Franco-Prussian War, the Germans had already abandoned costly frontal attacks and begun to use turning movements executed on the flanks, but in the winter of 1914, when the battle subsided into a deadlock of trenches from Switzerland to the North Sea, there were for the first time no flanks to turn, and the defensive weapons were even stronger. The use of artillery to cut barbed wire defenses removed the element of surprise from the attack and made the ground impassable, thus substituting one obstacle for another. Despite these realities, the Allies undertook most of the offensives in three fruitless years of a war of exhaustion, and as a result they lost two or three men for every German casualty. According to Churchill, they ignored the lessons of the great generals of history, who won by maneuver and unexpected stratagem instead of slaughter.

One political and strategic way out of the impasse was the vast turning of the flank that Churchill considered the Dardanelles expedition to be. The three main facts at the beginning of 1915—the deadlock in the main theater, the need to relieve Russia, and the possibility of great amphibious operations on the flanks—pointed to a move in the Balkans, where four small states with armies totaling 1,100,000 men were natural enemies of Turkey and Austria. With British guidance and naval supremacy, the Allies could have destroyed the 700,000-man army of a Turkey as yet cut off from Germany; seized Constantinople; turned the German flank and attacked the weakest foe (Austria) at its weakest point; opened the Danube; rescued Serbia; aided Russia; brought Italy, with her two million-man army, in on the Allied side; and saved countless lives. Also, Britain would have become irresistibly the leader of the alliance.

As early as August 1914, Churchill had thought of using the British fleet to clear Gallipoli for the Greek army, which had been placed at Britain's disposal, but politics supervened. In 1915 he counseled a cessation of offensive action in the West, where time would be on the Allied side if the Germans were allowed to wear themselves out with abortive attacks on the trenches. If troops could not be spared from the West, he proposed initially to force the straits solely with old surplus battleships and to withdraw should the attempt prove unfeasible. Such a naval attack would lack certainty but would involve limited costs and risks. Soon, however, the government drifted into an uncoordinated and dilatory military commitment, and Churchill claims to have denied responsibility for any army operations there. Three separate opportunities having been fumbled, the Dardanelles expedition eventually foundered, while, on the only front available thereafter, the Germans, he insists, were actually strengthened by each Allied offensive (from the July 1916 Somme to the November 1917 Paschendale).

A half-century later, Churchill's account (first written, as a vindication of his role in the tragedy, for the 1916 Royal Commission inquiry and probably the germ of this entire work) of what he thought one of the great campaigns in history is necessarily incomplete, its impressive eloquence notwithstanding. His version overstates a "good case," says R. R. James, and must be "approached with caution." It takes little account of the gulf between himself and his admirals and does not sufficiently indicate the utter lack of planning and preparation in an amphibious project requiring great coordination.

The controversy between the "Westerners"—the generals, who believed that there should be no diversion of forces from the main front in France, where the enemy had to be defeated—and the "Easterners"—the (mainly heterodox) politicians, who, eager to end the bloodletting in France, sought indirect routes into Central Europe through the eastern Mediterranean—raged during and after the war and has been continued since by historians. Noting that no supplies were available to be sent to Russia, that the loss of Turkey would have aided, not hindered, Germany, and that there existed neither an easy road nor an army to use it from Constantinople to Central Europe, A. J. P. Taylor describes Gallipoli as constituting no more of a back door into Germany than did the far better port of Salonika, in which a large mass of Allied troops idled the war away. Trumbull Higgins argues similarly that a victory in Gallipoli could have been obtained only by a complete halt of British operations in France, which Kitchener, like Lloyd George later, could not bring about for political reasons. Victory, moreover, would have sucked in yet more troops from the West, which, according to Higgins, was actually Germany's weakest front. Higgins claims that the basic fallacy of the "Easterners" in seeking a theater where the Germans could not get at the Allies was that the Allies would not be able to get at the Germans either; there was no alternative to "killing Germans." This "strategy of evasion," concludes J. F. C. Fuller, diverted nearly a million troops in the Middle East and Africa without affecting the German strength.

Many statesmen and historians, on the other hand, have remarked on the irony that Churchill's greatest failure may well have been a stroke of genius: the finest strategic conception of either world war, it was a potential turning point of history; had it succeeded, Churchill would have been the hero of the war. They blame Kitchener, Asquith, or the cabinet for the failure of Churchill's plan, because the fault lay not in the conception but the execution. James, ascribing this belief to the postwar reaction against the triumphant "Westerners" and the incredible toll of the war, believes that the rehabilitation of Churchill (which began with his massive and eloquent self-defense in *The World Crisis*) has led to a romanticization of an imaginative but tragically flawed idea. Everyone indeed agrees that Churchill should not have been made the scapegoat, but neither was he blameless, for, though more catalyst than villain, he forced the plan on a government unable to carry it out. His initial specious pleading caused his subsequent sound either/or advice to be disregarded, and the expedition could not succeed, Higgins declares, "on any of the terms actually available." Here is, then, according to Garvin, Churchill lacking the power to coordinate everything; or, according to Taylor, Churchill at his best and worst, persuasive, impatient, exaggerating, obsessive; or, according to Higgins, Churchill seeking political results without a military victory; or, according to James and to Marder, Churchill overestimating his own knowledge and capacity, overlooking the practical difficulties in the implementation of his grand strategy, rushing into an unsound gamble without preparation and coordination and without knowing what to do next. Here, at last, is the activist but erratic Churchill finding himself, like his father in 1886, completely isolated.[13] The resulting self-justification is the most comprehensive and plausible statement of a strategic alternative to the impasse in the West; whether that alternative was a pipe dream or a real possibility remains of necessity an insoluble question.

*   *   *   *

The political-strategical way out of the deadlock having been frustrated, Churchill, according to his tale, turned all his energies to a technological-tactical solution he had concurrently been working on. Obstacles created by machines could be overcome, he reasoned, not by preponderance of numbers but by other machines which would restore the offensive rights of the stronger side. If the superior fleet was paralyzed by the mine and the torpedo and the superior army by the machine gun, the solution was to interpose a plate of steel between the ship and the torpedo, between the soldier and the bullet. The practical applications of this principle were the monitor (or "blistered ship") and the tank and, used in conjunction with them, smoke and gas. Churchill claims to have thought about all this in 1914, but it was to be three years before his ideas were accepted and applied.

After three separate experimental tank models failed, the "high and technical and professional authorities" of the Ordnance Department returned a negative report in early 1915, and the tank idea seemed dead—except in the mind of Churchill. The three elements at hand—bulletproof armor, the internal-combustion engine, and the caterpillar system—had only to be fused. Withholding all information from the unreceptive Ordnance Department, the War Office, the Treasury, and even the admiralty, Churchill budgeted on his own responsibility £ 70,000 for this highly speculative experiment which no prominent official would have approved. Had the tank idea been abortive, "I could have offered no effective defence to the charge that I had wasted public money on a matter which was not in any way my business."[14] The gravity of the situation and his conviction that he was on the right track are his defense, but only the subsequent successes made that defense valid.

He concludes that, thanks to the new machinery, in 1918 the stronger armies recovered their prerogative to advance without undue losses. He was already involved in the closely contested scientific race with the foe which, greatly accelerated in the later conflict, he would call the "Wizard War." The moral of his tale is that he, with his curiosity, confidence in his own judgment, and willingness to run risks, played a central role; others had the ideas but not the authority or persuasiveness—or the audacity to lecture prime ministers, cabinet members, and generals on military matters and foreign policy. His consequent love of power was not for the sake of lording it over others, he claims, but in order to be able to get things done, to break through bureaucratic routines, to confront researchers with doers, to harmonize conflicting wills. In modern war, an official position connected with the services is like the command of an army. He sees himself as having rushed into "hazardous or forlorn" tasks because he alone could direct a complex enterprise which "otherwise would have had no common connecting center."[15] And, with only slight modifications, historians indeed credit Churchill's unique hospitality to scientific ideas and ability to translate thought into action with being the operative impulses behind the tank, one of the great developments in warfare. In turn, they criticize the generals for being blind to the value of the tank and to Churchill's brilliant advocacy of it.[16]

Not only does Churchill's analysis run counter to the military doctrines of the day, but he reinforces it with harsh judgments on the war staffs of every country and every branch of the military.[17] Though the officer knew well how to move his troops or ships, wrote Churchill, the limitation of his scientific knowledge and his entrenched ways made him inept in the novel situations created by technology which required "the aid of the Statesman, the financier, the manufacturer, the inventor, the psychologist."[18] The generals were so backward as still to think of cavalry break-throughs and to block alternative expedients like Gallipoli or the tank. The critique in the frontier war books of the military mentality is thus vastly developed in *The World Crisis* because the follies of the generals were magnified and costly in this long, bloody war. The championing of the amateur viewpoint against the professional, of the broad against the specialized, had more credibility in the postwar years, especially coming from the one minister who had studied war intensively and had offered strategic alternatives.

One problem of the military was the fact that many leading generals were ignorant of the battlefield conditions. Churchill himself took every opportunity to visit the front, where he observed the "ignorance of Staffs and Cabinets" amid the novel warfare, and he even attempted to become a pilot in order to understand certain questions of policy. Consequently he fears that the age of great commanders is gone forever. Instead of participating in battle like Marlborough or Napoleon and deciding the fate of empire by the gestures and resolves of a few hours, the modern generals sit in quiet, dreary offices surrounded by clerks reading disconnected reports while far away thousands of soldiers are slaughtered. War now drives away or destroys the sensitive, imaginative generals and leaves in charge the insensitive ones, who endure because they are "blockheads." Churchill's prophecy came true, indeed was fulfilled partly by him: "Next time the competition may be to kill women and children, and the civil population generally, and victory will give herself in sorry nuptials to the spectacled hero who organizes it on the largest scale."[19]

All this adds up to a portrait of the professional military mind as scathing as that in Tolstoy's *War and Peace*. (It is worth noting that the critique of Germany's taking on Russia, as well as Belgium and thereby Britain, amid unfinished business was to be ignored by Hitler.) As in the case of Gallipoli, the verdict of history on Churchill's thesis that, as J. M. Keynes puts it, the officers were wrong "on the weight of the argument beforehand and of the evidence afterward" is ambiguous. Everyone acknowledges that the generals—as usual—prepared for the previous war, and military historians criticize Haig's strategy. But the fact is, many have remarked, that Germany lost heavily in the West during 1915–17, and the suspicion remains that she could have been defeated only there. Moreover, as Esher pointed out in 1917, Churchill's attempt to curtail all offensives pending the arrival of the Americans overlooked the moral and political factor of doing nothing during a summer and winter from which the people expected results—an oversight, we may add, on the part of one who insisted that in war politics and strategy are one. Churchill, having attended prewar German, French, and British army maneuvers and having dreamed of—and several times asked for—the chance to lead armies, was in 1916–17 also in the curious position of being a former low-echelon army officer with the cross of Gallipoli presuming to lecture the top brass; his apparent dilettantism and temerity naturally irritated everyone.

But Lloyd George, Attlee, and Liddell Hart remind us that serving as the catalyst in 1915 for the two great attempts to break the deadlock in the war, he provided the only imaginative strategic idea (Gallipoli) and the only tactical weapon (the tank) of the war. In addition, one must point out, his ideas on war making were unusual; he actually made far more inventive and viable innovations in World War I than he did during World War II. Indeed his two major contributions to the latter war—the tank landing craft and the Mulberry artificial harbor, which were well used in the Normandy landings of 1944—date from his 1917 memos.[20]

The Binary Logic of a Pachyderm

Diplomats fare no better than generals in Churchill's book; the advent, conduct, and aftermath of the war bespeak their failure. But European diplomacy being, unlike military enterprise, a field to which Churchill has hitherto given little thought, his discussion of the subject lacks his typical clarity and surefootedness. Yet he does not rest content with his extended negative critique of both the military and civilian leaders. In addition to offering and implementing during the war concrete alternatives like Gallipoli and the tank, he now suggests a method of analysis to clarify men's thinking, a modus operandi applicable to the problems faced by all generals and statesmen. Both their failures and the way out can be delineated by this philosophical principle, which, having appeared sketchily in his first books, becomes a veritable obsession here. It is the first of the four grand themes that inform respectively each of his four huge works *(The World Crisis, Marlborough, The Second World War,* and the *History).*

The political failure of the Allied anti-Bolshevik drive, like the military failure of the original German onslaught in the West, Churchill accounts for by the principle of Either/Or. In the earlier case, Germany should have decided at the outset whether to concentrate on France while holding off Russia, or vice versa. Attacking Russia first would have been wiser, but having attacked France, the Germans vacillated. In order to crush France in six weeks by numbers and speed in a wheeling movement through Belgium, they should have cut the eastern forces to a minimum and yielded territories to the Russians and even to the French in Alsace. Instead Von Moltke shifted one-fifth of the invading force to the defensive in Alsace and acceded to Austria's desire for an offensive against Russia. The latter choice forced him later to move two army corps to the eastern front and led to the defeat on the Marne. By trying to do well on both fronts, he fumbled on both, whereas he could have succeeded in both, one at a time. "Prudence and audacity may be alternated but not mixed."[21]

This "commonest of all the great military errors," easy to perceive and yet difficult to avoid, was repeated on the Austrian front, where Von Hötzendorf had to decide between concentrating on Russia or Serbia. "To choose either, is to suffer grievously in the neglected theater. To choose both, is to lose in both. . . . A score of good reasons can be given not only for either course, but also for the compromises which ruin them. But the path to safety nearly always lies in rejecting the compromises." The Austrian, in lieu of making one of his armies fight *"somewhere* at the crucial moment," allowed it to drift; it left one front before doing anything substantial and arrived at the other in time to participate in defeat.[22]

The same error was at work in the Allied camp. Churchill had wanted Britain to lead the Balkan states against Turkey and Austria, while Grey had hoped for ties with Turkey. The resulting indecisiveness was fatal. "In the end we had all the evils of both courses and the advantages of no course": Britain was forced into war with Turkey without any Balkan confederation.[23] The supreme example of this mistake was the Dardanelles expedition. The choice was between using from the very beginning an army of some 150,000 troops, with excellent chances of success, or confining oneself, because of the rawness of the troops, to naval attacks alone. Instead, the government oscillated between the two plans. "Either course was painful; but both were sound and practical. . . . Kitchener did not make up his mind, . . . drifted into both, and was unable to sustain either."[24]

The reshuffled cabinet then hesitated between Salonika and Gallipoli. Asquith, committed to the latter, compromised by letting six divisions from France be sent to Egypt rather than to either Balkan front. Decisiveness would have disrupted the government, but better "let one section or the other carry out their view in its integrity"[25] than have makeshift unity paralyze executive action by causing the provisional adoption of half-decisions or the postponement of final decision. Britain had had to decide "one way or the other" about Gallipoli.

This principle was later operative in other Allied theaters. The Rumanians, unable to decide whether to seize Transylvania or defend themselves against the invading Bulgarians, moved ineffectively into the former and crumbled before the latter. The British campaign in Palestine, like Gallipoli, was a drain on the main front in France because "enough was sent East to be a dangerous dispersion, and never at one time enough to compel a prompt conclusion."[26] Similarly, in postwar diplomacy, President Wilson's attempt to play the role of idealist abroad and caucus politician at home "in double harness" undid him. In the Irish crisis, Britain made a sudden sharp reversal of policy which might seem foolish to superficial judgment, but, though a good case can be made for either a violent or a pacific approach, "nothing in sense or mercy could excuse weak compromises between the two."[27]

This, then, is Churchill's formula. Nearly all men strike the Either/Or stance at some time, and moral absolutists do so often, but hardly anyone else has done it so rigorously in one book. A central tradition of the West, as expressed in Judaism, in the mainstream of institutionalized Christianity, in Aristotle and Horace, in St. Thomas of Aquinas, in English and American political traditions, has stressed moderation, compromise, the golden mean. It was Machiavelli who, as a pioneer expositor of a secular political science, insisted (as Kierkegaard later did in the moral-religious sphere) that the middle way is fatal, that only extremes of severity or gentleness lead to success. In this respect, Churchill was a Machiavellian.

The failure to grasp the principle invariably leads, in Churchill's analysis, to a sad corollary, which he summarized in one of his World War II speeches as "too little and too late" or, in the words of a 1915 memo, "We have always sent two-thirds of what was necessary a month too late."[28] Thus, had Kitchener gone into Gallipoli with full force at the very beginning, he would, Churchill believes, have triumphed, and at a far smaller cost "than was afterwards wrung from him." Every ship, man, and ammunition round needed for the early stages of the Dardanelles campaign had to be painfully extracted from the plentiful supply on the western front; far greater amounts were subsequently sent "without evil consequence"—but by then it was too late. Two or three more divisions in the April landings could have broken the Turk defenses. "Where was the extra Army Corps that was needed? It existed. It was destined for the struggle. It was doomed to suffer fearful losses in that struggle. But now when its presence would have given certain victory, it stood idle in Egypt or England."[29] In short, the enterprise drifted because the opposition to it was too weak to obstruct each step fully but strong enough to delay it. Hence the army arrived "too late and ill-organized to deliver its own surprise attack, but in plenty of time by its very presence to tempt the Navy to desist from theirs."[30] When it finally evacuated, the government was ready to lose 40,000 troops, though it had earlier been reluctant to lose a handful of men and some old ships for the sake of an important victory. Churchill concludes sagely: "The risks that men are prepared to run in relation to circumstances present some of the strangest manifestations of psychology. One tithe of the hardihood they display to escape disaster would often certainly achieve success. . . . While time is young, while prospects are favorable, while prizes inestimable may be gained, caution, hesitancy, half measures rule and fetter action. The grim afternoon of adverse struggle alone brings the hour of desperate resolve."[31]

The corollary operated in other theaters as well. In late 1915, Britain offered Rumania and Greece a 200,000-man army. "Such a spirit manifested three months earlier would have prevented the disasters by whose imminence it had been evoked. . . . But now these immense offers, not arising from foresight but extorted only by the pressure of events, fell upon deaf ears."[32] In 1917, Haig prevailed on the cabinet to back his futile Paschendale offensive rather than to aid the Italians. The result was the Caporetto disaster, which forced the Allies to transfer ten divisions and two of their best generals to Italy—a group which, sent earlier, would have forestalled the debacle. In a late 1917 paper, Churchill urged the building up of reserves and tank forces in place of a sprawling army, but these unpopular proposals were adopted only "after the catastrophe of March 21. Taken in January, they would have prevented it."[33]

Politics and diplomacy were conducted no better. At the beginning of the peace conference, Wilson insisted on open meetings of all twenty-six allied nations. As a result, two months passed in which nothing was accomplished, while world crises simmered. At last, "guided by common sense and the force of facts," Wilson locked himself up with Clemenceau and Lloyd George and settled every important problem. Had the meetings taken place earlier, the peace conference would have thrived. "He had begun by rejecting the obvious and easy. He welcomed them warmly when they returned to him upside down after many days."[34]

The time to have given the Irish home rule would have been at the beginning of the world war, but the idea was resisted by statesmen who afterwards found themselves in much worse circumstances signing the Irish Treaty of 1921. The Irish conscription question was likewise so handled that "we had the worst of both worlds, all the resentment against compulsion and in the end no law and no men."[35] The postwar intervention in Soviet Russia failed because the Allies could not decide between full support of anti-Bolshevik forces or an honorable peace with the revolutionaries. "Half-hearted efforts to make peace were companioned by half-hearted attempts to make war."[36] The Allies decided at last to support General Kolchak, but had they done so six months earlier, when such a move was just as desirable, they would have had twice the power available. In all the hesitant foreign interventions in Russia, "enough foreign troops entered Russia to incur all the objections which were patent against intervention, but not enough to break the then gimcrack structure of the Soviet power"; they "did the utmost harm and gained the least advantage."[37]

The trouble is, Churchill implies, that men in general, politicians and military men in particular, are unable to face painful choices; what they can obtain early by acting quickly and taking some risk they are prone to forfeit later at leisure and great cost. Only the shock of adversity, of violent blows, awakes them from their illusions. The true statesman is one who initiates policies which may be disagreeable and unpopular but which he can still master, who acts early out of wise choice rather than later under duress and humiliation, when matters have passed out of his control. And greatness consists in seeing quickly the options and the need for action instead of indulging in wishful thinking; in having the courage to override the "experts," tutor public opinion, run the necessary risks, and face the consequences; in acting when one can, not when one must.

Devastating as this critique of human obtuseness and pusillanimity often is, it rests on the assumption that choices at either extreme were in the realm of the possible and that they would have led inexorably to success. With the wisdom of hindsight, Churchill overlooks ways in which, because of the information available or the mood of the moment, the alternatives were not really visible or viable and ways in which a move to one of the extremes he urges might have run into new and unforeseen obstacles or been foiled by fortuitous events. What the alternatives and the mean between them are, moreover, may be a subjective matter; perhaps the men who made the decisions Churchill disapproves of saw themselves as taking extreme steps. Nor can we be sure that there were not third or fourth options which Churchill, content with the oversimplifications into which his binary logic betrays him, may have conveniently overlooked.

He also ignores the possibility that civilization may have muddled through so far precisely because men have tended to compromise rather than hasten to the extremes in settling conflicting interests—and that it might indeed have done better if there had been more rather than less compromise. The air of sweet reasonableness with which the Either/Or principle is forwarded is, furthermore, misleading. We can well imagine the howl Churchill would have raised if history had taken him at his word and chosen the "no" end of the antithesis—not gone into Gallipoli or Soviet Russia at all. Churchill is really striking the stance of all idealists or absolutists (of the Right or the Left) who, confronted with a setback, assert that it is due not to their principles but to the fact that their principles were not fully tested or applied. As S. L. A. Marshall observes, Churchill's declaration, "not to persevere was the crime," is based on ignorance of the obstacles and, more important, is the "dangerous position of the man who has promised victory if things are done his way."[38]

The Either/Or principle was often and dramatically violated in wartime, Churchill believes, because Britain's parliamentary institutions underwent insufficient change. Different situations require different procedures; ignoring or postponing difficult decisions in peacetime may well be wise, because compromises and indeterminate courses, by satisfying various interests, often keep the nation undisturbed or allow apparently insoluble problems to fade away. But in war, when men are destroyed because their leaders cannot decide, when peace is won at the council but lost on the battlefield, "things explode" unless looked to.

War presents another difficulty. Since he is often told what he wants to hear, a leader inclines towards optimism. In peacetime, he is corrected by the parliamentary opposition, which zealously "assembles all the worst possible facts, draws from them the most alarming conclusions, and imputes the most unworthy motives."[39] In war, Parliament must not betray secrets, and the chiefs of services have no balancing apparatus comparable to Parliament. Their staffs, subordinate to them, are moved by loyalty and the desire to win favor. Hence many mistakes can be avoided only if the issues of strategy are fought out in secret sessions of Parliament.

Another wartime need, in Britain and among the Allies, was a strong centralized authority, such as Churchill and Fisher achieved at the admiralty. At the beginning of hostilities, there was no clearinghouse of problems, no conference of Allied civil and military leaders. Armies and navies dwelt in separate compartments; the Allies pursued separate courses. War, which, Churchill insists, knows no rigid divisions among services or nations, or between strategy and politics, was dealt with piecemeal. Because power was widely disseminated, "unsatisfactory compromises" were arrived at only after protracted discussions. A single leader is more likely to make daring Either/Or moves if given the elbow-room; Churchill himself was prepared to sanction the running of risks.

To enunciate the principles of Either/Or and of strong-man leadership results in, or springs from, a hardness of outlook, a no-nonsense, thick-skinned, sometimes obtuse attitude. This is indeed one of the most characteristic traits of Churchill, the tough-minded bulldog-faced opponent of "appeasement." In the prewar arms race, Germany, he insisted, could not be deterred from her course by Britain's abstaining from countermeasures; the Germans would only regard such passivity as effete. During the 1912 crisis, Churchill made a bellicose speech which raised an outcry in the Liberal press and in Germany, but a British emissary, he proudly notes, declared the speech to have been a great help in his negotiations with the Germans. When the climactic crisis began, Churchill, without consulting the cabinet, sent the fleet to its war station, in order to give every German authority "the greatest possible interest in avoiding a collision with us."[40] He insists that his seizure in 1914 of the two battleships being built in Britain for the Turks, much criticized as estranging Turkey, "nearly made her our ally."[41] After the war, and again after World War II, Churchill wanted the Allies to make a speedy settlement, for the power of the statesmen and the unity of the Allies would decline as their armies dissolved and domestic politics supervened.

He was always ready to retaliate doubly against the foe for any dastardly act or to use such an act as reason for tougher measures. In the Gallipoli campaign, citing Turkish massacres of Armenians and the absence of British prisoners, he criticized the "sentimental-ity" which forbade the British use of gas against the Turks. Nor would he scruple, as others did, at violating Italian neutrality (to attack a German cruiser in Messina), Dutch neutrality ("which kept the Rhine open for Germany and closed the Scheldt to Antwerp"[42]), or Turkish neutrality and the ultimatum period (to attack the *Goeben*). He implicitly defends the infamous Black and Tans' counterterrorist activity by likening it to the tactics Chicago or New York police use against gangsters, and he portrays himself as having been ready to advocate "the most unlimited exercise of rough-handed force" on the Irish. For Near East difficulties, the solution was not Wilson's idea of a commission of inquiry—however applicable that might be to American or British domestic problems—because statesmen in a crisis, like generals in war, must often act upon limited information. Similarly, Britain should have compelled Greece and Turkey to come to terms: "There are cases in which strong measures are the only form of prudence and mercy. . . . Knock their heads together until they settle. Such was my counsel. . . . Necessary minor but rough measures had to be taken."[43]

No misapplied democratic or Christian sentiments tempt Churchill in foreign policy. He lectures the pacifist in us: talking about and striving for peace is good, but understanding the causes which lead to war is better. If either side in a dispute reveals its desire for peace, it proclaims its "impotence of will and hand" and makes disaster certain. Hence he regretted the "disproportion" between British policy and strength, and he was the first to urge conscription, even before the war. The gathering of British forces against Turkey in 1922, he is sure, avoided a new war and won the respect of the Turks; had Britain declared that it would not fight in any event, peace would have been elusive. By contrast, Wilson's "idealistic" delay in bringing America into the war cost millions of lives.[44]

Thus his politics of firmness and militancy—already visible in his first books (notably the *Malakand*) and to become famous or infamous in the 1930s and late 1940s—becomes a leading motif here, in conjunction with the Either/Or principle. Churchill's analysis may well be correct, but his language is exactly like that of the nationalists and radicals he often opposed, and if he and they had their way, wars would probably be even more frequent than they are. He seems oblivious of the moral ramifications of his position. He blandly says of other prewar leaders, "Every statesman has been at pains to show how he toiled for peace, but was nevertheless a man of action whom no fears could turn from the path of duty. Every soldier has found it necessary to explain how much he loved peace, but of course neglected no preparations for war," without seeing that his own viewpoint makes him also an accomplice in the drift to war.[45] He overlooks the fact that bellicosity is just as likely to harden as to pacify the other side.

His thick-skinned attitude, no less than the shocks of the war experience, help render questionable the idea of progress. Perhaps because of his own role as stimulant and sponsor of technological advances in war making, Churchill exhibits here marked doubts about that popular idea. Severity is necessary because men have grown more destructive. When recording the aging Emperor Franz Joseph's scorn for the proliferating laborsaving devices and machines of speed, he observes that such "unfashionable opinions" have not yet been disproved. Civic strife in Austria Churchill ascribes to the gifts of modern times: universal education, democratic institutions, a wide franchise, compulsory military service. Rampant nationalism has replaced the vacuum formed by the decline of religion. The modern press, exercising power without responsibility, has whipped up public frenzy and discredited the political leaders.

Churchill begins *The World Crisis* with the reflection that in Victorian days, British statesmen thought they had come through great dangers into a secure and prosperous age. Yet since the Jameson Raid in 1896 (which nearly coincided with Churchill's Cuban trip and his entry into the arena of world affairs), "nothing has ever ceased happening."[46] On the very eve of war, many believed that the systems of alliances, checks, and diplomacy could achieve universal peace; war seemed antiquated. What followed instead of a golden age was "no ordinary war," but life-or-death struggle which aroused horrible passions and threatened civilization itself. Modernity and progress have in fact vastly increased the suffering caused by the "quarrels of nations." Having acutely predicted in 1901 that a European war would be long and exhausting, he now declares, as he will during the rest of his career, that in this "sinister" century, war has become for the first time the potential destroyer of the human race. Yet that threat has brought no end to the world crisis; this modern world in which the "affairs of Brobdignag are managed by the Lilliputians"[47] has merely "entered upon that period of Exhaustion which has been described as Peace."[48] There has simply been no more progress in diplomacy and statesmanship than in generalship.

In his frontier war books, in *For Free Trade,* and in *My African Journey,* Churchill, while expressing reservations, in the main subscribed to the belief in progress. In his "radical" phase, he was too immersed in trying to bring about social progress to bother much with the larger philosophical question. But World War I was as traumatic to him as to all the other thinking men of his generation, and, though he did not draw the grim conclusions many literary intellectuals did, his succeeding works would contain as a leitmotif—often in jarring juxtaposition with his scientific meliorism—the theme of a vanished world, an innocence lost, in contrast to the horrible century the human race has stumbled upon and must somehow negotiate passage through.

The Strategies of a Memoirist

Despite its obvious strengths, *The World Crisis* is an imperfect work. The shifts from impersonal, broad narrative to "the personal thread," from far-flung regions and gigantic events to the familiar furnishings and domestic ambience of Churchill's mind and of English council chambers are not satisfactory. If the book is autobiographical, the discussions of distant battles and fronts which did not impinge on Churchill's career are irrelevant, and his career as battalion commander is conspicuous by its absence. If it is historical, the minutiae of the narrator's life, such as what he was doing when important things occurred, intrude.

It is, above all, an amorphous work, which meanders because of Churchill's uncertain career during the war. Churchill spent most of World War II as prime minister, from which position he had an overview of worldwide events. This accident of history imposed a form and a central intelligence (in the Henry Jamesian sense) on the later memoirs.[49] *The World Crisis,* however, is shaped by the fortuitous changes in the author's career. Churchill is too near some events, too far from others. As a result, the six volumes differ from each other in scope and barely have a common denominator. Nearly equal amounts of space are devoted to the prewar situation and the five war months of 1914, to 1915, and to all of 1916–18; the admiralty days and the Dardanelles expedition obviously occupy a disproportionate position. Entire theaters like Mesopotamia and Palestine are disposed of in a few paragraphs, and the African events are not even mentioned. There are periodic references to airplanes and bombing raids but few details. Economic factors, politics, and diplomacy receive scanty treatment. The causes of the war remain vague. We are told of several treaties, alliances, crises, but what of the complex factors behind the treaties and crises? What moved millions of men in each country to throw their lives away so quickly? Even the individuals with whom Churchill came into daily contact remain ghostly presences.

Churchill's vanity sometimes disrupts the shape of the narrative. Amid the story of the Graeco-Turkish war, he presents a memo from that period without deleting paragraphs in it which relate to other issues altogether; having placed all his thoughts on record, he apologizes: "To return to our tale." Occasionally appended to that vanity is his old smugness, his inability to see his own bland assumptions. Thus, at war's end, he decides, for reasons of domestic economy, to continue temporarily the manufacture of weapons and ammunition. When he moves to the War Office, he urges the arming of anti-Bolshevik forces "from our own immense surplus of munitions."[50] The Poles should carry on for a few months "fighting and defeating the Bolsheviks on their borders"[51] rather than making a separate peace or engaging upon an invasion of Russia which would implicate the Allies in heavy commitments. The reader is left to wonder whether anti-Bolshevik idealism is at work here or merely old-fashioned warmongering to take care of the domestic arms surplus and unemployment problem. Churchill himself ingenuously concedes the materiel to have been an "unmarketable surplus," to keep which "would only have involved additional charges for storage, care and maintenance."[52] Thus, as head of the War Office, he disposed of the problem he had inadvertently created as munitions minister.

The same smugness allows him to brand the Germans as dastardly for inventing the flamethrower, using gas, sinking ships indiscriminately, letting the Bolsheviks loose in Russia, but to take pride in the British invention of the tank, retaliation with gas, use of false flags on ships, offer of Austrian and Turkish lands as bait to the Balkan states. Tottering Soviet Russia is reprimanded for looking after its own welfare by making a separate peace and releasing "a million Germans for the final onslaught in the West" as if Russia existed solely for the welfare of the Allies.[53] The humiliating terms it accepted from the Germans are shown to flout the ideals of "No Annexations," "No Indemnities," and "Self-Determination," but these had not been the proclaimed goals of

Russia (Tsarist or Soviet), which had been much more interested in seizing Constantinople; only victors can, in any case, enjoy the luxury of living up to such ideals.

In a 1914 memo urging a coalition of Balkan states against the Central Powers, Churchill uses for the first and only time the phrases "Christian states" and "Christian peoples," as though it were more moral to associate with one's coreligionists. Yet this is not a religious war, and, though he asserts here that Britain has always been the friend of the Christian states, he elsewhere claims as well that Britain has had long ties with Turkey and is in fact the largest Mohammedan power in the world. The intrusion of "Christian" seems mere hypocrisy adapted to fit the moment's needs and in any case sits badly with the adjacent proposal to carve large areas out of Austria (also Christian, though we are not reminded of *that*) and Turkey for the Balkan states. (The dissolution of the Austrian Empire he would attack in *The Second World War* as evil.) Similarly, he speaks of the Gréek leader Venizelos as the only man in the Balkans to discern the "fundamental moral issues of the struggle"—even while bribing him with an offer of Cyprus.[54]

For Churchill, World War I was simply a struggle between good and evil. The post–World War II reader of *The World Crisis,* especially in America, is likely to see World War I as a contest between two immoral imperialist power blocs and to regard Hitler and Nazism instead as the great bane of modern European life, but Churchill saw Germany as Satanic even then. The recent researches of Fritz Fischer, establishing the existence of a Wilhelmine grand design which Hitler merely carried on, would appear to vindicate Churchill, even though the modern reader may not be as ready as he to exculpate the British, French, and Russian empires. With his most patriotic rhetoric, he dwells on a melodramatic contrast between the pacific, innocent, unprepared Britain and the powerful, calculating, ruthless Germany. The survival of the British Empire is thus equated with that "of democracy and of civilization." But such noble rhetoric, along with his urging the Allies in 1917 to proclaim as a war aim territorial settlements according to the wishes of the people rather than of antiquated rulers or vengeful victors, sometimes seems mere window dressing. To W. S. Blunt, Churchill appeared to be becoming more imperialistic, and Asquith claims that if at war's end Russia, Italy, and France seized booty, Churchill wanted Britain to obtain Mesopotamia, Persia, and the German colonies as her share of the spoils; Grey and Asquith were the ones to suggest that it would be more seemly for Britain to gain nothing from the war.[55]

Churchill justifies the righteousness of the British cause in his account of his accidentally turning to a relevant passage in Scripture and the righteousness of his own course at the admiralty by the thought, "I had acted on high public grounds and on those alone, and I fortified myself with them"—though to do so he suppresses many facts relating to himself in the cases of the admiralty, Gallipoli, Russia, Ireland, and Turkey.[56] His version of the intervention in Bolshevik Russia gives only a limited picture of the turmoil he caused, of his obsessiveness, chicanery, self-contradiction, and of the venerable Churchillian affliction of projecting ambitious plans without the means of realizing them.[57] He does not see, either, that the Irish troubles were a local manifestation of the nationalism which spread over the world after the war and which heralded the eventual dissolution of the British Empire in the wake of the Austrian, Turkish, and German ones.

He insists naïvely throughout the work that if the war had drawn to an early close a true peace could have been won. Whether the many postwar problems would actually have been solved in such a case—any more than Bolshevism would have disappeared if it had been "strangled in the cradle"—is dubious. The tough-minded Churchill here reveals a chronic sentimentality, for he makes the same assumption in *Randolph Churchill, Marlborough,* and *The Second World War*—if only the protagonist of each tale had had his way, all would have been well. One would have thought that a realist like Churchill, conscious of the ambiguities of all human actions and the unlooked-for consequences of choices, might realize that problems always follow victories and that no sudden end to the human condition (here called "the European problem"), no sudden entry into the Age of Gold, was imminent.

His simplistic assertion has the effect of making the mistakes and inertia of others seem catastrophic. For someone else seems somehow always at fault. Churchill in fact has everything worked out too neatly: what went right in the war is due to his vision and work in the various departments; what went wrong is explained by the Either/Or formula, which implicitly strips everyone else of pretensions to prescience or prudence and reveals them as cowards and fools. And both success and failures Churchill had of course correctly predicted. When his didacticism and wishful thinking triumph over his good sense, the prophet threatens to become a whining, rejected suitor.

Critical reception of *The World Crisis* has been mixed. Scholars complain that the work lacks penetration, that it presents high-placed men in action without revealing their motives or their means of reaching prominence. Uneven, at times naïve, bombastic, dated, it is, finally, a personal account, an "entertainment," a piece of storytelling or fine journalism that often masquerades as a formal analytic history. Its premise seems to be that Churchill was so important that when he fell in 1915 mankind lost control of the course of events; its main theme is the truism that the folly of the world confounds its wisdom, and its refrain is the tiresome "if I had only been listened to" by one who often seems an amateur strategist with insufficient information, impotently wallowing in endless speculations on "what might have been" as a way of dealing with what was probably an insoluble problem.[58]

The style, which seems to mirror the book's substantive deficiencies, has been a major bone of contention. Though some find it rich, varied, and measured, many complain that the grand manner is too lush, verbose, melodramatic, too much influenced by Churchill's resounding oratory, in the tradition of Gibbon rather than that of Tacitus. Fine writing often veers into claptrap, resonant absurdity mingles with pithy matter. Isaiah Berlin has pointed out that in the late 1920s many intellectuals had come to regard Churchill as a hollow man displaying a puerile romanticism and militant imperialism; his rolling periods, especially in this work—somewhat archaic, artificial sounding, self-aggrandizing—were taken to reflect his character perfectly.[59]

One may conclude that *The World Crisis* is flawed, not only because it is uneven in form, quality, style, and reliability, but also—if we judge it as much as a literary work as a history—because of its content. The stories of Marlborough and World War II have tragic dimensions which even a slightly talented narrator can bring out. World War I, on the other hand, is an ugly, pathetic event. The frontier war books, for all their negative critical moments, offered an ordered vision and happy endings; though in *Randolph Churchill* the landscape darkened, the long-range view was bright, and Randolph's spirit informed the meliorist thrust in the biographer's volumes of "radical" speeches. But now the happy ending of victory barely relieves the bleakness of *The World Crisis,* the spectacle of European civilization fragmented, "progress" unmasked, professional expertise and traditional wisdom bankrupt. The agonizing postwar years during which the book was written exhibited few of the blessings of the peace which was to replace the war and which was the ostensible goal of the war. The "world crisis" turns out not to be congruent with the world war because crisis is now a permanent condition of which the war was only a phase. The world of Churchill's previous books has been rendered unreal; its order now seems contrived.

Though in World War II unbelievable horrors were perpetrated, the best as well as the worst of man was on display. The conflict was meaningful; three years of the triumph of evil were followed by three years of the resurgence and final victory of good. Certain values were upheld at war's end, however imperfectly, by indomitability and heroism. Respite and a prosperity of sorts was brought to many lands that had long weltered in wars and social chaos. World War I, on the other hand, was lugubrious fracas blundered into by all sides in a mixture of high-flown rhetoric and imperialist greed, without—Churchill's insistence to the contrary notwithstanding—clear causes, clear demarcations of good and evil. It saw a protracted stalemate with hideous slaughter; the inept politicians and generals on both sides seemed devoid of understanding, purpose, or leadership. And over the modern reader hovers the bitter awareness that all would have to be gone through again twenty years later. In this, there is matter for a *Dunciad,* an epic on human folly (rather than Hitlerian depravity), or for the theater of the absurd. But Churchill is not the man to write such works.

A historian cannot, of course, be held responsible for the course of events he narrates, but in this quasi-historical work, such order as Churchill has brought to the events contributes as much to mystification as to elucidation. His discussion of Gallipoli and the tank, his hardheadedness, and his binary logic are, in the final analysis, limiting and superficial, more attractive than convincing. They overlook the complexity of life and the uncertain consequences of all human plans and actions. His vision is ultimately too egocentric to be central or coherent, too simplistic and pathetic to be tragic. Perhaps because he was too Victorian and because World War I so disrupted his career, so overwhelmed him personally (as it did Europe), he could not look at it dispassionately, could not understand this watershed between Victorian and modern man.

4

The Fourth Phase: The 1930s

Belletrist, Reactionary, and Prophet in the Wilderness

He re-created an old and valuable link between literature and public life in England—Robert Rhodes James, 1970

Churchill always responded to the . . . call of drum and trumpet, perhaps most of all now, when he was writing the [Marlborough]—A. J. P. Taylor, 1965

Belles Lettres:

After Armageddon

The year 1929, like 1900, 1911, and 1922, marked a major juncture for Churchill as statesman and as writer. In 1900 he had turned from military affairs to politics, in 1911 to administration of various military services, in 1922 to full-time memoir writing and the road leading back to the Conservatives and to the treasury; 1929 saw him putting the finishing touches on *The World Crisis,* as well as departing from government posts and in effect from his high place in the Conservative Party. Like Lloyd George, he was, after great deeds in the earlier part of the century, on the shelf and without a following or, in a sense, a party. His many imprudences made men write him off, and, his career a "record of brilliant failures," he seemed, C. P. Snow says, the classical case of a man with a splendid future behind him.[1]

If the late 1890s were the years of war dispatches and war books, the 1900s the years of biographical work and radical speeches, and the 1920s the years of memoir writing, the 1930s proved to be, because of his political despondency, Churchill's most fertile and versatile decade as scholar and writer, during which he also prophesied the next war. He published seven books in ten volumes and wrote four other, unpublished, volumes. In these years he composed his most detached historical works, the only ones not about himself or his father, his only forays into the remote English past (*Marlborough* and the first draft of the *History*), and the books regarded by some as his best works *(A Roving Commission, Great Contemporaries,* and *Marlborough).* He also flooded the newspapers and magazines with several hundred articles, often on a biweekly basis. Supporting himself by his pen, remaining in the public eye, passing judgments (usually dour) on current social and political trends were perhaps not more important reasons for his prolificacy than indulging, amid the dearth of public duties, in the sheer joy of writing. After the labors of criticism and self-justification in *The World Crisis,* during the exhaustive and exhausting work on *Marlborough* or the ardors of prophesying doom, and while he was writing on past, present, and future wars, Churchill found relief in playing the role of armchair philosopher and chatting with his readers on a wide variety of matters, large and small. The comprehensive expositor of world-shaking events in multivolumed works proved equally at home with the informal essay and the miniature composition. Never before or after was he so much a writer of belles lettres.

In the welter of material, one can discern eight types of essays: (1) rehashes of World War I matter—whether used in or deleted from *The World Crisis*—under such titles as "Crucial Crises of the War" or "Great Events of Our Times"; (2) rehashes of portions of his autobiography, under such titles as "My Life and Times"; (3) celebrations of British grandeur and paeans to British monarchs, like "The King's Twenty-Five Years" (on George V); (4) character portraits of "Great Men of Our Time," mainly British; (5) brief studies in history; (6) paraphrases of works of literature described as the "World's Greatest Stories" but consisting mainly of nineteenth-century British novels; (7) general observations on science, current painting, society, manners, heroism, political memoirs, and travel, such as "What I Saw and Heard in America"; (8) small talk about himself, like "My New York Misadventure"; (9) and, of course, dissenting commentary on contemporary politics, with cautionary titles like "Plain Words . . . ," "Plain Speaking . . . ," "The Real Issue . . . ." Churchill shamelessly repeated himself, with or without revisions or additions. Articles published in newspapers in Britain soon turned up in American magazines; articles published in one newspaper appeared, only slightly revised, a few years later in another. A set of observations on the ruthlessness of modern war came out first in 1925 in "Shall We All Commit Suicide?"; it then appeared in *The World Crisis,* again in *Thoughts and Adventures,* and was quoted once more in *The Second World War.*

The two collections of miscellanies published in book form, *Thoughts and Adventures* and *Great Contemporaries,* are samplings of some of the best pieces. In the *Thoughts,* one group of essays treats of such matters peripheral to *The World Crisis* as Churchill's prewar observation of German army maneuvers, the U-boat war, Ludendorff's offensive, and the author's continuing critique of the generals. Another group records personal experiences like electioneering, flying, spy hunting, a prewar clash with criminal anarchists, and varied wartime experiences on the front. A third group consists of casual speculations, with—of course—personal application, on such topics as cartoons, hobbies, painting, and the perennial question of how one would relive one's life. A last group is on the two great problems of modern times—economic turmoil and the bewildering transformation by rampant science of a world still in the throes of primitive passions.

The pieces in *Great Contemporaries* are presented as the "stepping stones" or raw material for a historical narrative, presumably comparable to the sketches of his father by other writers which helped him in the composition of *Randolph Churchill.* Though concentrating on the prominent British statesmen of the turn of the century—Balfour, Chamberlain, Rosebery, Morley, Asquith, and Curzon—it includes, in no particular order, certain contemporary European statesmen, four generals, and two nonpolitical Britons, G. B. Shaw and T. E. Lawrence. The portraits are written according to a pattern. Each contains three sections, the first of which includes a brief description of the man and his role in world affairs. Then, usually, appears a sentence such as "I first had the honor of meeting him . . . ," for this book, like nearly all of Churchill's, is self-centered; it depicts not the great men of the age but the great men (with a few exceptions) whom Churchill has known personally. Usually a third section presents historical background, concentrates on a critical event in the life of the subject, or includes a narrative detail which appears in many of Churchill's books: "I have my last picture of him. . . ."

*   *   *   *

Before writing the huge *Marlborough*, Churchill dashed off *A Roving Commission*, a short autobiography limited mainly to the first quarter-century of his life, which neatly coincided with the last twenty-five years of the nineteenth century. The public had had many glimpses of Churchill, partly from his own previous books, and he now brought the "whole together in a single complete story." This slightly incredible tale of adventure ends—amid intimations of the turmoil the new century would bring—as the deaths of Victoria and Salisbury herald the close of an era and as Churchill, having run through several careers as officer, journalist, polo player, social lion, lecturer, finds his métiers of politician, orator, and author. Hence, despite the bleak vistas of a declining civilization, the *Commission* radiates a retrospective cheerfulness, for not only is the hero fortunate in everything he puts his hand to during his early adult years, but his success follows a most unpromising start.

The structure and tone of the autobiography are shaped by the substance. It ends at 1900 because, as the story of Churchill finding himself and his vocations, it is, like all such books, a tale of education, an extramural education obtained in the nineties, when many things "were in the making." With the creative writer's ability to evoke alien states of mind, Churchill recreates the "point of view appropriate to my years, whether as a child, a schoolboy, a cadet, a subaltern, a war-correspondent or a youthful politician,"[2] rather as in his other works he tries to convey through documents the authentic feelings of bygone days. This results in considerable irony and humor.

But another dimension exists as well. Although the *Commission* in part handles the same material as is treated at length in his first four books, it is not a mere iteration. The events and beliefs presented earlier with enthusiasm and innocence are now colored by experience; the sad afterknowledge, the fall of man into the twentieth century, throws a grim irony over those now distant events. Unbeknownst to the actors, World War I hovers over all their actions, and the manifold social turmoil of the postwar world in turn hovers over the war itself; trauma and disillusionment constantly hedge the narrative. If the noble Victorians in the story are at all representative of their era, man has rarely been so ignorant, deluded, vulnerable. The memoir is Churchill's somewhat patrician rendition of the "lost generation" outlook, his attempt to put together the fragmented pieces of his intellectual world by harking back to a vanished Victorian Eden. It is, therefore, at once his sprightliest and saddest book.

For a terrible revelation has come upon the world. One of the major themes of his writings of the 1930s is the vast contrast between the elegant, innocent world he grew up in and the hectic, anxious age which overtook it. The Victorians, living in an age of British splendor and unchallenged leadership, of peace, prosperity, and progress—the "British Antonine Age"—were certain that "much was well, and that all would be better" in a world free at last from "barbarism, superstition, aristocratic tyrannies and dynastic wars."[3] But in a few unbelievable decades, every aspect of life has undergone vast, quick, and unprecedented changes. No other generation experienced "such astounding revolutions of data and values." Hardly anything once thought to be permanent has lasted; everything "impossible has happened."[4] He candidly wonders, upon rereading his manuscript, whether the sense of ubiquitous anarchy is "but the illusion which comes upon us all as we grow older."[5]

The elegiac note, the nostalgia, the British love of tradition enters into everything which Churchill contemplates. For example, the automobile, whose annual slaughter (in the 1930s) of 10,000 and maiming of 250,000 persons in Britain is blandly accepted, has destroyed the country-house customs, and speed has vitiated the dignity and depth of life. Although a "fuller life" is, thanks to the much celebrated "Democracy and Science," available to vast numbers, the paradox is that, on the one hand, the improvement is imperceptible and "we all take the modern conveniences and facilities as they are offered to us without being grateful or consciously happier";[6] and, on the other hand, human wisdom and behavior have remained static. Man's physical powers outstrip his intelligence and nobility. To stop this avalanche of scientific progress lest we be "mastered by our own apparatus" appears impossible. Faced with western man's official optimism and confronting the great modern predicament as it has been delineated by writers and thinkers of our century, Churchill concedes that the answer to the old choice between Blessing and Cursing "will be hard to foretell."[7]

The perennial problem of producing sufficient food has, Churchill thinks, been solved, only to present man with the problem of distribution. Taste in consumption is now shaped by industrial leaders and the vulgar pressures of the marketplace. Churchill favors older things—the silent film to the talkie, the stage to the cinema, the newspaper to the radio.[8] Not without reason, then, has he grown conservative and found it difficult to believe any longer in change for change's sake.[9] He prefers the old spellings and pronunciations; he dislikes the revised version of the Bible and the alterations in the Book of Common Prayer. In a delicious aside, he offers us the possibility that, had he become a cleric, he would have preached "orthodox sermons in a spirit of audacious contradiction to the age."[10] The man who in the writings of his twenties celebrated zest for adventure, love of life, and the urge to reform, and who in the writings of his old age will exult in the will to survive and triumph seems now, in his fifties, an embittered soul estranged from everything.[11]

Peace in the 1920s and 1930s presented nearly insoluble political problems caused by progress. Large masses of women and working people had been enfranchised. Not only was Churchill himself a victim of these new political forces, but he was also perturbed by the philosophical ramifications. The representative and parliamentary institutions seemed to him to lose their authority when based on "universal suffrage." Although electioneering fruitfully exposes a politician to the variety of men and political currents, "so-called democratic politics" is full of "trumpery figures" whose follies Shaw has justly derided. On the continent, the "victorious democracies" drove out the "hereditary sovereigns" in the name of progress and left a vacuum which was soon filled by unrestrained dictators. Churchill therefore advises Spain to keep King Alfonso and to have "a limited monarchy and a Parliamentary Constitution mutually protecting each other."[12]

He likewise believes that a politician must have, as did Lloyd George and even Asquith, in the crunch, "that ruthless side without which great matters cannot be handled."[13] He goes so far as to concede that "something may be said for" dictatorships in critical periods. Fascism he accepts as that alternative to communism which transformed society and saved Italy, admittedly at the cost of her liberty. (He thinks enough of Nazi and Fascist encouragement of increases in the birthrate to want Britain to emulate it.) Yet he concedes that strong-man rule is a dangerous solution which "should pass with the crisis."

In Britain the problem is that the precious institution of Parliament seems less and less capable of dealing with the depression. The postwar issues have, he thinks, transcended mere politics; successive governments of whatever political stripe have failed to cope with the new economic imponderables: the absence of the jobs and prosperity promised by technology, the bad coordination of production and consumption, the breakdown of classical laissez-faire economics.[14] Britain's difficulties are part of a worldwide crisis: civilization itself seems unable to utilize the new abundance of basic commodities. "Have all our triumphs of research and organization bequeathed us only a new punishment —the Curse of Plenty?"[15] Churchill doubts that traditional electioneering and adult suffrage can cope with the "intricate propositions of modern business and finance," especially as the measures to be taken would be unpopular.[16]

At one point, he therefore urges the three ex–prime ministers— Lloyd George, MacDonald, Baldwin—to decide jointly on a way out of the crisis. This, like his suggestions that disarmament could be achieved or international monetary problems solved if only a half-dozen great men of the first-class powers conferred and gave the necessary orders, is a curious fusion of his perennial coalitionism, of his intermittent belief that individuals can shape history, and of his peculiar faith in strong-man rule, personal diplomacy, and summit meetings. At another point, he urges the formation of an "Economic sub-Parliament" of experts detached from public opinion. Such a proposal ignores the probability that the economists would divide along the same ideological lines as the MPs. Verging on a desire for government by an elite in order to circumvent the broadened franchise and to make Parliament impotent on the main economic issues just as it was being made responsive to all the people, the proposal is the nearest Churchill came to losing faith in democracy.[17]

Certainly Churchill has traveled a long distance from his "radical" days. His prewar shift from Tory to Liberal he now explains away as a sincere though lamentable act of youth; since the *Commission* ends with premonitions of the coming party change and *The World Crisis* begins with 1911, his radical years, 1906–11, have been expunged from his own official record. From 1919 on, he was, on questions like bolshevism and imperialism abroad or socialism and the unions at home, actually more reactionary than many Conservatives. He ignored or forgot the social evils he had once so eloquently decried. When the Liberals collaborated with labor and seemed to forsake the imperial causes, he finally left them for the last bulwark against socialism, the Tories.

That the Liberal Party was fragmented and that Churchill's party shift was once again followed by the award of high government office gave amusement to the cynical. Yet, though his frequent changes of party labels (five in all) aroused mockery and led many to believe that he was an emotional self-promoter with flawed judgment, Churchill remains at ease with his conscience. He is not ashamed that throughout his life he was "in disagreement alternately with both the historic English parties."[18] Every step he took seems to him inevitable, and he thinks himself "more truly consistent" than almost any other public man. Like Burke and Halifax of old, he exhibited, he insists, the right kind of inconsistency, for he was open to changing circumstances and reluctant to be a follower rather than a leader of the public. Though the party policies often change, he has always remained a "Tory Democrat and Free Trader."[19]

But resisting the India home rule scheme, defending Edward VIII, or warning about Hitler, he—a Tory in exile and without a party to join this time—is more alone than ever in a long political life. He therefore rests on the laurels he has won in legislation, administration, diplomacy, the three important fields of government—as a pioneer in peacetime social legislation and administration; as head of admiralty, munitions, and war offices; and as diplomat instrumental in the postwar Middle Eastern and Irish settlements. Although he is unsure whether he will ever be in office again, he writes not "Finis" but (prophetically) "to be continued in our next."[20]

So the aging Churchill, entering his sixties and apparently facing the sunset of his career, recapitulates and takes leave. Leading a "wonderfully happy and fortunate life," having built a house by his own hands, having a pen that makes him independent, enjoying the study of history and the amusement of painting, he resignedly looks back at four rich and varied decades in the limelight, at, despite many disappointments, a blessed life. Thankful for the "gift of existence" and for his successes, he launches into an apostrophe to life. Happier every year since he reached manhood, he has not had time, in the wake of entering upon the world stage at twenty-one, "to turn round. An endless moving picture in which one was an actor. On the whole Great Fun!"[21] Still, he would not want to live his life over again; his good luck might leave him. Content with what has happened, reconciled to the "mysterious rhythm of our destinies," Churchill accepts life, "good and ill . . . together. The journey has been enjoyable and well worth making—once."[22] Thus does he come to terms with his destiny and accept himself and his shrunken expectations—little realizing that the great climax lies yet ahead, that, passing in the 1930s through a "desert," he is soon to undergo adventures beyond his wildest dreams.

*   *   *   *

Besides adding a new dimension to familiar incidents, the *Commission* also provides at last some of the details of Churchill's private life. We see his parents, again, but in a different perspective. *Randolph Churchill* was written with reverence and imaginative sympathy by a young Parliamentary neophyte who portrayed his father as a fellow politician and a warm, gregarious man of the world. The *Commission* is written by a man who, at the age of fifty-five, has lived beyond the year in which his father died, who is in a somewhat valedictory mood, and who, in trying to recapture his own past by reverting to the child's viewpoint, remembers a typically stern, aloof Victorian father annoyed by the son's mental lethargy, a remote, solemn, self-absorbed person with little time for the baffled child. The pathos of the gulf between father and son is what the *Commission* adds to the detached picture painted by the dedicated but reticent young biographer. Moreover, the major theme in the biography of his father—that of the twists and turns of history—runs also through his autobiography and his brief portraits in the *Contemporaries*. It will become, in the *History,* the "disguised blessings" principle that shapes the historical process.

The *Commission* seems slight next to Churchill's major works and is indeed superficial in some ways. Yet perhaps precisely because of the absence of the prophetic stance, of literary or historical ambitions, because of the relief from the compulsion to vindicate a Churchill or prove Britain's mission, it is Churchill's most charming work. For once, he does not worry over memos, official records, and appendices. Relying mainly on his memory, the narrator roves freely, and his style, not bound by the carefully connected minutiae which characterize most of his books, relaxes. Colloquialisms and warmth replace the magisterial tone. The author is here as in the *Thoughts, en pantoufles;* despite his melancholy over the end of an era, the book radiates a playfulness and mellowness, a sense that it is all a jolly lark—to live, to recall, to record, and to read. In none of his works is a sense of humor so dominant or the style so lively. Unlike his other memoirs, which were written soon after the events, it is rich in historical ironies, for three decades of experience separate the author from his subject. His ability to identify with other persons no less than with the younger self results in poignant or amusing moments, as when he looks at the British presence in India through the eyes of the primitive frontier Pathans. Amidst many digressions and reflective passages, serious questions are raised only to be dismissed with jocularity, for the author is too content over having survived to look deeply into things. As in his major works, he scants methodical philosophy and psychology. His successful career betrays him into a facile personal optimism that sits ill at ease alongside his apocalyptic vision. The book seems to exclaim, "By Jove! It all happened to *me!* And it

worked out well. Isn't that wonderful!" Questioning some assumptions but not others, his is ultimately a conservative, tragic
sense, in that he mocks without intending to change.[23]

The *Thoughts* is also an engaging book, though it lacks the unity
and range of the *Commission*. Quite a few essays in it are as carefully
constructed as short stories. In other pieces, Churchill, little
concerned with apologetics, criticism, or sources, wanders nimbly
around and through his subject, like a Montaigne or a Lamb. The
flexibility of the style is striking. Whether sounding the dark *ubi
sunt* motif or descanting lightly upon hobbies, Churchill, as the
Times Literary Supplement reviewer noted, seems always a happy
young warrior enjoying himself and sure of his convictions.[24]

Great Contemporaries is another impressive small work, excited yet
balanced, warm yet urbane, incisive yet eloquent. It contains
touching last glimpses of the various prominent men, and it often
evinces sympathetic identification: The piece on the kaiser begins,
"No one should judge the career of the Emperor William II
without asking the question, 'What should I have done in his
position?' "[25] and proceeds to describe with sensitivity the predicament of the man. Every piece is well written. "Savinkov" plunges
the reader *in medias res* like a polished short story (perhaps by
Conrad): " 'How do you get on with Savinkov?' I asked M. de
Sazonov when we met in Paris in the summer of 1919. The Czar's
former Foreign Minister made a deprecating gesture with his
hands. 'He is an assassin. . . .' The old gentleman, gray with
years . . ."[26]

The character sketches make one realize anew that Churchill,
despite his adeptness at twentieth-century politics and war making, has his roots in an earlier age, whose leaders were cultivated
people, witty debaters, proficient orators, brilliant conversation-
alists, excellent writers. The importance to him of the British
statesmen of the previous generation is suggested by the vividness
with which he conjures up their physical appearance, manners,
habits of mind, and by his familiarity with their backgrounds and
milieux. Nearly all came from aristocratic or wealthy families,
went to the finest schools, and lived to ripe old age. But, as the
poignant scene of a confused John Morley on the eve of Armaged-
don suggests, these peaceable men, their dreams swamped by novel
events, were to be eclipsed by the dynamism of figures like Lloyd

George, springing from different backgrounds and attuned to the frenzy of the new century. Great as they were, Churchill confesses, these Victorians dealt with "minor things" and never "had to face, as we have done, and still do, the possibility of national ruin." It was an era of "great men and small events."[27]

In scrutinizing the moderns, Churchill enjoys parading the paradoxes of their careers: Shaw the respectable subversive, the wealthy Socialist, the free-spoken antidemocrat; Joe Chamberlain the radical and free trader turned imperialist jingo and protectionist; Boris Savinkov, "a terrorist for moderate aims"; Trotsky, whose devotion to communism was interwoven with great egoism and whose personal ambition was defeated by the very Jewishness he had rejected; Parnell, a Protestant leading Catholics, a landlord inspiring a "No Rent" campaign, a conservative "law and order" temperament exciting revolt;[28] Haig, a modest, decent man ruthlessly applying pressure on his troops. "Such are the mysteries of human nature!," exclaims Churchill, in a renewed outburst of romantic doubt of putative consistency in human behavior.[29]

Another characteristic pattern involves military men—French, Hindenburg, Kitchener, Haig, Fisher—whose careers, seemingly finished with distinction, were suddenly revived in World War I, only to end ingloriously. But Churchill, the foe of generals, is not unkind to them; his tone is elegiac. The political figures, on the other hand, do not pass by uncensured, and the judgments rendered on them reveal Churchill's study of, and preparation for, leadership. Asquith's simplistic view of life, for instance, led him to contemn arguments, personalities, and events which did not conform to his view of things, making him at times ruthless. Balfour, by contrast, always able to see both sides of all questions, lacked the decisiveness necessary in crises, when "most important things have to be done on imperfect and uncertain information."[30] For politics, Churchill prefers the activists to the deliberating intellectuals. Balfour, Curzon, Asquith, Rosebery, and Morley were specimens of refinement but not great leaders of men. Throughout his life Churchill would rail thus at the modern "intelligentsia" and harbor respect for those men of action, even Mussolini and Hitler, who could move nations.[31]

Three activists presented in a highly favorable light—perhaps because they reflect different facets of Churchill's own personality and career—are T. E. Lawrence, Clemenceau, and Lloyd George. Among the most effective portraits are those of Rosebery, clairvoyant about world affairs and foreseeing the Great War, yet detached and otherworldly both in political life and in his writings, with their typical "self-imposed limitations"; the kaiser, a shortsighted, naïve person in a prominent position; and, most poignantly, Curzon, the man who had everything except the certain something that makes for greatness. The scene in which Curzon is passed over for the office of prime minister, which he had seemed destined for, is handled with a novelist's deftness of manner, richness of analysis, and detached irony with a touch of compassion.

The *Commission* and *Contemporaries* are complementary works. The former evokes the late nineteenth century as seen in one private life; the latter presents, in part, the same world in its public, official demeanor through diverse (if mainly political) lives. In both, the author looks back with nostalgia to the vanished world of his youth. The autobiography, recreating the earlier period by recapturing the state of mind of someone growing up in it (as well as presenting brief glimpses of striking Victorian personages), makes the contrast explicitly. The later book, a mature assessment by a veteran politician of the prominent Victorian statesmen who were at their zenith at the time of the author's growing up, makes the contrast implicitly by juxtaposing the lives of possessed, classless moderns like Trotsky and Hitler with such unlikely contemporaries as Rosebery and Morley. This is Churchill's "Eminent Late Victorians" (written while he was immersed in the age of Queen Anne), and, even if it lacks the iconoclasm of Strachey, it is no naïve, sentimental effusion.

Praise for the *Contemporaries* has been high. Many critics remark on the balance, incisiveness, generosity, and justness of these trenchant essays on the public acts of great public men. The grand manner suits the eminence of the men, the defunct aristocratic values Churchill admires, and the conservative, disillusioned vision. Radiating a sagacity about men and politics, the book also betrays his own interest in ambition ("Curzon"), love of adventure ("Lawrence"), and obsessiveness ("Trotsky"), for, as a result of his egocentric selectivity, the author himself, "formidable, affectionate, lovable," often gleams at us, says Guedella, from twenty-five mirrors. The portraits of the late Victorian contemporaries of his father, whom Churchill knew well, are, to be sure, much better than those of the moderns (especially the vituperative sketch of Trotsky), but, along with the *Thoughts* (and *Step by Step*), *Contemporaries* is journalism at its best. Containing some of his finest writing, it may contribute more to our understanding of modern British politics than do his large, quasi-official works of history.[32]

Marlborough:

Redeeming an English Soldier-Statesman

Churchill's major literary work of the decade was, in fact, one of these ambitious books, the large-scale biography and history, *Marlborough*. This project took him back not to the politics of his youth but to the global conflict of another century and thus required mastery of the spirit of a remote age. Though it was a commissioned work, Churchill would not have invested nearly a million words and ten years had it not had special significance for him. For he wrote about a man who was not only his ancestor, an invincible general, the first of what became the Spencer–Churchill dukes of Marlborough, and a maker of modern Britain, but also a supreme example of heroism in the two vocations (besides writing) which mainly interested Churchill and in which ultimate triumph seemed to have eluded him—politics and war making. In narrating his own early life, Churchill had told of a series of sparkling but unimportant military adventures; in narrating his father's, he had traced a spectacular but unfulfilled political career; and *The World Crisis* was a tale of countless errors by military pygmies. Marlborough, by contrast, was titanic, versatile, and successful, having changed the course of European history after his years in the political wilderness.

Churchill had long thought of writing on Marlborough, but now he had the motives and the enforced leisure for visiting a hero in a heroic period. Apparently closing an exciting career that had failed to reach a long-desired climax, the author, his expectations contracting, found relief in telling a tale with a proper resolution. During his own political frustration and alienation, he wrote a work which served, like *Randolph Churchill,* as an act of family piety and a rehabilitation of an English worthy much slandered by critics. And after a world war in which the individual was swamped by the sheer flow of forces, he found it refreshing to contemplate an age in which a genius of war making seemed clearly to influence events. While many intellectuals responded to the traumas of the Great War and of the postwar dislocations by looking forward to a communist or fascist utopia, Churchill, with his predilection for the romance of history, sought his ideal society in the past, in the reigns of Victoria and Anne. His two large projects in the 1930s, the *Marlborough* and the *History,* venture further into the past (and uniquely out of the confines of his immediate family) than any other of his works. From the chaos of modern life and the ruins of his own career, Churchill, seeking a sense of order and of fulfillment, turned to the age of Anne and the successes of Marlborough. What reality denied him, the historical and familial imagination granted. The work was thus in many ways a recharging of his spiritual batteries.

The result was a multifaceted book reflecting its author's abiding interests: a biography which, in the absence of private documents, concentrates on the general and diplomat rather than the private man; a political history of England from the time of Charles II to the coming of the Hanovers; a close scrutiny of the reign of Queen Anne, depicted here as a crucial period in the parallel evolution of British parliamentary democracy and imperial power (an evolution which is the theme of Churchill's next work, the *History*); a monograph on the art of war in the early eighteenth century; a celebration of Britain's first becoming a world power and of the recurring British commitment to the cause of European liberty; a projection of what the general *manqué* and now politically inactive author wishes he had become (rather like the young officer's projection in *Savrola* of the politician he wanted to, and would, become); and, not least, a tale of an adventurous career as fascinating as any in fiction, a tale aptly told by one himself endowed with an adventurous life, immense political and military experience and study, and one of the most eloquent pens in the English-speaking world.[33]

Churchill adores the age he chronicles. This "great," "glorious," and "intense" period, contrasting with the milder, less dramatic years of Charles I and George I which preceded and followed it, had its "violent" and "seamy side," yet saw an "insensible but ceaseless march of culture and civilization."[34] Macaulay stressed the improvements in the quality of life since Marlborough's age; Churchill, though he sometimes speaks of changes for the better or offers contrasts without rendering value judgments, is conscious of the ways in which matters have worsened. As in his other works, his irony often pricks the smug modern sense of progress, and he relishes the many historical paradoxes. Only the few ran the country in those days but "with searching rivalry" and merit;[35] the sudden rise and acclaim of dictators was thus impossible. Men were more brutal yet somehow respected life more; though ignorant by our standards, they thoroughly digested the few books they read; instead of constant bustle and the frittering away of time with modern diversions, they knew leisure and companionship. Bleeding, now a "discredited old-world remedy, always seemed to have relieved [Marlborough]."[36] In war as well, a greater sense of decorum and civility obtained, not hatred, mob violence, or mechanical proficiency. A general like Marlborough, present at the battle rather than "working in calm surroundings," had to have an "almost godlike" combination of mental, moral, and physical qualities; the "sublime function of military genius . . . has been destroyed forever."[37] Churchill's inference is ironic, in the manner of Montaigne's conclusion to his essay on the cannibals: "Altogether they were primitive folk, and we must make allowances for their limitations."[38]

Marlborough thus functions not only as (looking back to the 1920s) a critique of the World War I generals and (looking ahead to the 1940s) a portrait of a heroic ideal Churchill would try to emulate, but also as another expression of Churchill's pervasive theme of the 1930s: the hideousness of modern life. Even in the remote, preindustrial age of Anne, life seems, when contrasted with the twentieth century, as dignified and noble as that in the more recent and "progressive" age of Victoria. But surely Churchill paints too rosy a picture of the past. His paean on the greater civility among aristocrats at war overlooks the lot of foot soldiers, just as on civil life he notes the amenities of the leisured and ignores the fate of those serving them. His simplistic assertion that the only values are the traditional ones of "fidelity to covenants, the honor of soldiers, and the hatred of causing human woe" skirts the problems raised by the complexity of human actions.[39] After all, within a few years he was to invoke the same principles of fidelity and honor in his eulogy for Neville Chamberlain, a man who lived by them but was adjudged by history—notably by Churchill's own memoirs—to have helped bring about World War II.

Churchill's increasing questioning of progress is concurrent with his growing belief in the somewhat archaic idea, expressed here as in the war memoirs and the *History*, that individual men and battles had an immense impact on the course of history. Notwithstanding current pacifism and modern opinion on the power of social forces, he insists that battles are "the principal milestones," creating new standards and conditions in every way. The victory at Blenheim, for example, settled the destiny of Europe for a century. Similarly, though Louis XIV was twice as strong in 1702 as in 1688, "the scale of the new war was turned by the genius of one man," whose will "outweighed all these fearful inequalities";[40] by 1708, in sum, "one man and three battles had transformed all," raising Britain to the summit of the world and beating Louis to his knees. In turn, Marlborough's deeds were cancelled, the alliance jolted, and the peace lost by something as trivial as a "bedchamber intrigue"; Abigail was the "smallest person who ever consciously . . . decided the history of Europe."[41]

The scholarship seems formidable, as in no other of his works. Picking his way through conflicting testimony and evaluations, Churchill, while leaning on William Coxe's 1818 biography of the duke, carefully weighs each writer's reliability. Yet the tone is not as detached as might be expected from an academic historian. Churchill refuses to abdicate judgment and lapse into a scholarly impartiality which treats Whigs and Tories, Hanoverians and Jacobites, Marlborough's war policy and Bolingbroke's peace negotiations as equally acceptable; in a world where men's acts may produce calamities for "millions of humble folk," he excoriates Bolingbroke's character, Harley's backstairs intrigues, and British perfidy. Marlborough, with his broad European view and his apparent sense of Britain's imperial destiny, is the fulcrum, and all the other characters, parties, and issues take their places accordingly. Hence the Whigs, though uncertain political animals, espouse ideas presented as normative and proper: the Protestant succession and the established church; the prosecution of the war against French expansion; Flanders and the Moselle rather than Spain or the sea as the decisive theaters; the credit system of financing; the nascent sense of Britain's overseas destiny; the court's reluctant but growing submissiveness to Parliament, and the Lords' to Commons. Hence, too, William III, for all his sins, is a good man; James, whatever his virtues, is bad; the Tories are unseemly; and the literati hostile to Marlborough—Pope, Swift, Thackeray, Macaulay—are harshly expelled from the witness stand.

Indeed, the disposal of various allegations, especially the notoriously hostile ones of Macaulay, causes Churchill's "impression" of Marlborough's "size and power" to grow "with study" and leaves us, as in the case of *Randolph Churchill,* with little less than the portrait of a saint.[42] Marlborough's "astonishing constancy" is established by his half-century of romantic love for Sarah; his thirty-year service to Anne; his fidelity to the Protestant succession despite the twists of fate; his steady friendships amid political turmoil; and his stable, continuous military association with Prince Eugene and others. The foremost of English soldiers and statesmen, he seems to Churchill a titan, "virtuous and benevolent," incredibly patient, "majestic, sagacious, . . . compelling victory, running all risks."[43] Making his way through the labyrinthine intrigues of five reigns and always emerging the successful champion of British and Protestant interests, as well as of his own, he comprehended all the factors and forces at work. Neither triumph nor disappointment distracted him from his task. The higher his fortune rose, the higher the virtue of this "stainless" "genius and hero," who was nothing less than the "greatest servant, who remained a servant, of any sovereign in history."[44]

*   *   *   *

Marlborough came to such greatness by means of the military vocation. In ten campaigns against the French, he obtained four classic victories, besides winning numerous important actions and taking thirty fortresses by siege. In the largest scale operations in history up to that time, against the main armies and the best generals of the first of military nations—Tallard, Villeroy, Vendôme, Villars—whom he defeated one after another, he never sustained a serious check, a convoy cut up, or camp surprised. Alone in military annals, he quitted war invincible, and disaster overtook his armies upon his departure.[45]

Marlborough's outstanding trait, Churchill infers, was his impatience with the traditional, cautious ways of making war. The allies seemed satisfied to protect the frontier passively and perhaps capture some Belgian forts. They aimed at geographical prizes, methodical sieges, textbook performances, delaying tactics, until the foe ran out of food or money. In place of this military chess, Marlborough sought, according to Churchill, the battle as the true resolution; not this or that town but the "annihilation of the French army in a great battle and the humbling of Louis XIV in the open field."[46] A battle under favorable conditions would be of greater advantage, he once declared, than the capture of twenty towns. Villeroy correctly described Marlborough as violating "every principle of war"—that is, every military convention of the day.

His bypassing of received wisdom required great confidence and a willingness to run risks. Churchill marvels that Marlborough's calculations were nearly always right and that he was never penalized, even for such a dangerous course as forcing the lines of Brabant with numerically inferior forces at one of the strongest points; but since Marlborough sought a battle and the French avoided it, they responded without fully understanding the situation and could not exact the forfeits due them. So confident was he and so much more desirous of a free hand in strategy and tactics than of mere numerical superiority that before the Battle of Blenheim he gladly rid himself of his ally, the margrave, and his 15,000 troops. Yet risk taking, Churchill clarifies, did not mean recklessness. Marlborough's audacity was preceded by calculation and succeeded by "sudden sober caution." Daring and prudence were separate states of mind, following each other (in line with Either/Or) in definite phases, or "tools to be picked up or laid down according to the job."[47]

Marlborough not only oversaw the battle on his horse from a short distance, but in critical moments—at Blenheim, Elixem, Ramillies—coolly took personal control at a danger point. After ten years of war and while in poor health, he still made personal reconnaissance within range of the enemy to make sure—as, we recall Churchill asserting, World War I generals did not—that his soldiers were not set impossible tasks. Contact with the hard facts of the battle had, however, to merge with comprehensiveness of vision. Even when detractors claimed that the credit for a victory was Prince Eugene's or when Marlborough needed a victory to silence the political wolves at home, he, as leader of the alliance, divested himself of troops for Eugene's use in a decisive theater and resigned himself to a limited campaign with a truncated army or, at the height of the Battle of Oudenarde, deprived himself of two separate forces for the sake of the general battle. Selfless, "serene . . . in stress, unbiased by the local event in which he was himself involved," he saw "the problem as a whole."[48] He is even shown with a Churchillian passion for using allied command of the sea as part of the main war effort rather than merely for trade protection; he toyed with ideas for amphibious landings north of Bordeaux or, later, on the north coast of France. Comprehensiveness of military vision includes, Churchill insists as always, nonmilitary factors. Marlborough's aiming in 1703 for the capture of the ports of Ostend and Antwerp was good politics as well as good strategy, for it accorded with Tory preference for sea operations.

Churchill concludes that no recent general even approximates the proficiency of Marlborough. We discern, therefore, in the record of Marlborough's consistent, successful application of the art of maneuver and of the military principles so badly violated by World War I generals the intellectual relief Churchill found in turning from the melancholy chronicle of the recent bloodletting to the military virtuosity of his ancestor. He is clearly still fighting the battles of the Great War, still defending his strategic views of that time, and *Marlborough* is, on one level, a parable or exhortative tale addressed to the "Westerner" generals. In the success of a soldier who flouted conventions and learned his craft by practice rather than by study of theory, Churchill the amateur strategist and perennial critic of "experts" has a club with which to beat the rigid minds of contemporary professionals. However, though Marlborough's preference for a mobile army in the field rather than siege operations seems to accord with Churchill's desire in

World War I for turning the flanks in lieu of continuing trench warfare, Maurice Ashley observes that Marlborough was, in World War I terminology, a "Westerner" and that Churchill circumvents this embarrassment by considering the Danube expedition Marlborough's (successful) Gallipoli and the siege of Lille as akin to the offensives on the western front.[49]

*   *   *   *

Ashley's is not the only dissenting view. Most historians doubt that bloody Malplaquet was much of a triumph for the duke. Ivor Burton, furthermore, questions Churchill's portrayal of Marlborough as thinking a set battle, with all its risks and especially under difficult conditions, to be always the best solution to a strategic problem; he also questions Churchill's own assumption that such a battle is always better than military chess. Still, no one challenges Churchill's depiction of Marlborough's farsightedness, organization, exploitation of weaponry, strategy, use of surprise, comprehensive vision, and tactical improvisation or his assessment of Marlborough as a supreme military commander, as a genius of warfare.[50] Less certainty surrounds Churchill's conviction that Marlborough was also an excellent diplomat and statesman.

Churchill's Marlborough is exhibited, as captain general and virtual prime minister, forcing or tricking the "foolish-frantic Parliaments, jealous princes, hungry generals, and bitter politicians" along the path he alone knew.[51] His headquarters in The Hague and his tent in the battlefields were the clearinghouses for the endless squabbling among the allies. His correspondence reveals his vast mental and physical energy, as, during battles and sieges, after a day in the saddle and under fire, he would grapple with the intricate relations of the allies and the intrigues at court, "conduct the foreign policy of England, decide the main issues of its Cabinet and of party politics at home."[52] Sometimes, at campaign's end, he wearily had to don his diplomat's hat and undertake, as in 1704, an eight-hundred-mile journey or, in 1705, a two-thousand-mile journey to various European courts to restore the cohesion of the Grand Alliance. On one occasion, he "met four kings in four days."[53] In 1707, the danger to the alliance came from the pressures exerted on the Germanic states by Charles XII of Sweden; while taking note of how Charles might be defeated by a traditional campaign of attrition, Marlborough personally helped turn Charles's ambitions toward Russia. Churchill considers this "one of his most notable successes in diplomacy," though not every historian would agree.[54]

But there was, Churchill points out, a central irony in Marlborough's career: each military victory weakened the alliance by allowing the members, with the common peril removed, to look more to their own interests. The glories of Blenheim, moreover, helped the Whigs gain control of both Houses of Parliament and turned a coalition into a party administration. Just as Marlborough the victorious soldier ironically added to the burdens of Marlborough the diplomat by weakening the alliance, so did he handicap Marlborough the nonpartisan statesman by disrupting the domestic coalition. Success in one field did not, as one would expect, make for success in the other fields. Forced to bring Whig pressures to bear on the Tory queen, Marlborough lost his influence at court, became estranged from eminent politicians like Harley, saw himself stripped of organized domestic strength, and later was ousted by the vindictive Tories.

Despite the general's fall, Churchill finds in these complex dealings, as well as in Marlborough's critique of the separate peace of 1712, a profound grasp of the European scene and of the principles of international relations. He is pleased to hear Marlborough using the very language that he himself was addressing to his contemporaries in the 1930s: the new Tory ministers "will be extremely deceived, for the greater desire they shall express for peace, the less they will have it in their power to obtain it."[55] Marlborough believed that Britain's safety lay in a resounding military victory followed by a good peace treaty rather than a seizure of towns, since the latter would, in his words, "create a jealousy both at home and abroad. I know this should not be the language of a general, but I do it as a faithful subject." To which, Churchill, seeing here his own perennial theme of "in war, Resolution; in victory, Magnanimity," comments, "It was also the language of a statesman."[56]

In fact, Churchill assigns a prescient Marlborough major credit for safeguarding the parliamentary institution, unifying the islands, opening the door to an age of reason and freedom, establishing Britain's naval supremacy and global empire, making a small island kingdom the linchpin of the Grand Alliance, and enabling it to humble a military colossus of which it had but recently been a satellite. But Churchill's attempts to prove that his ancestor was as great in politics and diplomacy as in generalship have not persuaded historians. They discern in Marlborough, sometimes in the face of Churchill's analysis, either a weakness as a diplomat or a lack of zeal for peace and justice. They assert that his obdurate desire for complete victory, his widening the aims of the war, and perhaps also his lurking personal ambitions made a settlement elusive. Though he could, unlike William III, implement plans for victory on the battlefield, he lacked a political and diplomatic grasp of realities, an ability to compromise, a formula for peace other than yet more military operations. He showed his diplomatic ineptness or duplicity in forcing on the allies the "No Peace without Spain" formula, which he knew was unacceptable to France. Not taking an active part in the negotiations into which Louis XIV entered zealously in 1709, he reduced himself, according to Ashley, to being a political and diplomatic onlooker. G. M. Trevelyan even suggests that taking Paris and forcing a peace on France could not have been as good for eventual European stability as a negotiated settlement.

Churchill may lament that Marlborough was not given his way, but the Treaty of Utrecht, which the general opposed, has been adjudged a good peace. Certainly preferable to the continuation of the war which should have ended in 1709, it suited the needs of the century. Because of Churchill's fascination with battle and with soldier's honor, Violet Barbour suggests, war, in this book, exists for its own sake, while "peace must give sureties for good behavior." Many have also noted that Churchill's disgust with the politics of the day, his opposition to fashionable pacifism ("let men bleat, 'war settles nothing' ") and to Conservative appeasement of Hitler at the time of the composition of *Marlborough,* render him bitter about the peacemakers of the 1700s. Deprecating the general's failures in diplomacy, he prefers the simple resolutions of the battlefield.[57] If Churchill's discussion of Marlborough's military strategy bears upon the fading quarrels of World War I, his discussion of Marlborough's diplomacy is partly shaped, perhaps vitiated, by the burning issues of the 1930s. This book is, among other things, a broadside at youthful pacifists and middle-aged appeasers no less than at old generals.

A Harmony of Interests

The uncertainty surrounding Marlborough's peacemaking efforts reminds us that we see him mainly as the public person, the soldier-diplomat-statesman; we are given only a few tantalizing glimpses of the elusive inner man. This is due partly to Churchill's temperament—his own war memoirs likewise concentrate on his official, public self—and partly to Marlborough's personality and the consequent nature of the documentation. It is a source of endless and understandable amazement to Churchill, whose adventurous life was littered with memoirs and apologias, that Marlborough, during years of leisure, maintained about his achievements and the disputed passages of his life a "complete silence." When in power, he often complained of his treatment in the press and conducted a large private and official correspondence, but once he became a private person again, he uttered nothing of reproach or self-pity.[58]

Such reserve, making him aloof and mysterious, was part of Marlborough's confidence, sangfroid, and commanding presence. When the Dutch vetoed his offensive designs, he quietly turned to alternate plans. When the post of allied commander-in-chief lay vacant, his composure before this "dazzling" soldier's prize astonishes Churchill; if he had reached for it, many would have objected, but his leaving The Hague without expressing interest in the command helped everyone else to see him as the only one for it. He even took his dismissal and subsequent abuse in 1711, as in 1692, "with unconcern."

Marlborough is presented as guided principally by obligations —to England, the Protestant succession, the Grand Alliance. Harassed by wracking headaches, Dutch vetoes, delays on the part of the allies, and London intrigues, he constantly spoke of wishing for peace and of wanting to retire to the country with his dear Sarah, but the higher goals kept him going. In terms reminiscent of Lovelace's famous Cavalier pronouncement on love and honor ("I could not love thee, dear, so much, / Lov'd I not honor more"), he wrote to Sarah: "I am sure you are so kind to me, and wish so well to the common cause, that you had rather see me dead, than not to do my duty."[59]

Such protestations cannot, of course, always be taken at face value; it is hard to know what motivates any man, and Marlborough's reticence on most topics compounds this difficulty. But from Marlborough's ambivalence about money, Churchill extrapolates a theory—for the general was not solely a disinterested public servant. In the various peace negotiations, he could not be bought; he would accept gifts, but "as a reward, not as an inducement."[60] This distinction, which the French could not be aware of and which posterity will not respect, Churchill applies to many of Marlborough's moral choices. Though with public funds his record was impeccable, he accepted many honoraria, provided they did not interfere with official policy or his sense of duty.

Money was itself only a means. Ultimately he seems to have dreamed of founding a powerful family in an enduring state, hence his desire for a dukedom, for proper income, for Blenheim Palace, for fame, and for a son. The raising of his family to first rank in England was no less important than raising England to the first place in Europe. "He was a builder for England, for posterity, and for himself"; the goals were not always separable, and "part of his genius lay in their almost constant harmony."[61] This idea of a "harmony of interests" Churchill sees at work in all sorts of actions that aided Marlborough's private aspirations along with his public "cause."

When, for example, Marlborough committed himself to obtaining for Princess Anne a large annual income from the crown and thereby estranged William and Mary, "it was his private interest that the matter should be settled so; it was his duty to the Princess; it was also the public interest. . . . Again we see in Marlborough's story that strange coincidence of personal and national duties at crucial times."[62] Similarly, his earnest support of the candidacy of Anne's husband, Prince George, for the post of commander-in-chief of the allied forces proved helpful to himself. Marlborough could not have gotten the post in competition with princes and veteran Dutch generals, but Prince George was "large enough to scare away the crows," and the Dutch, in order to retain control, wanted a foreigner who was not a prince. Marlborough's agreeing to the proposal that the elector of Hanover replace him in 1703 strikes Churchill as another unfathomable mystery of his character. Did he know that the Dutch would never agree to such a change? He could not be blamed for executing a mission merely because, if the mission failed, the results were good for him. Churchill portrays Marlborough doing everything that a man could be asked to do against his own interest and yet nonetheless advancing the course which favored his heart's desire; his duty proved to be his interest.

Again, when Marlborough was prevented by the margrave's delay from battling Villars, he apologized to the Frenchman for not having attacked him. This gesture of unusual ceremoniousness or of self-confidence was also a way, by means of the sounding board of Versailles, of fastening the blame on the margrave. When Marlborough sought a renewal of peace talks in 1708, he alluded to a bribe the French had offered him two years earlier. To introduce a question of private gain into a grave transaction might seem imprudent, but Churchill finds it another example of Marlborough's ability to combine national, European, and personal interests, as in many of his most questionable acts, for the suggestion had the effect of convincing Louis XIV of his sincerity. That his peace effort is tarnished for us by his pecuniary interest, Churchill explains, added in those days to its chance of success; that he probably was sincere in desiring the money detracts from his status as a man but not as a diplomat because the personal interest did not turn him from his task. He worked for a chastened France, a reconciled Europe, a glorious England; he delighted in the military successes that were the means of achieving these goals; "all these conditions being satisfied, and without prejudice to their achievement, he would take pains and stoop for a commission. Supreme vanity, profound comprehension, valiant, faithful action, and if all went well large and punctual money payments!"[63]

When the emperor offered him a principality in 1704, he desired it, petty as the desire might seem to us. But he handled it "with his usual art of having a solid and becoming reason at every stage for getting what he wanted."[64] Writing to London, he dwelled on the political embarrassment which would be caused by his refusing it. Even while representing himself almost as the "victim of inappropriate rewards," however, he put pressure on Wratislaw to make sure he received no mere title but also land and a vote in the Diet of the Reich. So, too, when Anne offered him a dukedom and Sarah tried to dissuade him from accepting, he informed his wife of his colleague's view that it was for the good of the cause, because, with many royal princes as allies and opponents, he needed aristocratic rank. His duty forced him to accede to the queen's desires and his own. "How typical is all this of Marlborough's method and demeanor," comments Churchill.[65] And how typical of Churchill is his calling one of Marlborough's "most memorable Parliamentary performances" an attack at once "spontaneous" and "dissimulating."

In sum, Marlborough took from his offices everything to which he was entitled "by warrant and custom" but nothing more. Though he was watched carefully by numerous enemies, they made few serious charges of corruption against him. When he was in disgrace for two years, not all the malice of faction, the power of the crown, and the investigations of his army records combined could unearth any evidence of the sale of commissions or any other wrongdoing in ten years of command. On the contrary, their quest merely established an incorruptibility rare in that age. No one, Churchill insists (and Trevelyan agrees), ever gave better value to England for every guinea he received.

Such a concept of a "harmony of interests" clashes with the idealist's severe standards of conduct and ready association of power with corruption. Though pettiness may accompany the climb to power and unworthy men of eminence may pay off minor scores, Churchill rejects the supposition that "the great minds of the world in their supreme activities are twisted or swayed by sordid or even personal aims."[66] He asserts, as he would again about his own ascendancy in 1940, that "the pursuit of power with the capacity and in the desire to exercise it worthily is among the noblest of human occupations."[67] This worldly attitude toward power is expressed frequently in his writings. He declares that a great man knows how to reconcile self-interest with probity. Only the naïve assume, Churchill insists, that the heroes of history were unselfish and altruistic, nor is care for one's interest a vice except when it becomes "slavish" or "ferocious," which it rarely did in Marlborough. The higher his fortune, the higher his virtue, and, later, his "conduct contracted with his power."[68]

This "harmony of interests," this acrobatic fusion of altruism and egoism, is the second of the four grand themes respectively of Churchill's four major works, but it also appears in his other writings. In the frontier war books, British imperialism is proudly shown to be a mixture of beneficence and profit; in *Randolph Churchill*, Tory democracy is held to rest equally on principle and expediency; in *The World Crisis*, British leadership is admittedly exercised on behalf of both European freedom and national interests. In the soon-to-be-composed *History*, the theme will be universalized and applied to the many molders of modern Britain as part of a conservative vision of history, even as in *The Second World War*, Churchill's personal charm, hedonism, and love of travel converge in a philosophy of personal diplomacy which, he strongly suggests, molded the alliance and, given half a chance, would have spared the postwar world many anxieties. This "harmony" also endows Marlborough with a special destiny, rather like the one Churchill felt in his own career. To portray a hero who was patriotic and beneficent without being pacifist or self-denying accords, moreover, with Churchill's pragmatism and his lifelong quarrel with purists and idealists. "The best obtainable was nearly always good enough for him."

Every politician is, of course, a pragmatist to a degree, but Churchill's ethical stance is peculiarly antithetical to that of literary intellectuals like Henry James and T. S. Eliot, profoundly conservative contemporaries who possessed a moral delicacy which Churchill despised. A certain kind of action that James (especially in his last novels) and Eliot (notably in *Murder in the Cathedral*) proscribe—doing the right thing for the wrong reason, having and eating one's moral cake—Churchill, in his apologia for his ancestor, elevates into a supreme virtue. He ignores the fear voiced by Eliot's archbishop that "Those who serve the greater cause may make the cause serve them / Still doing right" with the result that "Sin grows with doing good." His thesis is on one level merely a sophistic defense of an ambiguous hero, an argument which Churchill turns upon any last remaining criticisms of Marlborough's conduct rather as he used its logical opposite, the Either/Or principle, in *The World Crisis* to exculpate himself. It is also, however, a coherent philosophy, derived from political conservatism and romantic love of paradox. Especially as presented in the *History,* it is hostile to a narrow consistency and moral prissiness.

The reader may wonder, nevertheless, whether such a "harmony of interests" is not merely a felicitous combination of chance, pragmatism, calculation, and Churchill's generous retrospective rationalization; whether, in other words, Marlborough actually behaved so unexceptionably, or whether the fortuitously happy consequences of his egoism allowed Churchill to portray a qualified disinterestedness which the duke never had. Certainly to many historians Marlborough remains an avaricious, duplicitous man whose diplomacy was deficient because he would not exert himself in long-range national policy when his own interests were not directly concerned.[69] But to the conservative or the pragmatist, the debate as to whether Marlborough's mind in fact worked in this Cnurchillian fashion, whether this "harmony" is Marlborough's or Churchill's contrivance, is irrelevant. And whether the detached reader adjudges a given act of Marlborough's to have been elevated by a "harmony of interests" or tainted by selfishness depends on the reader's temperament. Some prefer to call a glass of water half-full; others, half-empty.[70]

*   *   *   *

The possible speciousness of the "harmony of interests" theme is a reminder that, in spite of the strengths of the *Marlborough,* not all scholars have been satisfied with it as a work of history. Some find it deficient in documentation and originality, simplistic on aspects of the age of Anne, and redolent with Whig myths. Churchill, they say, as is his wont, provides a vivid but superficial narrative of the flow of events. With its florid rhetoric and special pleading, the book is ponderous rather than exhaustive. While capturing the drama of battles and politics, of men in action, Churchill, like his intellectual foe Macaulay, evokes a world of simple good and evil. The complex character of Marlborough is simplified and sanctified, with the result that Churchill is more convincing on the soldier than on the courtier and diplomat. Nostalgic about old battles and hypnotized by glittering words, he takes liberties proper in the dramatist but forbidden the historian, and the book perhaps fails as biography no less than as history.[71]

Yet whatever its weakness as biography or history, nearly everyone accepts the *Marlborough* as a literary masterpiece. Effortlessly knitting together evidence and forceful argument, along with the varied locales, actors, and background stories, Churchill solves the narrator's problem of handling concurrent but geographically separate theaters of combat, London politics, and continental diplomacy. He achieves a splendid construction, a work "eminently readable" and lucid. Despite his partisanship, the book is often accurate, balanced, and convincing. Graphically depicting history as a struggle for power on the battlefield, in English ruling circles, and at European courts, this is a book on the colossal scale of works like *War and Peace* or Wagner's *Ring*. It has an undeniable grandeur. With gusto and generosity, it offers a splendid canvas of the age, a gallery of vivid portraits and scenes.

Although some complain that the style, despite its admitted majesty, seems infected by parliamentary oratory and debates, by "historian's English," by a plethora of adjectives, a favoring of sound over sense—what Guedella calls a "fatal lullaby"—many find it "muscular" and "rich." The spacious discourse, witty, ironic, pithy, with a sparkle lacking in *Randolph Churchill,* is as capable of Stracheyan disdain as of Carlylean eloquence. The immense resources of Churchill's narrative and expository art make the style and structure together seem comparable to the grandiose architecture of Versailles or Blenheim, to the massiveness and flourishes of the baroque art of the late seventeenth century.[72] Many have called *Marlborough* Churchill's best book: a supreme historical work which wears very well with the passage of the years, which assures Churchill a place among English writers, which ranks with the major works of Trevelyan, Neale, and Carlyle, and which is a monument worthy of the general and of the grand manner of his age.[73]

Churchill's exposition of political intrigues, like that of the battles, is marked by verve and intimacy. In recording the birth of the system of British party politics he knows so well, he catches every nuance. We feel that connoisseur and raconteur is taking us by the hand and, between hearty puffs on a sizable cigar and sips from a glass of brandy, leading us through the labyrinth, as if he were a government-accredited guide. His exposition is marked by the knowledgeable lifting of the veil at the appropriate places; the veteran's pointing to ground much gone over; the aficionado's criticisms of blunders and weaknesses; the ironies signaled by a secretive wink; the pedagogic pretense at being shocked or surprised over matters he is only too familiar with; above all, the relish of the charm and glory of it all. In a sense not only Marlborough but all of the politicians, including the vile Bolingbroke, are Churchill's ancestors.

Here the narrator is, however, oblivious to a discordant note. Having set out to clarify the reasons for Marlborough's fall and ill repute, Churchill discovers that the usual explanations—the general's alleged Jacobitism, avarice, warmongering—are false. The true causes, as in *The World Crisis,* are the incredible shortsightedness, stubbornness, and flabbiness of most statesmen and leaders and the confusion and intrigues which disrupt a nation in wartime. Unlike *The World Crisis,* this tale contains one man of genius who is able to bring the flood of events at least partially and temporarily under control. Yet he too is undone, and, not unlike *The World Crisis* with which it is meant to contrast, this romantic tale or Greek tragedy, this "classic instance of how far romance lags behind reality,"[74] leaves one with a jaundiced view of all politics. But Churchill is so rapt by the complexities, the sporting aspect, the glamor of politics, that this point eludes him, even as he is too engrossed in military strategy to notice the human suffering it produces. *Marlborough* leaves us with a compelling portrait of a supreme hero, though we remain uncertain whether this Marlborough with his "harmony of interests" ever existed. While it is a "masterpiece," we cannot classify it for sure as either a "historical" or a "literary" masterpiece.

Many have remarked on the special place of *Marlborough* in the political career of the author. Churchill had apparently come to the end of the road in politics, and he needed new sources of energy to get his career started again. From the story of the slander and hatred Marlborough faced all his life, he could learn to see his own disappointments in perspective, even while reminding a lethargic Britain of her past greatness. *Marlborough,* written at the nadir of his political life but the zenith of his intellectual powers, is thus in a sense autobiographical as well as historical; the vindication of a Marlborough suffering from neglect and contumely was a self-vindication, in a way even the start of Churchill's comeback.

The hostility it evinces to the "peace party" gradated into the author's campaign against appeasement in the 1930s, for as Churchill progressed with the project, he could see a struggle emerging in the Europe of his day very like that in Marlborough's.

While the two world war memoirs, looking to the recent past, were works of self-justification and even self-therapy, the two biographies, directed to a more remote past, were, as studies in one man's bold political campaign and another's bold military campaign, personally heuristic and prefigurative. When he wrote about himself, Churchill was retrospective, but when he wrote about his family, he adumbrated his own future. *Randolph Churchill* helped the author to find himself politically, or rather to delineate a program, a creed which crystallized his instinctive political reflexes and so armed him for the coming five-year legislative and administrative struggle on behalf of the new liberalism. *Marlborough*, in which he extended his military vision by means of the study of a single genius (rather than of the many recent military failures in *The World Crisis*), helped Churchill master the political and diplomatic nuances of managing a grand alliance against a continental military power. Presenting the world with a portrait of heroism, Britain with a reminder of her mission, and himself with a model and "prophecy," this exercise unwittingly prepared him for the imminent six-year war against Nazism. What began as a historical study, a vindication of a fallen statesman by a fallen statesman, became the preparation, by the future leader of Britain and forger of a new Grand Alliance, for the struggle which transcended all previous ones in scope and danger. What began as an alternative to the bad generalship in World War I became a blueprint for what he tried to be, or imagined himself being, in World War II.[75] And what began, in a way, as an escapist, nostalgic work proved terribly pertinent to Britain's present and his own future, as pertinent as his current speeches. Not just a dissertation written by a disinterested academic scholar and without impact on the author's own values or on the larger society, *Marlborough* is thus both descriptive and impassioned, retrospective and prophetic, personal and public experience, and rarely, concludes Commager, have author and subject been so made for each other.

Depicting in this work a fusion of political and military interests he had long been reaching for in his own life, Churchill has changed his hero-ideal from his politician father to his warrior-statesman-diplomat ancestor. His political exile turns out to be a disguised blessing, for its product, *Marlborough,* is at once a sort of self-revelation, an apprenticeship for the prime ministry, and a means of, and testimony to, the author's maturation as a statesman. Undergoing in the 1930s something like a dark night of the soul—as a result of his sense of a Victorian paradise forever lost and a personal climax missed, as well as the hostility greeting his current warnings—Churchill found in this book the means of recovering his destiny. Now at last he could study the broad field of European diplomacy and alliances, a subject which, absent from his writings until *The World Crisis* and superficially treated in that work, became central to his thought in the 1930s and thereafter. This next step in the enlarging of his interests was indispensable for his role in World War II, and *Marlborough* was a historical study which served as the necessary intellectual self-discipline. Hence meditation and action were one for Churchill, and his work as historian crowned his work as prophet and as statesman. A remark of Churchill's in "Moses," an interesting short paraphrase of Scripture, is of interest here: "Every prophet has to come from civilization, but every prophet has to go into the wilderness. . . . He must serve periods of isolation and meditation. This is the process by which psychic dynamite is made."[76] Thus Churchill's studies in history enabled him to be one of the first to see in Hitler the lineaments of a new and worse Louis XIV. And in 1940, the man with one face directed to the past and one to the future was the embodiment of British tradition because he saw the war under the aspect of history and fancied himself a Marlborough. He was indispensable partly because of the vision imparted to him by his own books, especially by this narrative in some ways strikingly parallel to the unknown events to follow. In an irony of history, the inspiration for a modern Grand Alliance came (with considerable help from Hitler) not only to a Churchill descended from an earlier leader of such a bloc but also to a man who on the eve of the alliance produced a study of that first Churchill.[77] Whether or not the "harmony of interests" idea applies to Marlborough, it certainly describes Churchill's own achievement in writing *Marlborough* between wars.

Foreign Policy Speeches and Articles:
Cries in the Wilderness

Writing his many books and essays was not Churchill's sole or even his most important activity in the 1930s. His look backwards was complemented by glances at present and future, for as the work on *Marlborough* proceeded, the contemporary situation began to approximate the one he found in the old books and archives. Without party or sizable following, he made a herculean effort during ten years to change the course of British foreign policy by means of a series of warnings and prophecies. It has in fact been little noted that only in his fourth decade of public life did European diplomacy and world affairs—as opposed to imperial matters, domestic reform, frontier or global war making—begin to occupy a large place in his writings and speeches.

Having returned in 1924, after nearly twenty years as a Liberal, to the Conservative fold in time to become chancellor of the exchequer for five years, Churchill fell out once more with his original party. Though they opposed Britain's first Socialist prime minister, the Conservatives supported MacDonald's "Little England" policy as it applied to the Asian empire. Churchill's *India* consists mainly of a series of his speeches of 1929–31 during the first part of the heated controversy over India, which resulted in his leaving the shadow cabinet and entering the political wilderness. His basic theme is that British policy will lead to the destruction of imperial authority and of Indian tranquillity. His paradoxical point is that his critique is based on abhorrence of bloodshed. He implies that the issue is not between violence and lenity, or rather that, given the ironies of human nature, it is really between his long-range pacifism and the government's pacific rhetoric and inept action, which will lead ultimately if unintentionally to severity and violence. Yet history has rendered an ambiguous verdict on this point of view, which is one of the most controversial of Churchill's political career. The strongest argument against him is that not only was he advocating a wrong principle but that his inability to see that the days of the British Empire were numbered vitiated the force of his prophecies in the later 1930s.

For the Indian phase was soon superseded by the German one,

as foreign policy continued to preoccupy Churchill. He eventually promised to accede silently to the India Constitution Act and turned his attention to a greater peril. Churchill's fame as the Demosthenes of his age warning against the would-be Alexander across the North Sea rests securely on the utterances collected in two volumes. *While England Slept* (or *Arms and the Covenant*) consists of speeches made from 1932 through 1938; *Step by Step* is a collection of some eighty newspaper articles, culled from a biweekly newsletter which commented on the state of world affairs from 1936 through 1939. The speeches represent four stages of his thinking on foreign policy. At first, when Germany was still disarmed, Churchill, like the American isolationists, urged his government to refrain from making continental commitments; then, when Germany began rearming, he turned to the League of Nations as an instrument of peace; later, with Germany becoming a threat and the league remaining impotent, he wanted Britain to arm and to press for a collective security alliance; finally, he excoriated the policy of appeasement, and, from having warned that German rearmament boded an expansionist foreign policy, he came to emphasize that Germany could be stopped only by firmness.

The newspaper articles provide a vivid portrait of the three climatic prewar years, when Hitler, after having in the first three years of his rule concentrated on developing a war machine, began to expand by means of diplomacy and bluff. Adding a preface, Churchill rushed the articles into print in book form almost on the eve of World War II, as though to provide the nation wtih a tract for the war about to be fought. The ideas and rhetoric are similar to those in his speeches of the period, but because the articles do not treat domestic issues, they show a greater concentration and continuity. In fact, chance has imposed on this work a structure which gives it some of the qualities of an intentionally literary composition. Quickly changing circumstances and unexpected events generate much suspense and excitement; thus, Churchill's joy over France's initial standing by Czechoslovakia is followed in the very next piece, "The Austrian Eye-Opener," by the electric effect on everyone of Hitler's sudden seizure of Austria. This is, in short, solid drama as well as a neat little history of the period.[78]

In these two books we find one of Churchill's major themes

(already explored in *The World Crisis*) and the most famous occasion of its expression. Platitudinous speeches and "short-sighted optimism" are useless, he believes, for the idea that aggression can be stopped only by the resolve to use force is a "mocking paradox." Had Britain armed in time, war "would not now haunt the capitals of Europe."[79] Passive resistance tempts the dictators into imprudent steps from which withdrawal by them will be impossible. To dwell on the horrors of war will not prevent a foe from beginning one, and Hitler's policy of aggression without war has succeeded because the mere threat of force suffices. Churchill sees himself as a figure easily derided—the "pacifist who is ready to fight for peace."

But Churchill's jeremiads are vitiated, critics have said, by three adverse facts. The first is that as secretary of war in 1919 and as chancellor of the exchequer in the 1920s, Churchill himself, disregarding military warnings and disappointing the younger officers who expected modernization of the army, reverted to his father's and his own original cause of retrenchment and disastrously weakened British defenses, especially in the new weaponry of air power and armor that he had fostered. British diplomacy was therefore, by his own logic, handicapped. The second fact is that Churchill's record of opposition is not as bold, effective, and clear as he makes it seem in his speeches and memoirs. Third, and perhaps most important, was the fact of Churchill's limited vision, caused by his fixation on the German menace and by his conservatism during the 1930s, which prompted him to regard the Ethiopian, Manchurian, and Spanish crises as diversions on which one should be neutral. This stance estranged him from the many to whom the imminent struggle was not a nationalistic one against resurgent Prussian militarism but an ideological one against Fascism wherever it might appear. But, as R. R. James concludes, even though he was wrong or imprecise on estimates, facts, forecasts, and remedies, he alone was right on the unprecedented pace of German revival, and his many past and present imprudences caused him to be ignored.[80]

Thus Churchill, seeing an imminent global struggle on a Marlborough scale, seeks the bases of a grand alliance like that led by his ancestor. But the occasion had not yet arrived. Upon the failure of the League of Nations, a Britain allied to France and

Russia would have posed a major obstacle to Hitler's "one at a time" method. Instead the Nazi and Communist regimes came to an agreement; this marked "the culminating failure" of the blundering British policy, which also forced the smaller nations to seek refuge in neutrality. Surveying the worldwide political situation consequently leaves Churchill depressed. He is haunted by the "supreme question" of modern war; the exposure of the entire population to modern weapons and tactics may see the ruin of European civilization.

Concurrent with this pessimism in Churchill's writings of the 1930s is a curious worship of generals and dictators and their "remarkable" exploits. Ataturk, "hero" and "father" of Turkey, with "far-seeing vision" makes "astonishing" reforms; Chiang is a "national hero" who through his "wise strategy" may well become a "world hero"; Franco could, by uniting his country, become a "great" man in the mold of Charles V; Mussolini is the "extraordinary" expression of the Italian soul, a Caesar-like figure admired by many. Even Hitler is praised as late as 1935. Though aware of the posturing—"the inimitable Führer in his grand and indispensable anti-Bolshevist campaign"[81]—Churchill at first willingly overlooks moral issues and international concerns to make pragmatic judgment of the German dictator as political animal, patriot, man of action. Were Britain defeated, Churchill would want such a man to restore her, and he wishes British leadership could be animated with "something of the spirit" of this obscure "Austrian corporal" who wrought such a transformation in Germany and Europe, this "extraordinary" man who holds the fate of the world in his hands. Hoping that success will mellow him, that the anger and hate are merely the traits or instruments of someone rising amid adversity, Churchill is willing even in 1938 to "welcome in a sincere spirit" some of Hitler's "assurances."[82]

Strange and even repulsive as these judgments now may seem, they grow naturally out of Churchill's outlook—not only from his ability to see a leader's viewpoint sympathetically and to give a man the benefit of his doubt, but also from a network of political principles. They are the counterparts of his conservatism on domestic matters. Much as he praised democracy and loved Parliament, he had, as we have seen, his reservations about universal suffrage, periods of electioneering, and the ability of the

Parliament to solve modern economic problems. These weaknesses, along with the turn everywhere in Europe to brutal dictatorships of right or left and, later, the lassitude of the democracies in the face of aggression by some of the dictators, profoundly shook his faith in democracy, as it did that of many in the 1930s.

Churchill always looked, furthermore, to the constitutional monarchy as providing a framework above politics, as though democracy would be vulnerable without a revered dynastic ruler formally at the helm. His continuing fear of bolshevism abroad and his growing domestic conservatism (everything to the left of him somehow seemed to lead to totalitarianism) caused him initially to see the strong men of the right as bulwarks against the left, even though he always distinguished between the dynastic interests of constitutional monarchs and the lack of constraints upon the dictators, and even though he soon came to dismiss the antibolshevism of the dictators. Add to these Churchill's growing belief, abetted by his study of Marlborough, that the exceptional individual may shape history ("one man and one man alone"[83]); his political philosophy of toughness, of calculated, limited use of force, of taking risks; his love of power as a means of getting things done; his personal delight in meeting great men and leaders; his activism, his hero-worship of men like Caesar, Marlborough, Napoleon (and, for a time, Lloyd George); his pragmatic judging of men (like the Mahdi) by their success rather than by the substance of their message or by the means of their succeeding; his suspicion of idealists and sentimental do-gooders—and Churchill's weakness for the strong man becomes inevitable. (But he could not, because of his imperial blinders, see the same qualities in a Nehru, or, on a spiritual, nonviolent plane, in a Gandhi.) The desire to emulate rather than only to worship and the desire to make himself a hero within the context of British democracy and decency were, like his patriotism, important factors in Churchill's own success and distinguished him at once from the cloistered dreamer living vicariously or the frustrated man turned zealot and demon.[84]

*   *   *   *

Churchill continued to cultivate his reputation as a prophet. Basic to his many valid prophecies was his vision of the coming war. Venerable anticommunist though he was, he saw clearly, unlike many Tories, that the Axis alliance was only nominally against the communism "of which they profess to stand in great dread" but aimed as well at the parliamentary democracies.[85] Foreseeing, even after the depressing Soviet-Nazi pact, that the interests of these new allies would inevitably clash, he was able to predict that the future lay in a Western alliance with Russia and that what was coming was not a new war but "resumption of the War which ended in November 1918."[86]

Among Churchill's long-range predictions one must mention the remarks that air bombardment of civilian populations would merely stiffen the will; that a Jewish state in Palestine would have to be "armed to the teeth"; that a victorious but ungrateful Franco would not join "his Nazi and Fascist allies."[87] (He was here, as on Russia, open to hopeful developments on an unpromising front.) In 1936 he foresaw the blitzkrieg, "the suddenness of a possibly decisive attack,"[88] as well as the turning of the Maginot Line by a "swing round through Belgium and Holland."[89] He saw that the Italians were being drawn into a war which would "end in their . . . rescue by Germany at a price fatal to their independence."[90] And, most important of all, he prophesied that "a period of suffering resulting from the air-slaughter of non-combatants may lie before us; but this, if borne with fortitude, will only seal the comradeship of many nations to save themselves."[91] He foresaw a triumphant Germany confronting a solitary Britain with a powerful air weapon by which the "destinies of nations" would be decided. So sure was he that he launched into a boast and paean that would become the great theme of his wartime speeches: "It may well be that the most glorious chapters of our history are yet to be written."[92] Had he not boldly (and prophetically) asserted in the 1930s that if Germany had defeated France in 1914 or 1918 and if the United States had not yet entered the war, Britain "could have repeated in the twentieth century the resistance which our ancestors made to Napoleon" and then, with an English-speaking alliance, won the war?[93]

And by his predictions no less than his pugnacity, L. S. Amery declares, Churchill earned his right to lead Britain through those chapters of history. The one man who had been ruled out in the 1930s as the prime minister of any party, but also the one man with a relatively clear record on appeasement, was now the only possible leader in the greatest peril. From having been, in the uneven quarter of a century that followed upon his initial successes, the scapegoat of Gallipoli, the ill-fated chancellor of the exchequer, and the reactionary on India, Churchill became the prophet against Hitler; and he would become the savior of his country.[94]

5

The Fifth Phase:
The 1940s

Wartime Supreme Commander

Churchill, I consider, was the greatest leader in war this country has ever known. Not the greatest warrior—Clement Attlee, 1965

The savior of his country—A. J. P. Taylor, 1965

Speeches:
The Roar of the Lion

Churchill's fame as prophet in the 1930s is eclipsed only by his fame as the indomitable war leader during the terrible years when a solitary and poorly equipped Britain outfaced Hitler by dint, it would seem, of its prime minister's defiant speeches and not much else. Never before had there been such scope for his rich oratory, a role so filled with challenge, urgency, drama. Now all the resources of rhetoric, the skill with words, the experience of decades of parliamentary debates, the rich sense of history, the wit, the courage in adversity were put to consummate use in a truly historic juncture. If ever the pen was mightier than the sword, this was the occasion.

Churchill's wartime speeches were published year by year. The resulting seven volumes (including secret session speeches released after the conflict) surely contain some of the greatest orations of all time. The finest, naturally, are those delivered in the earlier, critical part of the war, 1940–42. These speeches magically encouraged people at the time of delivery, and they dramatically evoke the supreme crisis when read today in silence in a relaxed setting. Here are many of the sonorous phrases and rallying cries Churchill coined or adapted;[1] the colloquialisms mingling amicably with orotund polysyllables; the homely, vivid imagery; the humor and understatement which, by keeping disaster at a distance, testified to his self-confidence and defiance, in contrast to the grim sarcasm and wild boasts of the hysterical Hitler.[2] Here, amid the rolling periods, is the recurring movement from stern survey of current duress, through resolve never to yield, to abiding faith in triumph and better times. Here, as well, is a patriotic rhetoric to match those forged by Shakespeare and Milton. The lines beginning "I see the spirit of an unconquerable people" capture the excitement of Milton's "Methinks I see in my mind a noble and puissant nation rousing herself," even as the "finest hour" peroration and the various passages which treat the grim present as a period of historical greatness to be long remembered are kin to the patriotic effusions in *Richard II, King John,* and especially *Henry V.* As President Kennedy definitively put it, Churchill "mobilized the English language and sent it into battle."[3]

Churchill's flair for the melodramatic and the superlative, for the impassioned rhetoric of patriotism and indomitability, at last sounded wholly appropriate. The erstwhile historian roused the nation to its best effort by conjuring up its glorious past. Invading Britain, he reminded everyone, was an old idea, and she had come through similar perils before. The current crisis being greater than those caused by the Spanish Armada or Napoleon in the "brave old days," his generation was, in its turn, "on the stage of history," under the scrutiny of posterity. Though the world thought that the "end had come," Britain stood alone against overwhelming odds and came through, in "this cardinal time," "the greatest days our country has ever lived, . . . memorable in the history of our race."[4] The achievement of a few thousand airmen was comparable to that of Drake and his hardy mariners; the "tremendous year," 1940, surpassed 1588 and 1918, surpassed the triumphs of Marlborough, Chatham, Nelson, and Wellington.

Tradition, by inspiring Churchill and making him see the present in perspective, reinforced his confidence. Anyone else would have been unnerved by the fall of France or by German penetration of Russia, but Churchill, with his experience of World War I, his study of Marlborough's wars, and his knowledge of a thousand years of European military history, well realized, as Plumb remarks, that encircling alliances have failed only temporarily. His sense of the past, in short, gave him a sense of the future.[5] The history he had always studied and courted now aided him in his leadership and thereby granted him a place of honor.

Toward the end of the war, Churchill observed that if, after V-E Day, the people were to put him "out to grass," he would understand, though he would like to continue to work for social progress and a lasting world peace. But whether or not his political vocation had been fulfilled, his writing vocation had not; he intimated his plans to compose his World War II memoirs. "There is no reason why persons in unofficial positions should not compile histories of their own activities during the war, and I trust I may be given the opportunity of making some interpolations of my own."[6] He had already placed his crucial decisions and actions "on the shelf, from which the historians, when they have time, will select their documents to tell their stories."[7] The elections of 1945, that "effectively disguised blessing," proved to be the circumstance which gave him the time to be his own historian once again.

The speeches bear an interesting relationship to the memoirs. They provide, as much as do memos or official records, the framework upon which the narrative is constructed; Churchill, never loath to quote himself, reprints large sections of them, duly introduced and commented on. (He had done the same in *The World Crisis,* but those speeches had not the power and fame of the later ones.) They dramatize the highlights of the war, while the memoirs provide the details. If the speeches as originally published are merely the mountain peaks, showing through a layer of clouds, of the story of Britain at war, they remain awesome peaks in the memoirs which clear away some of the clouds and reveal the valleys. They are, at the same time, the "official" or ideal version of the war; they present, of necessity, the aspect which it would do the British people, and the foe, much good to see. They rouse morale and cover errors, flaws, and dissension with a bold front, while the memoirs reveal, often for the first time, the fears, hatreds, and squabbles on the Allied side or within the British government. Hence, for example, de Gaulle and Chiang appear in the speeches as heroes and Stalin as a great, reliable, and even friendly leader, whereas the memoirs exhibit Churchill's numerous difficulties with de Gaulle and Stalin and his annoyance over the Americans' vastly inflated idea of Chiang's importance.

The Second World War

Churchill's Finest Years

The Second World War is a fascinating book because of the tale, the teller, and the telling. It is the narrative of a global cataclysm, composed in a personal style by one who was at the heart of things from beginning to end. No other wartime leader in history has given us a work of two million words written only a few years after the events and filled with messages among world potentates which had so recently been heated and secret. Britain was led by a professional writer. Since men of action are rarely writers, books have usually been written *about* the giants of history; the men themselves speak to us of their deeds only in fragments or at second hand. We have the formal battle reports of a Caesar, the obiter dicta of a Napoleon, the letters of a Lincoln, but nothing like a detailed exposition of a long sequence of events seen from the center of the world stage, together with an account of the interplay of one man's designs and the tide of history. Well may Churchill boast that no "similar record exists or has ever existed of the day-to-day conduct of war and administration."[8] Even as he came to his prime ministership well prepared by forty years of varied political and executive experience, of defeats and triumphs in peace and war, so had he, in exactly a half-century of journalism, oratory, historical and autobiographical writing, forged a style and sense of structure before he began to record the climactic years of his career.

Having immersed himself in nominally objective works in the wake of his autobiography of 1930, Churchill now returned to the memoir form. After the vicarious excitements of Marlborough's generalship and diplomacy and of the panorama of English history, studied in the years of his own relative inactivity, he told of his own wartime leadership and manifold activities, his own place in the unfolding pattern of events he had tried to elucidate. History itself had once again thrust him and his interests as a writer from the remote and objective into the present (or recent) and personal. Continuing from where *The World Crisis* ended, in the 1920s,[9] *The Second World War* is the usual Churchillian melange of autobiography, apologia, general history, and selected documents; of impersonal autobiography and personal history. But it is much more unified because Churchill was in a central position continuously and could observe events from a higher vantage point. The technique he had developed awaited only the climax of his political career to be put to supreme use.

Each volume contains an appendix of memoranda selected from a collection a million words long. Whatever their reservations on other aspects of Churchill's leadership or his chronicle of it, critics stand in awe of the versatility, keenness, lucidity, vitality, wit, practicality revealed in these minutes, whose author has been compared to a conductor sometimes trying to be the whole orchestra or a vast machine capable of picking up a safety pin or a locomotive. These communications may have been childish, tiresome, eccentric, trivial; they may have made life unnecessarily difficult for underlings; they may have contained considerable fakery, for Churchill often knew only a few details of a topic and not, as the recipient feared, the whole area on which the memo touched. But they kept everyone on his toes. Plumb believes that Churchill wrote them consciously as historical documents, while Whittemore sees them as deliberately wrought compositions by a man considering himself a writer and defining statesmanship in terms of the ability to express oneself. The result, adjudges Howarth, is something, composed in "urgent, imperious good English," that is above "literature" or "style." For some readers, the documents, with their record of resilience, forthrightness, intelligence, and war making proficiency, *are* the books.[10] Although it is the culmination of a literary genre Churchill had practically invented in 1897 and had cultivated thereafter, *The Second World War* is, then, decidedly a unique work.

*   *   *   *

Becoming the top man during this war, which, he was sure, he alone knew how to finish, was indeed the climax toward which his four decades in politics had been moving. "I felt as if I were walking with Destiny, and that all my past life had been but a preparation for this hour and for this trial."[11] He now appeared fortunate to have been excluded from Baldwin's government, despite his chagrin at the time, for he was thus dissociated from the compromises of the ensuing years, from party antagonisms, and from responsibility for the inadequate national defense. As the years in the wilderness proved to be propitious, the successful man is certain that fate watched over him: "Over me beat the invisible wings";[12] man little foresees the results of "wise or unwise" action, he says, applying to himself a recurring theme in his books. "Great was the service [Baldwin] was doing me. . . . This was not the first time—or indeed the last—that I have received a blessing in what was at the time a very effective disguise."[13]

Similarly, since the first twenty-eight months of his prime ministership saw an "almost unbroken series of military defeats" without precedent in English history, it was a marvel that, under heavy political fire in the summer of 1942 and on the eve, as it happened, of an unbroken chain of successes, he was not removed from office, as he had been in 1915. "I should then have vanished from the scene with a load of calamity on my shoulders, and the harvest, at last to be reaped, would have been ascribed to my belated disappearance. . . . All this shows how much luck there is in human affairs, and how little we should worry about anything except doing our best."[14] When later addressing the U.S. Congress and referring to his being half-American, he found the coincidence another sign of "some appointed plan," "some great purpose and design."[15] Such talk may well be self-deluding, but, as Nicolson remarks, Churchill's daydream had long been to become prime minister in a dangerous war; few daydreams have ever been so fully realized. He found himself with unprecedented power, at the age of sixty-five and after an endless political career, at last able to make good the claims forwarded in *The World Crisis* and to apply to the most crucial hour of British history what he had learned by writing the now terribly germane *Marlborough*. Given his belief in his own greatness and in Britain's, his varied experience and knowledge, and his way with words, his whole life might well seem a preparation for this juncture. For once, concludes Amery, a democracy had a leader who could both express its spirit and be a master of war.[16]

He certainly behaved like a warrior. Having, like Marlborough, attained supreme command—albeit through a political rather than a military career—and considering himself, by dint of study and wide military experience in previous wars, a strategist, Churchill often ventured into purely military questions and clashed with his own generals and Roosevelt's. The memoirs are therefore filled with detailed technical discussions of activities in all the services. No other prime minister could have participated in such discourse with confidence; a retired general aptly said to him, "You . . . have the enormous advantage, rare amongst politicians, of being able to talk the same language as sailors, soldiers, and airmen."[17] As head of the admiralty, Churchill frequently offered the prime minister detailed counsel on army, air force, and general supply matters; as prime minister he found his colleagues "increasingly disposed to give" him "latitude . . . in the military conduct of the war."[18]

He presents himself as continually looking for new theaters, whether to aid Russia or provide combat experience for raw American troops. This aggressiveness, although Churchill did not fully realize it, maddened his generals, for it often sprang from political causes: the need to be doing something for home morale, or to try to match the Russian effort, or to silence American isolationist opinion. In his insistence that a policy is as real as a bullet, he overlooked the complex requirements of a mechanized army. Churchill therefore leaves us with distinctly unfavorable impressions of his first two Middle East commanders, Wavell and Auchinleck. Only toward the end of the war was he able to feel, like Lincoln, that he had found fighting, risk-taking commanders in men like Alexander and Montgomery. One must ask, however, whether Churchill is not using the earlier generals as scapegoats for the unproductiveness of his first years as prime minister. General

Brooke, his army chief of staff, believes, with some historians, that Churchill is guilty of exactly the errors he condemns: judging commanders by results rather than "the quality of their effort" and forgetting their prudent preparation against dangers which, as a result of such foresight, did not materialize. Churchill is too depressed by defeat and elated by victory to see that Wavell and Auchinleck did as well with their limited manpower and supplies as Alexander and Montgomery were to do in more affluent days. Interfering throughout the war with the field commanders (even, thanks to modern communications, in tactics) while lacking firsthand knowledge of the frontline conditions—the very thing he had accused World War I generals of doing—he pressured them into the offensive prematurely and excessively. When they resisted him, he called them tired and defeated.[19] *The Second World War* also perpetrates an injustice on Air Marshal Dowding, the unsung hero of the Battle of Britain. His blocking the assignment of the last squadrons to France (which Churchill was tempted to do for political and sentimental reasons) and his subsequent resolute defense strategy were rewarded with oblivion because he had successfully resisted Churchill and offended the air marshals committed to the bomber offensive.

For when he came through the worst of the enemy's air and undersea offensive and turned the corner toward victory, Churchill thought that the fighter planes had been the salvation of Britain but that only the bombers could win the war. With overwhelming mastery of the air, Britain could destroy the industrial and scientific basis of the German war effort and economy. An expanded bomber force therefore had priority over the tank. This decision is curious, considering that German bombing had not broken British endurance and that Churchill himself had predicted during World War I and again in the 1930s that the bombing of civilian centers would enhance resistance rather than creating panic. He now gives the bomber offensive much credit for final victory and says little about contrary postwar findings on the subject.

He is in fact laconic about what became one of the major military and moral cruxes of the war, and history has taken him to task for his role in it. Advertised as retribution for Nazi wickedness —though Britain had begun the bombing of civilians without reference to immediate army needs—the bomber offensive, a legacy of the days when Britain stood alone and had no other offensive weapon, proved self-defeating. At first it brought about Hitler's terrible counterstroke; eventually it outdid German "frightfulness" in the slaughter of civilians but without useful results. Making only a slight impact on German war production and morale, the "terror raids" exacted a huge price in British airmen killed, production diverted, and resources wasted. The emphasis on the manufacture of bombers left the army and fleet (notably in the Far East) with insufficient fighter plane cover and thereby prolonged the war. Men and materiel sent on disappointing raids against U-boat bases and building yards could better have been used at sea for mine laying and convoy escort and on land for transportation and dive-bombing.

If offensives in the West were the military obsession of World War I, the bomber offensive was that of World War II, and here Churchill was an accomplice rather than a wise critic. He did not understand that the invention of radar revolutionized the air war or that the Luftwaffe was valuable because it was used in conjunction with the army. His lifelong distrust of the army seemed to culminate in his 1941 belief that it was not even necessary for victory; he accepted instead the air force's faith in "victory through airpower." The independent air offensive was allowed, like the Mediterranean campaign, to starve the preparations for a second front. It was in a way a new Gallipoli, and thus his World War I strategy of keeping casualties low by avoiding frontal assaults led, Trumbull Higgins believes, to the policy of indiscriminate bombing—in spite of divided public opinion and the objections of various eminent men—and ultimately to the American use of the atom bomb. Churchill felt scruples at times, but he seemed to grow indifferent to civilian suffering; when the public expressed moral revulsion, he made Air Marshal Harris the scapegoat.[20]

Churchill's discussion of weaponry is, moreover, vitiated by his failure to keep abreast of military developments in the 1930s. An enthusiast of war making, alert to modern developments and bureaucratic obstructionism, he continued to dwell heavily on World War I and still thought in old quantitative terms of rifles, machine guns, and battleships rather than of tactical forces, mobile armor, and aircraft carriers. In the wake of the Spanish Civil War, he discounted the growing power of the U-boat and the plane vis-à-vis the battleship, even though many experts were arriving at the contrary conclusion. Thinking of the tank in slow motion, he regarded it (like the U-boat) as obsolete; thinking of the plane as a bomber of cities, he did not see it as, working in conjunction with sea and land operations, a threat to the foot soldier. The man who prided himself on being an iconoclast and innovator actually held rather archaic notions of war making, as reflected in his use of phrases like "feat of arms" and "capital ships." The disasters in Norway, Greece, and the Far East were attributable in part to his romantic notion of traditional naval supremacy and to his commitment to heavy bombers at the expense of fighters.[21]

Many charge that traditionalism also impeded his military thinking with reference to the second front. If the issue of the bomber offensive is skirted or slighted in *The Second World War*, that of the second front is confronted, and Churchill's defense against the widespread belief that he opposed it is one of the themes of the book—although scholars complain that he obfuscates more than he clarifies. He notes sarcastically that in June 1940 Russia had remained neutral in the face of a live second front; he concedes that his World War I experience made him prefer flank operations to head-on onslaughts and that he was haunted by thoughts of Gallipoli, especially with reference to the Salerno and Normandy landings. He shows his commitment, however, by quoting his early memos on the creation of the immense apparatus necessary for landing one million men with armor on the beaches. The Russians did not understand that such an operation required an armada of specially constructed landing craft, not to speak of air supremacy, neither of which was available in 1941, 1942, or even 1943. During the long preparations, North Africa was liberated; Hitler's decision to make a stand in Tunisia prolonged the African campaign into 1943 and postponed the Normandy invasion to 1944. Churchill came to see this as a blessing, for a 1943 invasion, however pleasing to Russia, would have led to "a bloody defeat of the first magnitude," but he emphasizes that it was American military opinion which ruled out 1943 at a time when he himself was still in favor of that date. As postponement became inevitable, he pressed instead, against American reluctance, for an invasion of Sicily and Italy so that something be done to help Russia. This "third front," this roundabout route, from North Africa through Sicily to Italy did in fact, he claims, wear out the Axis powers, tie down twenty German divisions, and deflect German reinforcements meant for Normandy and Russia.

The second front was indeed the most controversial aspect of World War II, rather as that earlier second front, Gallipoli, had been of World War I, and Churchill was intimately connected with both. The earlier war saw a great debate between the politicians and the military over eastern (Mediterranean) as against western (France) strategy; with the failure of Gallipoli, the western strategy prevailed despite continuing civilian criticism of the bloodshed in France. In the later war, the British military leaders, having learned their lesson or having their options limited, agreed with the civilian leaders on an eastern strategy. This time, the American military was hostile to such a policy, and it divided into Westerners (Marshall and his followers) and Far Easterners (King, MacArthur). Although it threatened unintentionally to give the Far Easterners predominance in American councils, the British Easterner viewpoint in the end prevailed. So Churchill, having the support of his own military by default and winning over with great difficulty the American military, at last obtained, a quarter of a century after first propounding it, his large, successful, amphibious flank-turning movement in the Mediterranean. His strategy was essentially the same as in the previous war, with North Africa, Sicily, and Italy in place of Gallipoli. While threatened invasion held the Germans pinned down in France, the Allied operations in the Mediterranean produced "freedom of manoeuver" and made use of Allied sea mastery. A major theme of Churchill's career was thus fulfilled. But whether the results in fact justified the operation, whether it proved a shortcut or a detour, remains almost as much the subject of debate as does Gallipoli.

Some generals and historians see the operation as part of traditional imperial strategy, followed by Marlborough and by Chatham and elaborately studied by Churchill in his recent work on the *Marlborough* and on the *History*.[22] The Mediterranean was seen as the main theater of operations and the enemy's weakest flank; by limiting the land war in Europe and heavily aiding the

Russians, the venerable policy of fighting mainly with foreign troops would result in low British casualties (and, according to some Americans, would deviously retain imperial influence in the Balkans). Others trace this strategy to Churchill's revulsion from the bloodletting on the western front in World War I, to his desire for maneuver, surprise, and speed in the use of small forces in lieu of the old mass land war, or to his putative obsession with redeeming Gallipoli and vindicating his Balkans strategy. One may add that, with the postponement of the second front, Churchill was realizing another World War I strategic idea of his—to strike a defensive posture (in 1917) pending the arrival of the American troops. Still others see it evolving from even more recent circumstances: the prewar Anglo–French strategy which aimed at sensations of war and victory on the cheap, or the circumspection of a Britain standing alone, or the early Anglo-American war councils, in which a war-toughened Britain with a preponderance of troops on the front exercised a natural ascendancy over the virginal, as yet unarmed Americans.

All of these explanations are probably apposite. As Hitler's crushing of France had proved a blessing by preventing the repetition of a western front like that in World War I and of the need to defer to an important ally, Churchill seized the opportunity to project a traditional strategy. Victories at the perimeter, a bombing offensive, and sporadic small landings on the continent coordinated with local risings would, he thought, so weaken Germany by the gradual tightening of the noose around her that a second front would be a reaction to a German collapse rather than a forcing of one. This strategy rested on vast overestimation of the effect of bombing and of the extent and military value of European discontent with German rule. Based also on the belief that the fall of Bulgaria caused Germany's collapse in 1918 and that Italy was an important Axis ally which would prove to be a "soft underbelly"—continuous with his World War I Balkans strategy—it imposed on the Grand Alliance in 1942–43 a defensive, opportunist, restrained war strategy which had met the needs and limited resources of Britain in 1940–41. There were, according to Taylor, two Churchills: the one who held together the Grand Alliance and the one who directed a purely British strategy without relation to the alliance, who desired a theater where

Britain could win (at least at first) without major American forces. Beating Rommel became a personal compulsion, out of harmony with the larger considerations of strategy.[23] Gallipoli seemed an example rather than a warning, and Churchill still sought a back door into Germany. Churchill, concludes Higgins, was neither a hero nor a villain, but simply a man who did not grow with the war.

The result of this Mediterranean strategy strikes many historians as costly. Initially it stretched British, not German, supply lines. The diversion of shipping caused one and a half million deaths by starvation in India. It created shortages of materiel in the Far East which led to British debacles and, ironically, thereby accelerated the postwar dissolution of the British Empire. The supply-shipping and landing-craft shortages, which postponed the second front and which Churchill claimed to be the causes of his strategy, were in fact the results of it. While the Russians bled the Germans to death on what Barnett considers the real second front, the western Allies pursued a peripheral campaign that engaged a small German force from Egypt to Italy. Like Gallipoli, Salonika, and Mesopotamia, and like the bomber offensive, this "strategy of evasion" probably weakened and certainly postponed the decisive and unavoidable onslaught in the West by proving to be a substitute rather than a preliminary for a 1943 second front. Italy, far from being a "soft underbelly," became the most frustrating theater of all for the Allies. It prolonged the war, sapped British resources, alienated Russia, played into Hitler's hands, and left the Allies dependent on a Russia which emerged in a sense as the major victor of the war. And when, in 1944 debates over Berlin and the Adriatic, Churchill began to warn of what he thought was the nascent danger from Russia, the Americans, like the Russians, had learned to distrust him—even as in the 1930s his hyperbole on India or on German rearmament made it difficult for Britons to heed him on the question of appeasement.

Some historians, on the other hand, dwell on the many practical obstacles in the way of an early second front and so justify in part Churchill's decisions: the U-boat campaign had first to be defeated; a shipping armada and fighter plane force had to be developed (a process delayed, we saw, by Churchill's bomber offensive); complex plans and new devices had to be matured. In the meantime, the North African campaign produced military and moral results as momentous as those in Stalingrad and at far lower costs. The Italian campaign drew German forces away from Russia and from the excellent line of communication in the West and in Central Europe (though how much is a matter of debate). D-day came, according to this view, at just the right moment. In 1942 it would have been a disaster; in 1943, uncertain. Even if some of Churchill's arguments against the second front in 1941–43 are a rehash of those against the western offensives in 1915–17, in fact far fewer men fell in the later war. Final judgment on the Mediterranean campaign, therefore, hinges on whether one believes that the second front could have succeeded earlier with the means then available, just as judgment on Gallipoli depends partly on the question of what strategic and political dividends victory there could have brought.[24]

*   *   *   *

What, then, caused the Allies to triumph? The war actually was "a damned close run thing." Perhaps a major reason for the German defeat is to be found in the character of Hitler, which Churchill does not sufficiently probe. To the conjecture that a more slowly moving Führer might have had a greater war machine, he responds that Hitler "was resolved to hurry, and have the war while he was in his prime."[25] Churchill thus bypasses a possible answer: a dictator who sets a war machine in motion is carried by forces which are soon beyond his control. "Could he . . . afford to retreat after living so long upon prestige?"[26]—anymore than could Napoleon (or, we recall, the Mahdi)? The decision to invade Russia was therefore the turning point of the war, but Churchill does not clarify what even he himself called an "outstanding blunder of history." Having failed to break Britain by air, Hitler had to embark on an invasion, but he recoiled like Napoleon from such an attempt until he had removed the threat from the East. Churchill advances this as an example of the "one at a time" policy—"1939, Poland; 1940, France; 1941, Russia; 1942, England; 1943—?"[27]—but it is exactly the reverse. The invasion of a quiescent Russia meant turning his back on an already aroused enemy who was bombing him. Surely, Hitler would have had less to worry about at his back by first invading Britain, especially if he feared her so little as to turn elsewhere, and especially since a nervous Russia had hitherto not acted while France was still in the field. After he had promised his generals to avoid a renewal of the kaiser's two-front war, Hitler's decisions led to just such a repetition and indeed, if one counts his move into Italy and even his fears about Norway, to a three- or four-front war.[28]

Perhaps Hitler's mystique of the *drang nach osten* and his racist theories of Slavic inferiority prompted his abandonment of the "one by one" policy and so undid him; perhaps he had no great designs on Britain and, since Germany was a land power, he felt greater confidence in invading over a wide front a large nation like Russia than in hazarding a short sea crossing against the smaller Britain; perhaps he sought slave labor, oil, and grain in the East; or perhaps, since an amphibious operation against Britain could not be mounted for some time and since a dictator must keep moving, invading Russia would be an outlet for the concentrated, crouched energies of his people. But Churchill, intent on depicting the Battle of Britain as the turning point of the war, has little to offer along these lines. He does not see that the very momentum which made Hitler broke him; he does not see this any more clearly in Hitler's career than in Randolph Churchill's.

The Old Statesman

If Russia was the scene of the neutralization of one peril, Hitlerism, it was also the place from which emerged what Churchill now considered a new peril. Toward the end of the war, the terrible prospect of the "Bolshevization" of a "broken and ruined" Europe grew to be his predominant anxiety, as it had been after World War I. He resumed his role as political prophet. Again he was ignored and criticized, especially by the American press, but a bare two years later his actions in Greece were "vindicated by events," and his views became "commonplaces of American doctrine."[29] He left his post as he had entered it, prophesying: "My appeal came to nothing. The world has yet to measure the 'serious consequences' which I forecast."[30]

Notwithstanding the Old Testament patriarchal tone, the tragic denunciations which begin and end the work, historians have argued over the validity of Churchill's later jeremiads. In his opposition to Russia, as in his stand on India, Churchill's conservatism, by safeguarding against one peril, brought about others; his intransigence helped the "hard liners" in Moscow just as it did the extremists in India. He had persuaded himself during the war, moreover, that Russia was less a communist society than a patriotic national state, and he now overcompensated. Nor did he understand the mood of an exhausted postwar Europe. In this last series of warnings, therefore, Churchill has seemed to some critics less prophet than instigator, issuing a series of self-fulfilling prophecies which alienated a friendly if understandably diffident Russia. We do not yet know, concludes Taylor, whether Stalin had become expansionist or was merely concerned with the frontiers and security of a Russia twice invaded in a quarter of a century; whether the Bolshevik peril, in short, was an invention of Churchill's designed to cement the Anglo-American alliance with a new common danger; whether Churchill, by his chronic sounding of the alarm against impending "unnecessary" wars, helped bring about the Cold War.

While Churchill, furthermore, presents himself as both prophet and victim of the new forces, some historians have asserted that he himself prepared the way for the postwar difficulties by his fixation on "victory at all costs" and on the destruction of Hitler. If he was relieved in 1940 to be spared an alliance with France like that which had clogged British strategic initiative in World War I, he little realized the far greater price he would eventually have to pay for alliance instead with the two giant powers on the periphery of European civilization, without whose might he could not obtain "unconditional surrender." Just as his adoption of "war socialism" at home unintentionally brought Britain closer to the postwar welfare state, so was his readiness to assist anyone fighting against Germany an act of expediency which helped continental Communist movements, and so did his placing the idea of the English-speaking alliance over that of a European federation—perhaps an inevitable choice—make Britain, in de Gaulle's words, a satellite of America.

Roosevelt's moral authority overshadowed Churchill's as Wil-

son's had Lloyd George's. In paying lip service to the unconditional surrender slogan that Roosevelt enunciated, Churchill
violated a principle he had himself set down with reference to the
Boers. Another of his favorite principles, that in war political and
military considerations are inseparable, had to be sacrificed to the
American belief that winning the war as soon and cheaply as
possible was the major goal.[31] Nor could he properly understand or
cope with the American suspicion that all Europeans were devious
imperialists. Though by dint of his personal correspondence, war
experience, and prestige Churchill obtained more concessions from
Roosevelt than any other British statesman could have, in 1944 he
became worried over Stalin and the postwar world at the same
time that Roosevelt, partly out of the desire not to repeat Wilson's
mistakes, was convincing himself that democratic America could
cooperate better with revolutionary Russia than with imperial
Britain. The president, not sharing Churchill's vision of an
English-speaking union, regarded Stalin as Chamberlain had
regarded Hitler and as Lloyd George had regarded Lenin—as a
man one could talk into reasonableness. Churchill had no choice
but to yield direction to the emergent superpower and try to steer
between the enthusiasm of Roosevelt and the cynicism of Stalin.
At Teheran and Yalta, he was, according to his lights, in a
Munich-like situation; beholden to Roosevelt, he yet sensed that a
military victory was intermingled with a tragic diplomatic defeat.
Of all this, the memoirs can say little, because of the author's
reverence for Roosevelt and his having to continue to deal with
America in his peacetime ministry at the time of writing.[32]

*   *   *   *

Roosevelt and Stalin function also as foils in Churchill's
assessment of his own achievement at home. They could order, but
the Briton (like Marlborough) had to persuade. He depicts himself
as gladly working within the limitations of British democracy, as
being responsive to the challenge of conflict and appreciative of
controversy. Historians have indeed praised the effectiveness of the
"war socialism" under Churchill; the absence of war profiteers; the
excellent handling of labor (a matter he left to Bevin). All this
contrasts with World War I. The Germans in 1942 stressed the

importance of eliminating the prime minister, that fountainhead of British morale.[33]

Proud of his administration for waging victorious war even while shaping in two years a reform program which would normally take five years, he ascribes his success to the substitution of his own idea of centralized responsibility in place of the widespread committee system, with its polite exchange of opinion, its gradually arrived at consensus, its concern for the acquiescence of every department and group. Seeking to coordinate the services, he made himself minister for defense and placed the chiefs of staff in direct daily contact with the executive head of the government to whom they were responsible. He kept a watch for the blunders of his experts and was probably an irritating but necessary gadfly who forced the generals constantly to examine their assumptions and consider alternate possibilities. But he had learned from Gallipoli that brilliant ideas are worthless if the military has no confidence in them, and he (unlike Hitler) usually yielded to them on purely military questions. At the juncture of strategy and politics, on the other hand, he could be obdurate, and the memoirs of most British military men indicate that Churchill's forcing upon them of military moves for political reasons—like the expedition to Greece in 1941 or the Anzio operation, the dispatch of certain convoys to the Arctic or of two battleships to the Far East—had a ruinous military effect.

He was, historians conclude, both necessary and dangerous. Though he claims to have made all the military decisions that mattered and to be more proud of them than of his 1940 speeches, he actually contributed more to morale than to strategy. To the public, the troops, and even the Commons, he was *the* leader under whom all would be well. With Churchill inspiring the nation and the military triumvirate in the main directing strategy, the result was, as he claims, an efficient war apparatus.[34] Yet, for good or ill, the course of the Allied campaign was to a degree the result of his thinking and advocacy. After Hitler made him, on May 10, 1940, a virtual dictator by thrusting on him far greater power and responsibility than anyone could have foreseen, Churchill committed, Taylor concludes, several great errors and numerous small ones, but the wonder is that he did not make many more, for no one else could have done all that he did and with such zest. In the crucial years, his instincts for once coinciding with the basic facts of the situation, he was the best wartime prime minister Britain could have had.

Above all, he provided the national leadership, the perfervid oratory, the animating spirit, the will to win; despite being wrong in many of his military decisions, he was to his nation, in Nicolson's words, the "God of War." Of his own role, especially in the dark days after Dunkirk, Churchill says, "It fell to me in these coming days and months to express [the people's] sentiments on suitable occasions."[35] He was, in other words, merely the spokesman for the firmness already there, merely the "roar" of the lion; he only gave "good reasons" for their resolve. He seems, like Savrola, to have been the expression of some greater force; of that mysterious entity called "Britannia."[36]

Yet his pride in his administration and in the morale of his people contains a good deal of self-deception. A knowledgeable observer-participant (and devotee of Churchill's), Harold Nicolson, took note of class feeling even at the height of the blitz and complained about the inept handling of the "publicity side" of government. And Churchill's lofty rhetoric does not leave room in the narrative for the revelation of the extent to which the two votes of censure in 1942, although handily won by Churchill, reflected widespread anxiety in Britain over the effectiveness of wartime leadership. Becoming increasingly out of touch with Parliament and the public, Churchill, remarks Thomson, treated the former as his privy council, the latter as his unseen audience, and felt responsible solely to himself and history. Only El Alamein and the North African landings saved his political life at a time when emergent social discontent fused with dissatisfaction over the military failures under his administration.[37]

Equally sketchy is his cavalier treatment of two other problems which exercised many Britons: war aims and the Beveridge Plan. In 1917, Churchill had urged the Allies to proclaim such war aims as government by consent of the governed, which, by looking to the future of Europe and the rights of her people, would appeal to many in Alsace, Poland, the Balkans. These were, however, nineteenth-century values, and in this war, he did not understand the argument that Germany was fighting a revolutionary war with clear objectives while Britain seemed to be fighting a conservative war with negative objectives. Oblivious to the new democratic spirit produced by resistance movements, he seemed to regard the war as merely a fight to preserve the old order and the imperial tradition recently celebrated in *Marlborough* and the *History*—not to bring into being a new world. As for social reconstruction at home, the publication in late 1942 of the Beveridge Plan for universal social security in Britain found Churchill so immersed in war matters and so wanting in the meliorist spirit that he only reluctantly accepted it in principle because of the enthusiasm it aroused and then dodged the matter. His memoirs barely mention it and are silent on the strong Labor vote affirming it, the only Labor revolt during the war.[38]

Churchill's obliviousness to these issues helps explain the astonishing electoral defeat at the zenith of his career. That setback seems to have left him for once speechless; in *The Second World War* he merely mumbles lamely something about the greater number of Tory than Labor MPs in the services. There were, in fact, many causes. Indifferent to what people fought for, devoid of a vision of the future, ignorant of the voters' new seriousness, Churchill seemed to lack the temper for the construction of a new Britain and, in foreign affairs, to be losing what judgment he formerly had. With an eye to the postwar situation, he had made himself leader of the Tories, but this, observes Taylor, may have been his greatest political error.

That kindred patrician soul, de Gaulle, who was no stranger to such an experience, has more to say on the fall than has Churchill himself. Churchill's identification with magnificent enterprise, he declares magisterially, became irrelevant to the postwar era of mediocrity. But a more populist explanation is advanced by Martin Greenberg, who says that the defeat was due not to British ingratitude but to a refusal to let great men impose themselves, to a political sophistication which, looking to the future, could calmly reject the brilliant past the hero embodied so well.[39]

The Diplomacy of a Sympathetic, Pragmatic Pilgrim

Churchill's profile of himself mingles political proficiency with two personal endowments—almost idiosyncracies—which are important catalysts of action. Besides seeming to possess a powerful intelligence, rich experience in politics and war, a style that fastens on the essential matter, familiarity with other continents and nations, a passionate devotion to empire and crown, and a zest for war strategy administered by an effective, deliberately assembled government machinery, Churchill flaunts his gregariousness and love of travel. These two traits combined to forge his philosophy of diplomacy and to play no small role—or so the book intimates—in maintaining the Grand Alliance. He does not tell us about the personal charm which made the gregariousness possible—although wherever he turns, he seems to see men won over by it—but his travels are lavishly portrayed.

In wartime, the love of travel could be catered to and justified on military grounds. When Churchill argued with the king and Eisenhower over his right to watch the Normandy landings in person, he advanced an opinion formed over the years and emphasized in *The World Crisis* and *Marlborough:* a war leader making grave decisions needs the "refreshment of adventure," needs the comfort of sharing in a small way the risks of the many he sends to their death, and needs to enlarge his scope of action by direct contact with events. In World War I, he learned that commanders must witness the battle conditions; "I had seen many grievous errors made through the silly theory that valuable lives should not be endangered."[40] Indeed, when he worried over Salerno, he recalled Auchinleck's error of remaining at his Cairo headquarters, "surveying orthodoxly from the summit and centre the wide and varied sphere of his command, while the battle, on which everything turned, was being decided against him in the Desert."[41]

Therefore Churchill often toured the front, seeking a "clearer impression of the modern battlefield,"[42] and even spent a day with a typical infantry battalion in order to see for himself why the units, after years of his bullying the generals on the matter, had so large a noncombatant tail. He found it educational no less than refreshing to leave the routine of office, to visit the bombed streets and be in contact with events; when he saw a family dispossessed during the blitz, he—such is the privilege of power or the delusion of his inflated ego—at once decided to initiate a system of state insurance and compensation for victims of bombing. This rationale for his enjoyable peregrinations is not without its persuasiveness, but one wonders what is cause and what effect. For when Churchill is sorrowing over not seeing Malta in its "struggle," is delighting in firing an army gun, being aboard a ship in combat, or being driven almost into the front lines, we seem to hear the young war correspondent, soldier, traveler—or is it the adolescent playing war games, the boy with his hundreds of toy soldiers? Life and war are still, as they were in his very first books, a drama to the climax of which he is invited. Visiting the Air Defence Headquarters at the height of the blitz, he found that the room was "like a small theatre. . . . We took our seats in the dress circle."[43] And between these forays into battle, he liked to inspect the troops in his thorough manner, "looking each man straight in the eye" or ascertaining whether they knew "Rule Britannia."[44] Churchill's visits to the Rhine battlefield especially make one think of Tolstoy's Pierre shuffling about bemusedly on the battlefield of Borodino or of the ingenuous Samuel Pepys and his voracious inquisitiveness.[45]

In the diplomatic realm, however, Churchill found even greater justification for his peregrinations. The grand theme of this vast work is that foreign policy is best conducted by means of personal diplomacy. The leaders of nations cannot come to a true understanding through intermediaries or impersonal dispatches which place days between the joining of question and answer. When communicating with other heads of state, Churchill himself, like Marlborough, drafted informal letters to "fellow workers." Problems insoluble at the second level could be settled quickly by such direct contact at the top. When he sent messages in April 1941 warning Stalin of Hitler's impending invasion, the reaction was nebulous because of the Byzantine intrigue needed to get them delivered to the aloof dictator. Churchill's conclusion is that "direct contact" with Stalin would have prevented the worst of the disaster. By contrast, in 1944, with the Allies reeling under the Ardennes counterstroke, Eisenhower wanted to send Tedder to Russia to obtain the aid of an offensive in the East. Weather delaying Tedder, Churchill telegramed Stalin and received an affirmative reply the next day. "I quote this interchange as a good example of the speed at which business could be done at the summit of the Alliance."[46]

Better than informal correspondence, however, was the personal meeting. This required leaving the old habitat for exotic places; dining and wining in grand, ceremonious fashion; conversing genially with the great of the world; and arriving at the most satisfactory agreements that the arts of persuasion, Machiavellian cunning, and, not least, personal charm could contrive. Churchill had, of course, been a confirmed traveler all his life. At the beginning of the war, when Britain stood alone, there were few places he could visit other than bombed-out city streets. But when Britain took the offensive in North Africa and the enemy brought the Grand Alliance into being, opportunities for travel appeared on all sides. As soon as he awoke on December 8, 1941, he "decided to go over at once to see President Roosevelt." The same day, urging de Valera to join the war, he wrote, "I will meet you wherever you wish."[47] When Allied coordination became necessary, Churchill was skeptical of the value of a conference of experts or officers who would continually have to refer back to their capitals and who would become enmeshed in the Soviet refrain of "Second Front." "This sort of argument, of which I had plenty in Moscow, requires to be met by principals. . . . Only the heads of States face to face could settle the fearful questions that were open. . . . How difficult everything becomes once one cannot talk together!"[48]

After the Casablanca conference, Churchill visited Cairo, Algiers, and Tripoli to settle many things "on the spot" and see others with his "own eyes." As the problem of factionalism in semiliberated countries arose, he decided to go to Italy to meet Tito, Papandreou, and the Italian politicians. "The telegram and the telephone more often than not only darken counsel."[49] When the Greek situation deteriorated, he abruptly left a Christmas celebration "to go and see for myself the situation on the spot" and take the measure of the principals; when on another occasion, Inönü of Turkey seemed reluctant to visit Cairo, Churchill was more than ready to rush to Adana. As he said once in a telegram to Roosevelt, "Let me know if I can help matters by a journey."[50] Upon Roosevelt's death, Churchill's first impulse to fly to the funeral was overcome by pressures not to leave the country at a critical moment. Yet he came to regret this lapse; never having met Truman, he felt that unhurried, informal personal talks on the spectrum of issues would have made a difference.

It was Churchill's genius to see that modern communications made it possible for a prime minister to go anywhere and still do his administrative work, and he is indeed often credited with having, like Marlborough, by his traveling, tact, and diplomacy, built and kept together the Grand Alliance. The list of Churchill's wartime trips is as impressive as Marlborough's. Oscillating between the reluctant voyagers Stalin and Roosevelt (with the latter he conferred nine times), he was the prime mover behind summit meetings at Moscow, Casablanca, Cairo, Teheran, and Yalta.[52] On such trips and others, he inspected troops, picnicked in the desert or the Atlas Mountains with his generals, bathed in the Mediterranean with his soldiers, met old friends, did his only painting during the war years, and dragged the sedentary Roosevelt to see the Sphinx or the Marrakech sunsets.

His cabinet, solicitous over the risks he was taking and perhaps envious of his wartime tourism, opposed one such venture. The comedy of the chief being overruled by his subordinates, of his obvious relish in travel being only thinly masked with the pretext of "affairs of state," is brought out by Churchill's comment, "I got quite upset by the obstruction of the Cabinet as I lay in my luxurious bed in the Taylor Villa looking at the Atlas Mountains, over which I longed to leap in the 'Commando' airplane." Between attending a session in the Commons or meeting General Wilson in Cairo, he had only one choice: "We are just off over the Atlas Mountains, which are gleaming with their sunlit snows. You can imagine how much I wish I were going to be with you tomorrow on the Bench, but duty calls."[53] He later even tried to lure out Eden, one of the nervous cabinet members: "Can make you very comfortable."[54] He seems, as in his first books, an ingenuous character in a fairy tale, an eternal tourist: "From Cairo," he says in one of his speeches, "I proceeded on my magic carpet to Tripoli."[55] The trip encompassing the Cairo–Teheran conferences took him out of Britain for over two months—two months' absence by a leader during wartime is surely unique in modern history! Perhaps he was only half-joking in the message to Tito, sent with his son Randolph, when he said, "I wish I could come myself, but I am too old and heavy to jump out on a parachute."[56]

Something of Churchill's manner at the tête-à-têtes is suggested by the description of his vain attempt to persuade Pétain to fight in 1940: "I recalled to [him] the nights we had spent together in his train at Beauvais after the British Fifth Army disaster in 1918, and how he, as I put it, not mentioning Marshal Foch, had restored the situation."[57] Or, when the decision was made to postpone the second front and everyone was anxious over Soviet reaction to the news, it was settled that Churchill should propose to visit Stalin in Russia, on the way, as it were, to Cairo. He would "have it all out face to face with Stalin, rather than trust to telegrams and intermediaries. At least it showed that one cared for their fortunes."[58] This first meeting in Moscow as Churchill presents it is a masterpiece of personal diplomacy. He tames the enigmatic Stalin by use of cunning (giving the bad news first and only then revealing to the resigned Russian the forthcoming North African operation), allegory (drawing a picture of a crocodile's soft belly to justify operations in the Mediterranean),[59] promises (talk of a direct assault the following year "marked the turning point" in the discussions), and tact (not asking what Russia would have done if Britain had gone under alone). When Stalin is surly the next day, Churchill masters him by abruptness and sulking self-pity and by threatening to depart. The narrator concludes that imparting the bad news personally forestalled any serious rift.[60]

Such conferences had official sittings and agendas, but Churchill found the dinners, formal and informal, of considerable importance in helping the progress of the gravest affairs. Though formal settlements and the routine communications among the foreign services have an impersonal, legalistic air about them, their basis is the everyday psychology that comes into play when men break bread together. Table talk and even toasts create the atmosphere conducive to agreements and vivify "bonds of unity," for personal diplomacy is most akin to a casual meeting of friends.[61] Whether a dinner was held in the desert near Cairo or amid lavish surroundings in wartime Moscow, or even if it was simply a picnic with a general in desert or mountain country, Churchill was surely in his element on these occasions. In a manner reminiscent of the name-dropping and hedonism in the frontier war books, he evokes the Cairo conferences at the "Kasserine woods thickly dotted with the luxurious abodes and gardens of the cosmopolitan Cairo magnates"—his kind of world—or a dinner ordered from

Shepheard's—"a gay occasion in the midst of care."[62] The September 1941 British mission to Moscow accomplished little, he believes, because of the cold mood prevailing at the one formal reception at the Kremlin. What it lacked apparently was Churchill himself to melt the ice. At one point during a later Moscow conference which Churchill did attend, when Stalin suggested going home for a couple of drinks, "I said that I was in principle always in favor of such a policy."[63] In such convivial surroundings he could go to work.

The theme of personal diplomacy naturally grows out of Churchill's varied preoccupations and values. Finally holding supreme power, Churchill adopts unashamedly the idea that the individual shapes history, an idea he had so far intermittently entertained and in the 1930s had seriously questioned. It becomes here fused, in a "harmony of interests," with his egotism and his love of travel. Just as he once graduated from toy soldiering to real soldiering, so in a half-century have the adventurism and peregrinations of his youth been magnified and transferred onto the world stage. Finding himself at last in the highest office, confident of his charm, eager to take the road, he easily persuades himself that all his gadding about and chattering mattered, that these two peculiar traits of his have, through the medium of power, changed history, that he, in effect, won the war. This is, at any rate, a theory of diplomacy; whether it is based on historical fact is another question.[64] It overlooks the role of historical forces, of the Foreign Offices and their sense of continuous policy as a necessary backdrop for, or better alternative to, the intervention of the whims of prominent but transient individuals or the moods of the moment. The bypassing of a departmental bureaucracy and of diplomatic channels may be sometimes salutary and sometimes not.

Whether or not personal diplomacy is a procedure applicable to all situations, a query may be raised as to whether it even worked for Churchill himself. Presenting his personal diplomacy as a series of triumphs, he overlooks the possibility that, at these tête-à-têtes and dinners, *he* might have been the manipulated one. Certainly many bystanders have remarked on his naïveté or self-delusion in his encounters with Greek Communists, with Italians, Americans, Germans, as well as with Roosevelt, Truman, and Stalin.[65] When he asserts, about his losing of a telegram debate with the Americans over the invasion of the Riviera or about the failures of the Potsdam Conference without him, "I was sure that if we could have met, as I so frequently proposed, we should have reached a happy agreement,"[66] we find ourselves uncomfortably close to the claims made at the conclusion of this work (and of *Marlborough*), that his (or Marlborough's) "removal from the scene . . . rendered it impossible for satisfactory solutions to be reached" and ruined "our best, and what might prove to have been our last, chance of durable world peace,"[67] that all problems would have been resolved if Churchill had been reelected and allowed to charm the conferees and flex his muscles at Potsdam. At such moments, Churchill's realism about the human condition and the course of history is swept aside by the most shameless hero worship and self-love, and we begin to suspect that

> Nowher so bisy a man as he ther nas
> And yet he semed bisier than he was.

Churchill's personal diplomacy, as well as his vanity, leads him to account for abrupt turns in Stalin's behavior with the theory that Stalin is more genial and less powerful than the world believes. "The most probable [explanation] is that his Council of Commissars did not take the news I brought as well as he did. They may have more power than we suppose."[68] Churchill italicizes what he takes to be the revealing words in a memo Stalin handed him: "It appears to me *and my colleagues.*" Then, as the war draws to a close and Anglo–Soviet relations deteriorate, Churchill wishes again to meet Stalin, to whom he feels "new links" and with whom he can talk man to man. This suggests again a difference between Stalin and "the Soviet leaders, whoever they may be."[69] Taking note of the ease of conversation, the "personal relations," and Stalin's "several expressions of personal regard," Churchill becomes again persuaded of "strong pressures in the background, both party and military"; he writes to his cabinet, "Behind the horseman sits black care."[70] At this point, one cannot tell whether Churchill is percipient—and the world too severe on Stalin—or fatuous. By separating Stalin from the anonymous Politburo, he is justifying his own commerce with a Bolshevik (this is a rare "good" Bolshevik), providing a rationale for his personal diplomacy (it works, and if he could have had informal access to "the others" over dinner or brandy, he would have won them over also), and exculpating his role in the Cold War (the evil "others" overruled a friendly Stalin), not to speak of fondling his own vanity by thinking that Stalin's warm words were sincere and that he, the charming anti-Communist and monarchist, had melted even the cold, calculating Soviet leader.

The successes of the personal diplomacy, whether specious or substantial, sprang from his quickness in understanding another politician's position. Churchill sensed, and made others sense, that leadership entails problems which transcend nation, tradition, or ideology; that being a leader makes one a member of a small, elite club. Hence the dining, drinking, and intimate conversations, and, throughout this book (as in *The World Crisis* and indeed all his books), the sympathetic identification with prominent politicians in alien and difficult positions. This understanding is a matter of prudent policy, even cunning, as much as of human warmth and imagination; "in war and policy one should always try to put oneself in the position of what Bismarck called 'the Other Man.' "[71] Belgium, for example, had erred seriously in insisting on her neutrality instead of forming a common front with France and Britain, but considering American aloofness, British pacifism, and Anglo–French appeasement, no man of responsible position in those lands is free to criticize.

Such sympathy, without which no history or fiction can be written, is not withheld even from the enemy. Perhaps also because of his worship of power, Churchill makes a sagacious exposition of Japanese history and mentality, of Hess's mind, of the reasons for Mussolini's Abyssinian adventure, of Darlan's typically French behavior. While conceding their logic to be "wrong and evil," he thinks it foolish to ignore "the secret springs of action to which [others] respond." Of Molotov, Mihailovic, Laval, Ciano, a Japanese admiral, and even Truman, he makes such observations as "those who have endured a similar ordeal may judge him."[72]

His correspondence with world leaders, in addition, reveals a fine sense of his addressee, an ability to assimilate the other's national conditioning and assumptions, to utilize his own knowledge of history. In several pre–Pearl Harbor communications to Roosevelt are locutions which, his footnotes remind the reader, had been used by Wilson in 1917, when the two nations fought side by side. In submitting his naval ideas for the Pacific theater to Americans, he conjures up the "invention and ingenuity" that created "the extraordinary fleets and flotillas which fought on the Mississippi in the Civil War."[73] In a speech to the conquered French, he tactfully mentions that Hitler had subjugated, among other places, Corsica—"Napoleon's Corsica"—and then quotes Napoleon's contempt for the Prussians, as well as an apposite remark by another "great Frenchman."

With this sympathetic identification, he brought to his personal diplomacy a pragmatism, an ideological flexibility or "realism" which enabled him to work with any bona fide member of the club—any person who could speak for masses of people, wield power, or obtain the submission of large enemy forces. Such willingness to cooperate with all sorts, to the dismay of many, sprang in part from his belief first expressed in *Savrola* that, since life is imperfect and most men are frail reeds, one must do the best one can with the choices available, especially under the duress of war. Though disgusted by Pétain and the Vichy regime, he was eager to give them a chance to redeem themselves. "There is no room in war for pique, spite, or rancor. The main objective must dominate all secondary causes of vexation."[74] When the Allies began to move into North Africa and southern Europe, they found themselves confronted with leaders who, tainted by contact with collaborationist regimes, changed directions when they saw which way the wind was blowing. The purist recoils from such persons, but Churchill wanted to save lives and shorten the war. Hence he seized the opportunity to work with Darlan—anglophobe, Vichyite, turncoat, and all—in the face of criticism from many who asked the idealist's question: "Is this then what we are fighting for?" Churchill's reply was that in war one deals with the possible: Darlan, and not the patriotic de Gaulle or Giraud, had the obedience of the African French forces; cooperation with him was in any case only a "temporary expedient."

Whether this pragmatism embraced, in France, Spain, Germany, and Italy, right-wingers or, in Russia and Yugoslavia, left-wingers, Churchill was prepared to allow men to redeem themselves. Not a Hitler, to be sure, but a Darlan, by his fortuitous collaboration with the Allies in Africa; a Franco, by his unwitting, indirect, passive help; a Badoglio, by his turning over the Italian fleet; a Ciano, by his confession of error; a Hess, by his deed of "lunatic benevolence"; a Rommel, by his joining in a plot against Hitler; a Doenitz, by his bringing about German surrender; and implicitly, classically, a Stalin, thrust by history into the common struggle. In all these cases, Churchill's conscience was at ease, for, he declared, "I have only one purpose, the destruction of Hitler, and my life is much simplified thereby."[75] His leftist critics, on the other hand, were reminded that the inconsistency was theirs, not his: "I do not know whether there is more freedom in Stalin's Russia than in Franco's Spain. I do not know how I can depend on a de Gaullist France."[76]

This attitude goes hand in hand with his perennial distaste for idealists, detachment from moral issues, and advocacy of stern war making. It is the nature of pragmatists not to become frozen in any stance, as idealists do. "We must not let our vision be darkened by hatred or obscured by sentiment."[77] Hence he did not care what was done with war criminals so long as military advantages were not subordinated to vengeance. His pragmatism shaped his response to Roosevelt's "unconditional surrender" demand and to the growing Russian influence. He did not want the disintegration of the Nazi machine arrested by Allied harping on a slogan which would unite the Germans into a desperate block; again, saving Allied lives was uppermost. Nor should that demand be made of Italy, Rumania, or Japan. On the matter of Russian encroachments, he likewise made distinctions. Whereas the fate of Rumania and Bulgaria was not a British concern, that of Poland and Greece "struck us keenly," and in one conference with Stalin he resurrected unofficially the old "spheres of influence" policy, that bane of idealists and mainstay of worldly pragmatism.

Thus we behold him coming to conferences with crafty politicians like Roosevelt and cynics like Stalin fortified by his pragmatism, his sympathetic identification, and his own charming, gregarious, loquacious, well-traveled personality. His personal diplomacy in World War II—his gift of himself to history—was, in a sense, the fulfillment of much that he lived for and wrote about.

From Sword to Pen

Though tragic in scope, this huge tale has many amusing aspects. Churchill's sense of humor appears not only in the narrative written from the secure vantage point of the afteryears but also in his utterances during times of crisis and adversity. Few other memoirs or history books are so filled with comic scenes and sparkling wit, so rich in an abiding sense of proportion. And it somehow sits well with the cataclysmic and lugubrious matter of the story, for Churchill does not allow the humor to take the sting out of the events or reduce war to a mere game. He simply refuses to overlook the light side. His cavalier description, for instance, of the blitz as a lark rather than a grim, heroic ordeal is in the best British tradition of the stiff upper lip, of understatement, jocularity, avoidance of heroics. Such a tone, markedly different from the histrionics of the other side, may well be a secret of survival. As Shaw said, he who laughs lasts.

The Churchillian posture in the speeches, of determined resignation, is therefore spiced in the retrospective narrative with a *joie de vivre,* a veritable enjoyment of the adversities. As in the days of his youth, he confesses to an aesthetic appreciation of the "stimulating but disagreeable conditions of war."[78] The period of the expected German invasion "was a time when it was equally good to live or die"; during the blitz, life at Downing St. was exciting, for "one might as well have been at a battalion headquarters in the line."[79] Even the coming of the flying bombs was turned to morale boosting: "The people at home could feel they were sharing the perils of their soldiers."[80] The joint church service at the first meeting with Roosevelt "was a great hour to live."[81] And through the worst of the storm, one retained one's dignity and chivalry, even to the enemy. When Churchill used a ceremonial style in declaring war on Japan or lauding Rommel in Commons as a "daring," "skillful," "great" general, people took offense. "This churlishness is a well-known streak in human nature, but contrary to the spirit in which a war is won or a lasting peace established."[82] Hence he does not regret his remarks; "when you have to kill a man it costs nothing to be polite."[83] If buoyancy facilitates endurance, chivalry ensures that rare quality, dignity in victory.

Part of the greatness of *The Second World War* is also due to its dramatic quality. A good deal of the writing is admittedly discursive and expository, with much analysis of plans, many clashes of abstract ideas. Churchill sometimes seems to be tediously wading through piles of documents dealing with minutiae.

Periodically, however, the narrative comes vividly to life. The naval and military battles were, as always, of great interest to him, not merely as incidents on which victory or defeat hinged but—especially in retrospect—as having an aesthetic, impersonal beauty of their own; the interplay of strategies and armies is like the moves and countermoves in a planetary chess game. And as in *The World Crisis* and the *History,* he is far better as the colorful chronicler of the flow of events than as the analyst probing into the motives and ideologies of men and movements, least of all his own motives.

There are also great scenes in which the narrator's eye for telling detail, the evocation of setting, mood, and character, is that of a first-class novelist. Such is the eerie sense of *déjà vu* and *ubi sunt* upon his return in 1939, as first lord, to Scapa Flow, exactly a quarter of a century after having, at the start of the other world war, paid the same visit during the same season in the same capacity. Or, with the crisis mounting and the repetition of the 1914 offensive through Belgium, his being summoned to power and his rushing to Paris, where the French leaders and generals stand about in confusion and dejection. The collapse of the venerable and once mighty France and Churchill's agony are beautifully rendered by the sensuous detail of the old gentlemen industriously carrying French archives on wheelbarrows to bonfires. Another powerful scene is that of the vote of censure, moved by Churchill's critics in the wake of the Singapore and Tobruk disasters, even as the battle rages in the desert. The ensuing debate, reminiscent of the one in 1915 which ended with Churchill's fall, was an "accompaniment to the cannonade"; a climax was being reached in parliamentary and desert fronts simultaneously.

One of the pleasures of this work is the glimpse it affords of the leaders in moments of relaxation. Usually at dinner, with their political masks down, they behave like the "triple pillars of the world" in the "party" scene of Shakespeare's *Antony and Cleopatra* —that is, much like the rest of us. Irrelevant to the conduct and course of World War II, such details are wonderful reminders of the sameness of human nature at all levels of the social pyramid. At one Moscow conference reminiscent of various scenes in Shakespeare, large areas of land are casually carved out and distributed as "spheres of influence" in a sort of grand poker game. The last of the Big Three meetings at Potsdam has its Swiftian aspects: the minor crisis caused by the demands of the press (significantly incomprehensible to Stalin); the discussions, which are really three monologues; the final banquet, at which Stalin collected on his menu card the signatures of the participants and Churchill taught him how to drink brandy from a large glass while continuing the diplomatic poker game; the revelation to a jovial, innocent-seeming Stalin of the existence of the atom bomb; and the abrupt forced departure of Churchill.

Near the end of the work appears one of the greatest, though briefest, scenes of all. On the way to the Potsdam conference, Churchill flies to Berlin and its "chaos of ruins." Taken to Hitler's chancellery—until a mere few weeks earlier the center of the Third Reich—he walks through its shattered halls for "quite a long time." A Russian guide shows him Hitler's air-raid shelter and the locales of the suicide and cremation. Long ago, Churchill refused as a private individual to confer with the German chancellor, and Hitler, having before his ascendancy once "missed his only chance" of meeting his opponent-to-be, was therefore curiously the only maker of twentieth-century European history Churchill never saw face to face. Now, at last, they meet—beyond the reaches of personal diplomacy. The great duel is over; Churchill, the victor, stands on the site from which so much evil originated. This climax of Churchill's life as warrior-statesman is also an event in his avocations of avid traveler, connoisseur of front lines and vantage points, and curious tourist: "We were given the best first-hand accounts available at that time of what had happened in these final scenes."[84]

*   *   *   *

In such a large work, there are naturally more than a few weaknesses. The historical accuracy it will take generations to ascertain, and the critic must confine himself to questions of construction and logic. Besides minor flaws like the excessive superlatives, the welter of memos, the loose strands in the narrative, there is the suppression of inconvenient facts. Taylor finds the work to be often slanted, albeit not deliberately so, while

Moran observes that Churchill, unable to admit to an error, deceived either others or himself. On questions like the second front one is unsure which kind of deception is at work; Churchill sometimes confuses reportage with self-justification. Plumb and Ashley also remind us of the silences and emphases unavoidable in the writings of a chronicler with a romantic imagination, a weakness for florid rhetoric, and a passion to be adjudged to have surpassed Lloyd George's war ministry, a chronicler who is also a still active politician-prophet with an eye on the future.[85]

The narrative art is uneven. Before a military operation is consummated, there is much tossing about of data and plans that eventually turn out to be irrelevant, and the dramatic effect falls short of that achieved by a simple historical narrative of events. The official war historians, confining themselves to what happened, are silent on projects not implemented, whereas Churchill sometimes (as in *The World Crisis*) is more interested in plans never carried out—in the contour of his imagination—than in anything else. Periodically in the later volumes, his procedure produces an anthology of documents loosely stapled together with an occasional sentence or brief explanation by one perilously close to relinquishing his job as narrator. At other times—as in the endless deliberations of May 1943 over whether to attack Italy next—the documents clog the development of the story, and Churchill is in the position of the legendary preacher who tells us what he is going to say (Churchill's strategic ideas), then says it (Churchill's memos), then tells us what he has said (the rejection or implementation of the plans). This may be one reason why the first volume, in which the detached narrator is at all times in command of the material (rather than of the historical decisions), reads best.

One might likewise complain about the shadowy quality of the characters. After holding the main office of the land, Churchill simply will not be distracted from his . perpetual self-contemplation. The impact of war on Britain, high and low, is left vague; even the activities of fellow ministers and the nature of cabinet meetings are hazy. The non-British campaigns are summarily dealt with, and the epic story of the Russian front, perhaps the key to Hitler's defeat, is barely looked at. If the structural defect caused in *The World Crisis* by the narrator's varied positions is avoided here by a central and consistently held vantage point, another defect, incipient in the earlier work—namely Churchill's egoism—becomes paramount. Churchill alone seems to grapple with Hitler's hysterical demands, Gandhi's self-disciplined nationalism, Russian duplicity, or American differences of opinion, and every instance of adversity becomes an occasion for the narrator's triumph. Thus his reaching the zenith of his political career saved the nation, fulfilled his personal aspirations, and, not least, solved the memoirist-narrator's technical problem, but so inflated him as to turn history into a mere foil for the self or into a solipsist's revery.

The point is best made in the excellent critique by Reed Whittemore, who concludes, "Few of us have the grand opportunity for self delusion that fate has afforded Churchill, and his delusion here . . . is surely understandable." This emphasis on his own role is a climax of his Carlylean view of the impact of the individual on history (as seen especially in *Randolph Churchill, Marlborough,* and the *History*); superimposed on the objective, detailed account of the war, it pushes the memoir dangerously close to romance.[86]

Equally annoying is Churchill's occasional moralizing about the fate of dictators and of "calculating" empires, and his concurrent ignoring of the survival of Franco or the unhappy fate of many decent, presumably noncalculating democratic leaders. This moralizing is unrelated to the truly unprecedented moral problems of our age. The concentration camps (hardly mentioned in the text), the Dresden fire raid, the atom bomb, the Nuremberg Trials are passed over. Is not, for example, his old principle of "soldier's honor" undermined or qualified by the refrain at Nuremberg, "I was under orders"? Gandhi's attempt to appeal to British consciences by fasting and civil disobedience did not reach Churchill, who worried only over the political repercussions. Nor did he see that the Indian troubles—and World War II itself—were a harbinger of the end of the old empires. Instead of the Cold War, he actually feared a new postwar alignment of the empires—British, French, Dutch, Belgian—against the large nonimperial powers—Russia, China, America. He offers no way out of the logic of meeting force with force, or out of the endless cycle of power blocs, rivalries, ideological clashes, periodic wars. He is oblivious to the possibility that he may have helped bring the Cold War into being or that when he boasts of his efficiency in the Greek crisis—"there was no time for the Cabinet to be called"—he is merely showing how power can be misused.[87]

His confidence in his prophecies, leadership, strategy, and personal diplomacy results in a swollen self-assurance, as if he alone could have forestalled the Cold War. His certitude about himself, Britain, and the English-speaking world as the beacons of mankind is irksome. This is history on the "official" level, with a rhetoric of pure motive, an admixture of justified vaunting and unfounded smugness. Britain's nobility is a little too much taken for granted, too divorced from any possible thoughts of vested interests, strategic necessity, pride, or power politics.

Churchill's outlook on race is Victorian. He speaks of the British Empire's seventy million people—that is, Caucasians—and he advocates retention of the color line in the services. Europe is the center of everything, the "parent continent" of civilization, and the League of Nations existed mainly for its benefit. The fate of Norwegians and Czechs means more to him than that of Russians and Chinese. The big powers are, moreover, to have a free hand in running things in the postwar world because, he explains obtusely, they were satisfied and "wished nothing more for themselves than what they had. If the world-government were in the hands of hungry nations, there would always be danger."[88] The smugness is never so insufferable as when he sloppily juxtaposes his stand against any concessions to India with a discussion of how he was much disturbed by reports of Soviet territorial ambitions in the Baltic states. These contiguous lands had in fact belonged to Russia for two hundred years, exactly as long as remote India had belonged to Britain, yet he blandly avers, "The Baltic States should be sovereign independent peoples."[89] Apparently the principle of self-determination cannot function so well in tropical regions of Asia as in cool Europe. "The greatest comfort on such occasions [differences with America over Indian independence] is to have no doubts."[90]

Besides being sketchy on economic, social, and psychological forces, the work lacks speculativeness. Why did the Germans fail to invade Britain, a lapse all the more enigmatic if, as Churchill asserts, their land-oriented military staffs had no idea of the problems presented by a sea crossing? Why Hitler's arrogant decision to invade Russia while Britain still stood at his back—a fatal abandonment of his "one at a time" policy? Why did the democracies rather than the dictatorships obtain the atom bomb—was it fortuitous? The will of a beneficent Power? The self-destructiveness endemic to repressive societies? Why does a Napoleon or Hitler have his hour and yet not achieve world hegemony? The lack of philosophic and historic perspective is marked by the absence of comment on the curious repetitions in history. The Russian Revolution was as terrifying to Europe as the French Revolution. Corporal Hitler rode to power on the reactionary currents in its wake as in a sense did Corporal Bonaparte. Hitler's subsequent career, notably vis-à-vis Britain and Russia, was a bizarre duplication of Napoleon's. Are men doomed to repeat history?

Perhaps most missed is a sense of the course of modern events. The beginning of the tale depicts the rise of the Nazi menace, and the close depicts the rise of the Communist menace, both of which Churchill opposed and warned against. But what is the relation between the two? Are they part of a historical cycle? It is now clear that a basic pattern of twentieth-century political history has been the confrontation between single-party, Communist and multiple-party, capitalist states. The encounter began in 1917 but was postponed by the emergence, on the extreme anti-Communist wing, of Fascist and Nazi movements which turned against their source as well as against the common enemy. These movements—unwanted children of quarreling parents, as it were —have disappeared from prominence as speedily as they appeared, taking with them the temporary détente between communism and capitalism in the face of aggression. The distracting interlude over, the confrontation between capitalism and a communism now entrenched is likely to be the course of the rest of the century. Communism, with its universal appeal to the downtrodden, and not aberrant Nazism, may endure a thousand years and pose the ultimate challenge to "western," "Judeo-Christian," "democratic" tradition. This means also, in one of the ironies of history, that Hitler, the supreme anti-Communist (though in a sense spawned indirectly by communism), was the man who brought communism out of its Russian confines into Eastern Europe, indeed into half of Germany (and, via the Axis alliance, into China); that Hitler forced Stalin into the quasi-Troskyite position of consolidating communism at home by spreading it abroad. In invading Russia, he shattered her isolation and introspection, and when she became triumphant, she naturally put her new power to use. "After Hitler, our turn," the old Communist slogan, proved true after all.

Something of all this should have been apparent to Churchill writing in 1950. But beyond some vague remarks about fascism and Nazism as the "ugly" children of communism, about the unfortunate fall of the dynasties, and about modern wars being between peoples rather than monarchs, he offers no analysis. He is so busy groveling before military strategies and his own personality that the larger patterns elude him. Thinking in an archaic language, he sees only a holy war against Prussian militarism, German nationalism, and the ambitions of an insensate but influential evil individual, not a war of ideology, a clash of socioeconomic forces, a stage in a historical cycle. Though it may be unfair to ask a politician or chronicler, especially a participant, to be also a philosopher, we expect a larger vision of things to present themselves to the would-be statesman, prophet, and historian.

And what is the meaning of this global cataclysm? While sympathetically explaining Japan's rise, Churchill ignores the significance of Japan as an outstanding example of the new Asian nationalism, of the taking to heart of the European lessons of industrialism and autonomy. Although she lost the war, her conquests diffused the will to drive out the white man and resulted in the postwar dismemberment of the European empires, the liberation of hundreds of millions of Asians and Africans. On all this—and the question of whether the end of the empires is only coincident with, or significantly related to, the rise of communism, or of what part the new states may play in the thirty-year-old confrontation of the two great ideologies—Churchill, the putative prophet and seer, is silent. Beyond some lofty rhetoric about not presiding over the dissolution of the empire, he has nothing to say about the closing of the imperial age, about the meaning of the revolution in thought and action since the heyday of empire in the 1890s. Nor does he grapple in this book with the momentous fact that Russia and America have replaced Europe as centers of world power.

To Malcolm Muggeridge, *The Second World War,* useful mainly as a reference work, is therefore "historic rather than historical." It is a record of history made rather than written, a monument to Churchill rather than work of history, a piece of impassioned oratory or vivid journalism rather than reasoned exposition or narrative literature, and, like *The World Crisis,* a collection of fading photographs rather than a lasting painting.[91] Yet despite these flaws one may conclude that *The Second World War,* when viewed beside the achievements of its statesman-narrator, remains not just a unique revelation of the exercise of power from atop an empire in duress but also one of the fascinating products of the human spirit, both as an expression of a personality and as a somewhat anomalous epic tale filled with the depravities, miseries, and glories of man.

6

The Sixth Phase:
The Late 1940s
and the 1950s

Leader of the Opposition,
Moderate Conservative Prime Minister,
Chronicler Summing Up

He sees life in terms of war, and his high and turbulent spirit is entirely happy only when politics and war are merged in one theme—A. G. Gardiner, 1926

The past which Churchill served died with him—J. H. Plumb, 1969

Speeches
The Postwar World at Mid-Century

Churchill's resounding and surprising defeat in the election of 1945 abruptly brought the wartime coalition leader and colleague of Stalin and Roosevelt into yet another novel role: leader of the opposition, peacetime chief of the very Conservative Party in which he had never been at ease. He was seventy-one years old. The elderly erstwhile backbench rebel who had found himself conducting military and diplomatic affairs during a global crisis became once again merely a partisan critic of other men's governance. He apparently remained in politics in order to win the peace, vindicate his policies, redeem the 1945 electoral humiliation, and perhaps prove to himself that under him the party could reverse the verdict of the electorate; later he desired to achieve a détente with Russia. When, after six years, he became prime minister again, with almost the final ambitions of his political life fulfilled, his politics turned atypically nondramatic, his utterances on the Soviets, the welfare state, and the empire sounded less strident. Though his main interest remained foreign affairs, he sought reconciliation with the trade unions no less than with Russia, in a vaguely progressive conservatism.[1]

In the wake of the war, he turned to writing his memoirs and resuming the role of outsider and prophet. This time, however, the world was his audience, an appreciative one which lapped up his every grunt or bon mot and quickly came to accept his views on the Cold War. Despite many defeats and frustrations, he had had as much success as is given any man, and he was honored everywhere. A national hero and a vindicated prophet, he spoke now like one assured of his place in history. Yet the speeches of this period, collected in five sizable volumes, are not on a level with those of his three great phases. The sources of inspiration were gone, for events had bypassed Britain, which, like the rest of the world, had become an onlooker at the activities of the two emergent superpowers. Instead of the rhetoric of indomitability, we hear again the satiric sallies of the polemicist. As the nation turns from mortal peril to postwar problems of domestic recovery, the orator reverts to his prewar vocation of excoriating inefficient government and asinine policies, with his wit as sparkling, his rhetorical weapons as honed and deadly, as before.

His typical use of hyperbole and his resentment of the 1945 defeat lead him to depict the Socialist government, with its historic reforms, as a major threat to Britain and civilization. After his invective against the "Nar-zi gang," however, his scolding of his colleagues seems like only sporting combat. Though he may really believe that Britain is going down the drain and that the Socialists are handmaidens of the devil, he is half of the time winking at us and joining us in admiration of his wit and rhetoric. His voice may be raised, his metaphors outraged, and his periods earnest, but it is good clean political chaff, the sort of thing that he had had thrown at him in the past or would have had again, had he won the election. Did he really expect people to think that Aneurin Bevan in charge of Housing was as dangerous as Rommel's Afrika Korps or Hitler's V-2 rockets, that the 1945 election was "one of the greatest disasters . . . in our long and chequered history,"[2] or that Britain faced a crisis as severe as that of 1940? For once legitimized and even surpassed by reality during the war, those superlatives he had reveled in from the days of his first utterances now lost much force from overuse or sounded like attempts at humor through exaggeration and caricature.

If there are no great orations here, there are some famous (or notorious) ones, notably that delivered at Fulton, Missouri (on the "menace of the Soviet power") and the short one delivered at Zurich (on the need for a United Europe—an idea actually broached in a speech at Metz and in a 1930 article). These two became *loci classici* of the last phase of Churchill's career and standard statements of Cold War thinking to which he would often recur. Among other interesting speeches is the brief, moving one on Lloyd George—the words of which can be applied to Churchill himself—and the one on his own eightieth birthday. The massive national celebrations on this occasion, which would have brought out of most men—notably politicians—platitudes and cant, stimulates his sense of humor, which is indeed rich and varied throughout.

In domestic matters, Churchill's program is the same as that forwarded in his "radical" years of the 1900s, but the great opposition came then from the Tories resisting the new social reforms and now comes from the left, which wants to extend the welfare state into a socialist society. Churchill's attack on the Laborite attempt to destroy the House of Lords—for which, ironically, he himself had prepared the ground with his bitter sallies against the upper house in 1910—is a measure of his change. In politics as in everything else, Britain prefers, according to Churchill, tolerance, decency, and tradition to system, logic, or even sheer ability. Although always changing, Britain, "like nature, never draws a line without smudging it."[3] One of the charges against the Socialists is that they dismiss the coherent British past he celebrates in the *History*—with its steady evolution of liberty, its rich traditions, its heroes of thought and action—as merely the "mess of centuries." Part of the special British message being the Burkean one of "slow and noiseless" organic growth, he favors long parliamentary recesses because, just as trees can more easily be cut down than grown, many of the new problems brought by the terrible twentieth century cannot be solved merely by passing laws.[4]

Churchill's criticisms are really variations on the partisan theme that the Laborites should have set country above party and shown themselves Britons first and socialists second. But this sophistry ignores the fact that the Laborites thought they were doing the best for Britain by being socialist. Distorting the truth in attributing losses to nationalized industries, Churchill provides a poor analysis of what is generally regarded now as a period of great social reform. In a difficult time, the Laborites made a herculean job of recovery, and they probably lost in 1951 only because the Korean War and consequent British rearmament forced them to impose new austerities.[5]

If Churchill's statements on domestic affairs seem anachronistic, cliché ridden, or intemperate, the cause may be that, after an absence of forty years from social legislation, he was not eager to return to the subject at a time when the war brought him such stature on the international scene. While indulging in the party politician's undignified fights with the Laborites—fights reminiscent of those with Balfour's Tories at the beginning of his career—he was more interested in the reconstruction of Europe, in playing the role of elder world statesman. And in foreign policy, he at least approved of most of the Labor government's decisions—introducing rearmament and conscription, resisting the Soviets, acting in concert with the Americans, joining NATO, sending forces to Greece and Hong Kong, participating in the Berlin airlift. The story of postwar diplomacy—of British alertness, American participation, western firmness, Korea instead of Munich—is therefore for Churchill a parable illustrating how men and nations should have acted in the 1930s, and the history of Europe in his lifetime is a narrative of redemption.

When Churchill suggests, however, that the time for a rapprochement is limited because once the Russians obtain advanced nuclear weapons, the West would not so easily be able to make "just demands" and a "lasting settlement," he exhibits a rather naïve faith in the efficacy of merely reaching an agreement on paper, especially since at other moments he warns of the unreliability of nonagression pacts. Once western strength is built up, moreover, Churchill, despite having been a leading cold warrior and a lifelong foe of communism, is responsive to signs of change. The spread of communism has been stopped, and he is willing to "forget old scores." Just as after the war he worked to bring Germany back into the European family, so in the 1950s he seeks reconciliation with Russia. He says, as he had nearly thirty-five years before, of Soviet Russia, "Time may find remedies that this generation cannot command." Prosperity may make Russia more amenable to living in peace with other states.[6]

In the early 1950s, therefore, he considers the current troubles in Vietnam to be related not to Soviet policies but to "local circumstances." He grows sympathetic to Russia's "reasonable" and "sincere" anxieties about future invasions, her desire for prosperity after a half-century of war, revolution, and famine. With Stalin's death, the growth of a "milder climate" in Russia, and his own return to power, Churchill hopes for more friendly contacts. Trade and exchange of personnel and services will ease tensions, but the best way of achieving reconciliation, he insists now as always, is by summit meetings. Accepting a "peaceful coexistence" that is not appeasement, he rejoices, by 1954, that he, often "abused" as a warmonger, has a reputation as a seeker after peace.[7]

*   *   *   *

A recurring theme since *The World Crisis* has been the horror of living in this "cataclysmic" modern world. Churchill has seen a "frightful half century" of the most terrible events in history, a period when the bright hopes of the past were dashed. Perhaps, he speculates, we should call a halt to discoveries that "our immature civilization is incapable" of employing well, for if the internal-combustion engine is no improvement on the horse, if even the march of medicine and its lengthening of our lives is of ambiguous import, what will result from entrusting the atom bomb to a human race indistinguishable from its "predecessors of the so-called barbarous ages"? Modern man, still "struggling, ill informed," bewildered, almost helpless, is, with all his "finest theories of freedom," adrift in the vast new world he has created.[8] Nursing the "illusion of growing mastery" of his own fate, he has in fact become "far more helpless than he had been."[9] Yet even though his "perverted" science threatens a return to the Stone Age or total destruction, its advance cannot be resisted; it is like destiny, and when Churchill speaks of "all time," he must qualify: "whatever time may be left to us."[10]

Nevertheless, undergoing a dark night of the soul, as he did in the 1930s, Churchill arrives at some glimmer of hope after confronting all the modern terrors. If the existence of weapons able to destroy the human race leads some to consider the "daily round" of life meaningless, a hopeful sign is that in conventional warfare "the more efficient fire-arms have become, the fewer people are killed by them"; the automatic weapons may have put an end to the "very mass attacks they were devised to destroy."[11] Similarly, awesome as is the hydrogen bomb, it has paradoxically diminished tension and the chances of a world war, despite the accumulation of incredible weapons of destruction. These doomsday monsters may oddly enough "bring an utterly unforseeable security to mankind."[12] To ban modern weapons, as Churchill shrewdly perceived as early as 1934, would merely send men back to clubs and spears; since wars come from the quarrels of nations, not from arms, if the pacifists' dream of a dissolution of all arms took place, "war would follow at once."[13] But now, when everyone can kill everyone else, no one will want to kill anyone; a war in which both sides will suffer the worst is less likely to begin than one in which ambitious persons see lurid prizes to be gained. Though moralists lament "that peace can find no nobler foundations than mutual terror,"[14] perhaps at long last war will now be outlawed. "Our perils may prove our salvation."[15] The old ironist revels once more in the paradoxes of history: By a "sublime irony, . . . safety will be the sturdy child of terror, and survival the twin brother of annihilation."[16] Lest Churchill sound too bloody minded, we should recall that in 1948 no less a person than Bertrand Russell suggested threatening Russia with imminent atomic war in order to force nuclear disarmament on her and that, long before, Kant had likewise argued that the union of nations will be brought about by the very thing it would abolish—wars.

Churchill is as conscious as ever of the "astonishing twists and turns" of life: "The principle of the boomerang . . . is . . . increasingly operative in human affairs."[17] If Stalin began the Cold War, he also unwittingly consolidated the English-speaking alliance, united Europe, and brought Germany back into the family of nations. The Korean War actually made general hostilities less likely by arming America and by enhancing the "hope of settlement with Russia following on the defeat of aggression."[18] Precisely because the situation was more tense, with blood being shed and with massive rearmament, "durable peace" was possible. In the face of all reason and experience, therefore, Churchill cleaves to the promise of the future. With Stalin gone, the Korean fighting ended, the U.S. mightily armed, and tensions slackened, he, at career's end, can find something cheerful: "The long period of suspicion and abuse may be ending."[19] His last speech as prime minister, urging men not to flinch, weary, or despair, can be the motto of his life, and among his last public expressions is his excited reaction to the nascent space age. The lunar rockets are not "merely ingenious bids for prestige" but products of great scientific strides which will "reap a rich harvest" for those with imagination "to probe even more deeply into the mysteries of the universe."[20]

In an epilogue to *The Second World War* written at the time of the publication of the last volumes of the *History,* toward the end of his sixth decade as a participant in and commentator on world events, Churchill surveys the dozen years which followed the war. Like the last of his published books, this epilogue ends on an optimistic note, as if harking back to the exuberance of his very first books. Signs of progress abound: Britain is united on basic policy; old enmities in Western Europe are dying out; the Cold War is thawing; the imagination is stirred by man's presence on the threshold of the space age. The efforts of Britain and the Allies in World War II were not after all in vain. War seems likely to be postponed because of the threat of mutual extermination. Russia is becoming commercial and prosperous; Marx is dated. The Russians are "fellow mortals" to whom he wishes prosperity and a splendid part in the guidance of the human race. "And it may well be if wisdom and patience are practised that Opportunity-for-All will conquer the minds and restrain the passions of mankind."[21] So, on February 10, 1957, at his Chartwell country house, he writes one of his last sentences, sixty years after beginning his career as adventurer and writer. It is the last of his long list of prophecies, and we still do not know if he is right in this matter.

A History of the English-Speaking Peoples:

A Postponed Summing Up

The *History of the English-Speaking Peoples* is the final major work of Churchill's to be published, but in order of composition it stands just after *Marlborough.* Most of it, his preface reveals, was written during 1938–39, and only after the distractions of sixteen turbulent, climactic years, during which the author was occupied first as wartime leader, then as war memoirist, and lastly as peacetime prime minister, could he revise and publish it.[22] The many references in his books and speeches to British history and tradition are now correlated and explicated in a coherent narrative; the many incidental laudatory remarks on British civilization are fleshed out and dramatized in what is a treatise no less than a history. The repository of much of his thinking on politics, statecraft, tradition, and national history, this work, like his other major ones, seems an inevitable outgrowth of his career.

He narrates the glorious rise of the British Empire and the English-speaking world—on the eve of the struggle that would see a climactic manifestation of the power of the latter and the eclipse of the former—because, as he says, to confront the present trials, the English-speaking peoples need to fortify themselves by a "contemplation" of past tribulations. The manner in which they form a single community may also be a model for other blocs of people and may aid in forming a world community. Though every nation of course "has its own tale to tell," this one is especially meaningful, a triumphant story of world primacy and of an exemplary evolution of democratic government and liberty.[23] Having come through a second world war, the Anglo–American alliance bears a "postwar common duty to the human race" and a primary role in the destiny of the world. The theme of the *History* therefore has "grown in strength and reality."

This may well be the first history book to treat jointly England and the U.S. after the American Revolution, or to consider the English-speaking peoples as a family or bloc. Churchill is uniquely qualified for such an approach, being himself the product of family strains from both sides of the Atlantic and having often visited America and worked closely with its leaders during both world crises. These circumstances lead to his idiosyncratic historiography and philosophy of history as well as to many of his actions as prime minister. He quotes a paean, from a little-known book by his ancestor Winston Churchill, on the English civilization "extending to those far-distant regions, now become a part of us and growing apace to be the bigger part, in the sunburnt America";[24] clearly he is proud to be a Churchill, a namesake, a Briton, and a semi-American. The closing pages of the *History,* like those of *The Second World War,* resound with the grand theme of Anglo-American solidarity, the vision which is his political last will and testament. His subject is the inevitable convergence of the two titans, and he sees himself as a Vergilian prophet, finding in the past the promise of the future.

As in his war memoirs, his aim is not to give a comprehensive objective narrative nor to rival professional historians but to present history through the filter of his own rather special experience of recent "historical and violent events." His various observations on, say, Ethelred's foreign policy or James I's "appeasement" of Spain are of interest less for the light shed on those recondite subjects than for what they tell us about the historian-statesman's own values. He writes of what strikes him as important and cavalierly overlooks large areas of historical experience. Where *Marlborough* is meant to be an original contribution to scholarship, this work remains a popularization. It is a personal testament, a patriot's gift offering, a politician's handbook, a prose epic, a would-be prophetic effusion.[25] It is also an occasion for renewing some of the controversies, especially in the military sphere, which bedevil *The World Crisis* and *Marlborough.*

Churchill presents the main story of the English-speaking peoples as the evolution of their domestic liberty and their rise to international prominence. The one involves the development of liberal institutions embodied in what he generally calls the "Constitution"; the other involves the struggle, at first, of the various ethnic groups on the islands to arrive at a political unity and, later, of the nation to obtain imperial possessions abroad to which the concurrently growing liberties are exported. That peculiar development is a product, Churchill thinks, of geography —Britain's detachment from the continent and mastery of the oceans—and, even more, of the national character, with its characteristic aversion to abstract theory. The slow growth of case law and precedents ultimately achieved the same freedoms as are abruptly proclaimed by the American Declaration of Independence and the French Declaration of the Rights of Man.

These developments are not without their anomalies, which are embodied in the monarchy, a central English institution necessary for unification but also sometimes a hindrance to individual freedom. The early stages of British history required a strong king, who would impose his will on conflicting petty local rulers. The potent ruler must, however, be just. He must set down a code of laws, as did Alfred; he must submit himself to the laws whereby he ruled, as did Canute; he must maintain them for the good of all, as did William I, Henry II, and Edward I; and he must, as both Saxon and Elizabethan England believed, keep the church in its place.[26] Then, in the advanced stages, the powers of the crown had in turn to be curtailed by a Parliament which came gradually to represent the middle and working classes. The monarchy in the days of its strength was a necessary part of a transitional phase, but in its modern suprapolitical existence, it retains great importance as a unifying symbol.

Such a reading of events has not found favor with most scholars. Churchill assumes that present British institutions are nearly perfect and that British history is a record of "firsts," of the evolution toward that perfection; hence he often uses the word "experiment," usually with reference to the initiation of new modes of politics. Churchill writes history, G. K. Lewis aptly remarks, as a playwright does a play, working his way to a denouement known from the beginning and using a chorus (the narrator) to voice the lesson of the story. This teleological approach to history has been rendered problematic by modern experience and revised theory. What Churchill designates the rise of "liberty" many see as a Whig myth, adherence to which causes the author to distort history. What really happened, they claim, is that the English gentry won *their* liberties from the crown and from the old aristocracy and then came into new money and an empire. "Liberty" is thus basically a political-constitutional matter, a freedom from feudal restraints upon commercial exploitation. Churchill's faith in the special destiny of Britain and his belief that liberty has fully matured are also parts of what seems to be the mythology of the British ruling class.[27]

Like Burke, Churchill praised a supposedly British gradualism in most of his works, and in this connection we recall Churchill's father attacking Gladstone (on Irish home rule) for being "an old man in a hurry." Historians, however, ask whether this "national character" may not reflect only the feelings of the ruling class or a transitory national mood, whether English character and taste have not in fact often changed. Churchill, concludes Lewis, being uninterested in the adventure of ideas, adheres to the conservative myth that political doctrines are alien to British politics and blithely ignores the great theoretical debates in the Anglo–American revolutionary tradition.[28]

Disguised Blessings

In attempting to assess the ultimate significance of events, Churchill grapples with the problem of historical perspective. Incidents have one meaning at the time of their occurrence and another when they have become part of history. What later seemed to be the "Great Charter of Liberties," for instance, was to the contemporary (as it is again to the modern scholar) merely a "Long List of Privileges of the nobility at the expense of the State,"[29] because the later centuries thought of law as an evolving human construct, while the Middle Ages regarded it as a "fixed standard" in a society "settled by custom or Divine decree." Similarly, "Wyclif's failure in his own day was total," but, having planted a seed, he, as Milton said, "wanted . . . nothing but his living in a happier age" to see his ultimate success.[30] The difficulty in evaluating events is further exemplified by Disraeli's negotiated "peace with honor" at Berlin. Though conflict was averted for the moment, the treaty has been criticized for leading to World War I. Churchill's rejoinder is that, the Eastern Question being "insoluble," any settlement would have been temporary, and the Congress of Berlin at least gave Europe a thirty-six-year respite. Final evaluation thus seems impossible, and tentative judgments depend on whether one focuses on the number of years of peace obtained or on the eventual coming of war.

The question of perspective is inextricably bound up with the equally knotty matter of the relationship between individual design and the pattern of events. History seems to show a direction, a thrust, but when looked at closely it reveals, like an impressionist canvas consisting of a riot of polychromatic dots, an anarchy of individual wills. Many historical milestones turn out to be, in Churchill's vision, mere by-products of selfishness, the results of the actions of men with eyes only on the moment. We are ignorant puppets of the historical process, often obtaining the reverse of what we want. The loss of the "distracting" Angevin Empire in France under King John, for example, Churchill considers a boon which allowed England to turn her energies within; "these consolations did not however dawn on John's contemporaries, who saw only disastrous and humiliating defeat."[31] The last years of Henry III and the reign of Edward I were the "seed-time" of the parliamentary system and of land reform, but hardly anyone foresaw the results. Pitt, having eradicated the French menace in North America, little knew that he had eased the "final secession" of the colonies from Britain. The revolt of the American colonies, bringing to light many inequities in the existing social system and leaving rebel arguments lingering in English minds, in turn begot another cycle of reform. Similarly, neither the French National Assembly nor the French army of 1789 with its liberating zeal could dream that its work would lead to the first modern ruthless dictatorship, nor could Napoleon in turn realize that the spirit of nationalism and freedom spread by French arms would "baffle and betray" him and lead to the rise of Germany "in the hour of his downfall," or that he would be succeeded by the reactionary Congress of Vienna, which repressed the popular movements for "nationality and freedom."

This motif is, of course, familiar from Churchill's other books. The theme of the unexpected twists of fate which pervades the portrait of late Victorian politics in *Randolph Churchill* is now applied to the panorama of modern European history. Somewhat more novel for Churchill is his emphasis on the discrepancy between intent and result; often "capable rulers by their very virtues sow the seeds of future evil and weak or degenerate princes open the pathway for progress."[32] Churchill makes an implicit contrast between the most popular and militarily successful of English kings, Henry V, whose winning of an empire in France ushered in a century of wasteful, tragic campaigns on the continent and who, while uniting the nation, persecuted the

Lollards; and Edward IV, who allowed revelry to keep him from pressing the foolish intrigues on the continent urged by Warwick. Though he was a "Little-Englander and a lover of ease," Edward by his policy happily enabled England to recover from the civil war.

So also did noble acts like Catholic or Negro emancipation turn out to stem from the expedient desire to avert an Irish revolt or to win over British public opinion by turning the sagging American Civil War into a "moral crusade," even as the Fifteenth Amendment, universalizing suffrage, was passed less out of love of liberty or of the ex-slave than to sustain the carpetbaggers. The failings of George I and George III were "fortunate" because they generated the modern "Parliamentary system of government" and helped develop English liberties, however "formidable and far-reaching" the immediate disasters.

In the amoral perspective of history, more is owed "to the vices of [King] John than to the labours of virtuous sovereigns."[33] John's antagonists, the barons, likewise concerned with their own class interests, only dimly groped toward a basic principle. Magna Carta merely addresses itself to "current abuses" affecting a discontented feudal ruling class, but ultimately it secured rights for all landowners and established guidelines to be even further extended. Though it was a privileged concession exacted from the king by a "reactionary" aristocracy, it set custom and law above the king, and this half-understood precedent made the barons' demands imperishable. Again, in turbulent reigns like those of Henry III, Edward II, or Richard II, Churchill discerns long-range salutary developments. The last of these kings, by canceling the gains that Parliament had made in the two previous centuries, unwittingly prepared the way for a reaction in which his successor, Henry IV, would be dependent on Parliament. Thus, for Churchill, benefits cannot but flow from selfishness, whether it be the potent ruler's or the rebellious barons'.

Other classic cases of private vice making for public virtue are the Reformation in England, brought in by "an opportunist King," and the Puritan rebellion, in which a strange amalgam of intolerant zealots desirous of purging the church, tenant farmers and parliamentarians resentful of royal paternal rule, and new middle-class, city-money power contended with the old aristocracy and landowners. Though these selfish rebel forces were wrong on the "ship money" issue, they precipitated a quarrel crucial for English liberties, toppled a king, and indirectly laid the groundwork for freedom of religion and of the press, even as Charles I (no martyr he: "His own kingly interests were mingled at every stage with the larger issues"[34]) helped preserve English liberty by dying while trying to limit it. Indeed, religious movements, in spite of their leaders' intolerance, often unwittingly generate political progress. The Lollards' challenge was ultimately to the nobility as well as the church, for the privileges of the one had no better title than those of the other; the Reformation's cry for liberty of conscience became transformed into the French Revolution's cry for equality of opportunity.

The Restoration, a step forward from the extreme of military dictatorship, was brought about when the circumspect, self-serving General Monk, "with the appearance of great propriety and complete self-abnegation," moved cautiously "forward towards the obvious purpose of the nation."[35] The next cycle of liberalization was wrought, ironically, by Parliament's desire to oppress Nonconformity, in spite of Charles II's inclination to tolerate it. Parliament thereby unwittingly "consolidated Nonconformity as a political force" with the objective of abolishing the church's privileged status, assisted in the foundation of political parties, and bound together all the dissenting elements in the nation. Just as Charles II's tolerance of Nonconformity sprang from his "easy indifference" rather than from any deep liberal principles, so also did James II appeal to this power bloc later not out of any love for toleration but as a cunning prelude to the revival of Catholicism. Thus circuitously—and, by design, temporarily—did an Englishman arrive for the first time at the idea of "toleration among all English Christians." In the same way, the slowly developing freedom of the press was never deliberately inaugurated but was helped along by an issue raised by the writings of the scurrilous and rakish John Wilkes; Parliament, in turn, did not act on any high ground of principle but because of the "inconsiderable reasons" that the detailed working of the Licensing Act was causing vexation.

These moral paradoxes mean that both long and short views are necessary for a proper understanding of history. What is bad in the short run or to the historical participants may be good in the long run and in the opinion of the detached student of the past; what is selfish in root may bear sweet fruit; what is personal vice may also be social virtue. Although one reviewer found no trace of it in Macaulay and only intimations of it in Stubbs, this idea (actually explicit and iterated in Stubbs)[36] has a venerable intellectual history. It originates in the Judeo-Christian reading of history as the working out, in sometimes unintelligible ways, of the will of Providence; even Pharaoh, Judas, or Satan, by trying to foil God's will, are inadvertently fulfilling it. This concept of *felix culpa* next appears in secular and nonteleological form in Machiavelli's *Prince,* a work which dissociates private from public morality by teaching that the health of the body politic may well depend on vicious action by its rulers. Machiavelli's analysis of politics is applied by Bernard Mandeville and Adam Smith two centuries later to political economy and social psychology. "Private vices" like selfishness, pride, luxury, Mandeville asserts, result in "public benefits" like a thriving economy and the refinements of civilization; Smith speaks of the working of an "invisible hand" in commercial relations which guides men's selfish acts to an end favorable to society. The idea is also reapplied to history—albeit with the idea of progress sometimes replacing theodicy—by Vico, who sees man often desiring one thing and making something quite different or finds that many contentions have good results unintended by either party to the dispute; by Kant, who teaches that neither individual nor nation knows the end his actions promote, that passion rather than reason is the motive force of history, that nature achieves its rational goal by means of men's antagonisms; by Hegel, who asserts that man's clashing, selfish passions, the springs of human action, are taken in hand by the "cunning of Reason" and used for ends unintended by the actors, that the World Historical Individual overrides the existing morality in ruthless pursuit of his selfish aim without awareness of being the agent of Reason; and by Marx, who substitutes "dialectical materialism" for "Reason" and classes for individuals. The idea became a commonplace of nineteenth-century historians; the New England school, for instance, spoke of the "strange moral vehicles" used by God or historical fate, of extreme forces blended by conflict into a moderate progressive advance.

Although probably unaware of this intellectual background, Churchill, ever a keen student of historical ironies, makes the "cunning of Reason" (or, to apply a phrase he uses elsewhere, "disguised blessings") the shaping principle, in conjunction with the Great Man theory, of the *History*. It is also the last of the four grand themes informing respectively his four major works. So had he in *Marlborough* delighted in his hero's ability to serve Britain and Europe while simultaneously serving himself, and this theme is indeed nothing but Marlborough's putative "harmony of interests" universalized.

Clearly, then, Churchill prefers intuition to conscious will, continuity to innovation, organic growth to deliberate reconstruction, pragmatism to general theorizing, gradualism to prompt reform, selfishness to starry-eyed idealism, paradox to reason, impulse to consistency, feeling (especially for class, country, and king) to abstract universal loyalties, tradition and spontaneity to design. This full-blown Burkean romanticism posits an overall progression, inscrutable to all but a few, which is apparently inevitable but which takes place by means of the interplay of conflicting individual wills, by means of detours and digressions in a typically British "muddling through." It bespeaks a conservative diffidence as to mankind's ability to master its destiny: his judgment being terribly frail, man little knows where he is going, what he really wants, or what will be the consequences of his actions. Since he is most dangerous when most altruistic, forward-looking, and rational—in other words, when he is consciously redesigning society—the individual had better confine himself to cultivating his own garden and respecting the legacy of the past. Fanatical idealists looking for instant utopias are at least as responsible, in this reading, for the number and size of the bloody detours as are those impervious to all ideas of change.

Churchill's surrender to the drift of things, one might suggest, veers dangerously close to antirationalism, fatalism, and political passivity in the individual, as well as blind worship of the status quo and of rampant individual self-interest in the society. It takes too little account of the moral energies and the creative reason which have played an important role in the dynamic of history. Taken seriously, it would have undermined the bases of Churchill's own activist political career—if the results of our public acts are often the reverse of what is desired, why bother?

This conservative reading of the past, moreover, sits awkwardly with Churchill's sense of the fortuitous, his belief that history could easily have taken a number of different courses. Churchill concedes that Parliament is a "very delicate plant," with "nothing inevitable about its growth"; once it "took root," its authority was stabilized "by a series of accidents."[37] The sovereign's no longer presiding over cabinet meetings was "a most significant event, though . . . only the result of an accident"—George I's inability to speak English—for the ministers came to regard themselves as responsible only to the prototypic prime minister, the "commoner" Walpole.[38] The role of chance is seen again in the fact that the "untested" American republic was established by the inauguration of its first president a bare week before the French Revolution plunged the world into new stresses. Britain likewise had a narrow escape in 1812—the language here recalls that in *The World Crisis* on the three momentous events in the spring of 1917—when the United States declared war on her only a week before Napoleon invaded Russia. Churchill never does reconcile this sense of the fortuitous with his Great Man theory of history and his ruling thesis of the apparently inevitable evolution of liberty.[39]

He has equal difficulty in harmonizing his own conflicting views on the role of violence in history. His sense of "disguised blessings" and of paradox makes him acutely aware that one of the greatest catalysts of progress is bloodshed. He often implies that immoral, illegal, or bloody acts may be necessary for the greater good and the longer run, and most of his judgments have, as in his other works, the toughness we associate with the sad wisdom of Machiavelli. He imputes the military mismanagement of ninth-century England, for instance, to an "undue subservience to the Church," rather as Machiavelli blamed Christianity for eroding martial prowess. He rejoices that St. Edward the Confessor's place as the English patron saint was taken by the chivalric St. George, who better reflected English "needs, moods, and character." Churchill clearly likes his Christianity in small doses and without cheek turning. Theology, he states, may have to "wait upon" arms, and conquering men of action receive his respect.

Illicit or violent acts have their place. The execution of Strafford "threw odium upon his pursuers," who were unable to convict him, but had he had his way, Churchill notes, he would have curtailed civic freedom. Similarly, though the Boadicean rebellions against the Romans were "horrible" and destroyed an incipient "higher civilization," Churchill, the hardy war leader, finds exculpating reasons in men's right to "die and kill" for their land and to severely punish turncoats. The Germanic tribes settling in England abandoned ties of kinship to form societies based on land tenure, a change which arose "like so many of the lessons learned by men, from the grim needs of war."[40] The unification of England was brought closer to fulfillment when, as a result of political intrigues among the kingdoms, "for the first time . . . British and English fought side by side [and] politics for once proved stronger than religion or race."[41] Parliament grew in stature when Edward III needed money for his French wars, when Henry IV needed support for his seizure of the crown, and, when, in the troubles under Edward II or during the Wars of the Roses, the contending factions turned to it, as a body representative of the nation, for public sanction for their actions. War, in brief, is not only a stimulus to self-preservation or a part of civilization; forcing men, in the face of greater dangers, to modify old enmities and routines, it even brings out the best in them. Churchill's love of making war thus modulates, in combination with the "disguised blessings" motif, into the Machiavellian–Nietzschean vision of the necessary bloodshed at the heart of civilization and nearly makes a shambles of his conservative, gradualist philosophy.[42]

His inconsistency is barely resolved by his distinguishing, in analyzing the Plantagenet age, a violence "of vigor" from one "of decadence." Presumably revolutionary violence is of the decadent sort, for on it Churchill and the intellectuals reverse their positions. In the 1790s, Wordsworth, like other writers, scientists, and "progressive" political thinkers of the period, responded enthusiastically to "foreign revolutionary ideas," just as, Churchill sneers, occurred "in our own day." When the Greeks revolted in 1822, "enlightened circles in London" wanted to aid them, but before Byron died, Churchill amiably records, he "was deeply disillusioned."[43] Almost as a challenge to leftist intellectual assumptions, Churchill proclaims that "revolts do not break out in countries depressed by starvation."[44] Citing Froissart's belief that the fourteenth-century peasant rebellions were caused by ease and plenty among the survivors of the plague, Churchill insists that France under Louis XIV was not, as is often claimed, oppressed, but prosperous and liberal. Notably obnoxious to him are the nineteenth-century historians who overlook Cromwell's deeds of "frightfulness" and, in "safe, comfortable" days, "gape . . . in furtive admiration" and eagerly lap up Cromwell's excuses.[45] Churchill (like Machiavelli) favors violence only in certain cases and as a last resort, not as an end in itself. For shedding "innocent blood," he dismisses the capable Shaftesbury and strips Cromwell "of all title to honour," whether as captain or statesman.

As a result of the role of the disguised blessing of violence, progress does not occur without interruptions. There are bad turns, misfirings, and, especially, swings of the pendulum. Though the men of the Puritan rebellion may have been intent on advancing the cause of Calvinist theology and middle-class politics, among them appeared radical ideals of social and political egalitarianism, of natural right, universal suffrage, and land held in common. Some of these ideas were worthy and would be fulfilled in later times; others were fortunately unheeded. But for a while the sequence of events had saddled England with a dictatorship, and, however legitimate the issues which caused the rebellion and however valuable its consequences, Churchill sees the Protectorate as an unfortunate, evil, un-English interlude—though he virtually grants it to have been a necessary bloody detour.

Here Churchill comes perilously close to ignoring another historical crux. For how can we tell whether a war or dictatorship is merely a digression from, or even an unwitting contribution to, the march of progress, or whether "progress" itself is really only a progressive interlude, a part of a larger cycle, a distraction from human stasis? If, as we saw, evaluation varies with the temporal vantage point, how can we arrive at an objective idea of "progress" in the first place? And may not progress be one of those many things that men of good will have striven for, only to bring, because of the dialectic of history, evil on themselves and the world? Can we ever adjudge anything (for instance, Disraeli's "peace with honor") to be good, without getting lost in the opposition of short- and long-range views and the thicket of "ifs" on all sides? And if in the grand design of the evolution of liberty, whatever was, was right, how can Cromwell, or anyone, be condemned?

In fact, the *History,* like Churchill's other works—signally the

Marlborough, which similarly involved an immersion in the remote past—radiates an ambivalence about the course of history. On the one hand, postulating a "forward march of liberal ideas"[46] and empire, it finds in history a clear design and a British destiny which somehow benefits the world. Even a "reign of turmoil" or a discarded institution like feudalism was in its day the "instrument" of human advancement. On the other hand, Churchill drifts into philosophical deep waters as his narrative approaches the Victorian period. The belief in progress having become by then a central tenet of the age, often naïvely invoked, he hedges it with the irony and patronizing tone suffusing the *Commission* and *Contemporaries.* The old optimism seems now to him a terrible illusion. The nineteenth century, "a period of purposeful, progressive, enlightened, tolerant civilization,"[47] might well have thought, he says, that persistent problems were being at last resolved; but then came the twentieth century.[48]

Churchill's doubts on the idea of progress actually appear throughout the work, and they imperil his teleological vision. He enjoys pricking the modern reader's complacency with suggestions that the quality of life in Roman Britain may have been superior to that in modern Britain. He remarks on the descent of many leading nations into despotisms which are dressed up with double talk. Even amid the brutalities of the Wars of the Roses, the people retained the faculty of horror, whereas dictators with modern science at their disposal easily manipulate popular opinion and vastly increase the amount of violence and the efficiency in killing. In this area alone, progress has been indisputable.

Churchill often notes the much less bloody working out of political contentions in the earlier ages, as in the "rigorously" yet "evenly fought out" clash between Henry II and Becket. Simon de Montfort, when he achieved power, could have consolidated it by brutally executing his foes in the modern fashion, but in those cruel days matters were not taken "to the last extreme." The persecution of the Wat Tyler rebels, of the Puritans under Charles I, or of the Royalists under the Protectorate was as nothing compared with recent or imminent "animal barbarism." The French Revolution led to the first modern "ruthless dictatorship," and in the ensuing hostilities, "for the first time in history the entire man-power and resources of a state were being marshalled for total war."[49]

History is, then, a record of growing liberty, creature comforts, and destructiveness. A compromised progress, this. Manifestly, our offense lies in our pretense to being modern, progressive, that is, better than earlier ages which actually were "comparatively civilized and refined." With little left now of the qualified optimism of his first books, Churchill inveighs, like an angry prophet, "What claim have we to vaunt a superior civilization to Henry II's times? We are sunk in a barbarism all the deeper because it is tolerated by moral lethargy and covered with a veneer of scientific conveniences."[50] Nor is there an end in sight. Human nature will not allow it. When, after the first civil war, England seemed close to a settlement, "it was too good to be true. Not so easily can mankind escape from the rigors of its pilgrimage."[51] For all of his teleology, or perhaps because of it, Churchill can envision nothing much better than the present state of society (aside from some minor improvements). Conservative piety accepts what is and seeks no utopia. Churchill, as a matter of fact, finds secure and prosperous periods of peace usually drab. "Man has never sought tranquility alone. His nature drives him forward to fortunes which, for better or for worse, are different from those which it is in his power to pause and enjoy."[52] The blessings often remain effectively disguised.

Past Politics and Wars

Despite its many interesting facets, the *History* remains a flawed, even irritating, work. One weakness is of course the teleological pattern. In tracing a long evolution, something he had not had to do in any of his other works, Churchill falls into the trap of making everything point to fulfillment in the present. A strong ruler unifies the nation, codifies the laws, and protects the people from the predatory aristocrats and the church. A baronial reaction to a weak or vicious ruler brings about the establishment of political principles which take their place in the developing tradition of English liberty. Thus Richard II's follies prepare for the constitutional monarchy of the Lancasters. Churchill then sides with the House of York, and lo! it achieves ascendancy. When it in turn falls on bad days, along come the Tudors just in time to make their necessary contribution in a period when stability is more important than liberty. The follies of the Stuarts lead to the harshness of the Protectorate and both disasters generate more liberty for Britain. There are no lasting mistakes or detours. Whatever is, is right.[53]

This approach radiates the very optimism Churchill derides in the Victorians and makes him callous to the sufferings along the way. Pride in Britain's pioneer role in the Industrial Revolution is not balanced by awareness of the awesome price in degradation and horror paid for this step forward, a price the young radical Churchill had been more conscious of. Britain seems, at the time of writing, to have attained a perfect political system (though not perfect politicians); further putative democratization is ill advised. Such smug satisfaction with the status quo hardly accords with the essay in the *Thoughts* intimating that in modern economic crises, the parliamentary system may well be breaking down altogether.

His closing three pages are equally complacent on foreign policy. He accepts the arms race at the beginning of this century, Germany's aping of Napoleonic France, and the silent, gradual buildup of the British navy (just as in 1945 he readily sees the Russians displacing Germany as a threat to civilization) as though these were merely part of a natural, necessary rhythm in history or the deeds of evil or foolish leaders, when they in fact are not natural, inevitable, or idiosyncratic but rest on ideas of national sovereignty, empire, power politics, military preparedness, and war which he refuses to examine. There is an unholy zest in his continual casting about for foes—and Britain's foes are always, conveniently, against the liberties of the world. Monumentally smug is his description of his nation: having been carried to "the leadership of the world" and having striven hard for peace, "at any rate for herself," Britain "would have been content to rule alone in moderation." He does not see that, possessing most of the available colonial spoils, Britain could urge peace on those howling wolves of Europe (Russia, Germany, Italy) who were jealous and hungry; the millionaire likes his "law and order." Irritated by Germany's temerity, Churchill finds her "sole objective" to be the will "to fight on till victory was won," as if this were not a quality which he often praised in Britain and her allies. (But he withholds from Germany that favored word of his, "indomitability," which is reserved for "good" nations.)

Perhaps the most archaic element in his thinking is his recurring though not consistently held conviction, now (as in *Marlborough*) at its most refulgent, that "almost every critical turn of historic fortune has been due to the sudden apparition in an era of confusion and decay of one of the great figures of history," that history is mainly the tale of "the impact upon events of superior beings."[54] "Bold ideas" either are expressed through "a man and a leader"—a Simon de Montfort, an Edward I, a Pym—or remain only ideas. Individual actions by, say, Lord North or the kaiser had "incalculable" impact on European history. This venerable belief, expressed by Plutarch, Machiavelli, Burke, Carlyle, Nietzsche, and many others, and attacked by Tolstoy, is now held by few historians or philosophers. Churchill ignores all modern theorizing about social processes and economic forces, and, for that reason, his writings, and particularly this work, seem rather dated and limited.[55]

Many of Churchill's judgments are parochial, being as usual distinctively British, Protestant, imperial, occidental.[56] He speaks of the union of the crowns of England and Scotland as "the obvious and natural solution," and his belief in the indivisibility of the United Kingdom is unshaken by the persistence of separatist movements in Wales, Scotland, and Northern Ireland. He blithely accepts the Reformation as a sure sign of progress, for the Catholic church seems "to conflict with the forward movement of the human mind" and Mary's reign represents "Old England in terrible counterstroke."[57] The spread of English tradition and liberties justifies the acquisition of empire. Though he rarely used the discredited Victorian phrase, "white man's burden," Churchill hints at something very like it in response to modern antiimperialist sentiments, especially on the vexed question of India. Criticizing native writers for calling the Sepoy Rebellion a "struggle for freedom," he quotes an unidentified modern historian to show that British rule ended Indian "bloodshed, tyranny, and anarchy." As with his zeal in *The Second World War* for the liberation of the Baltic states, he is eloquent on independence when it concerns Spain vis-à-vis Napoleonic France. Napoleon, considering himself a liberator, "could not understand a people who preferred misgovernment of their own making to rational rule imposed from without," but concerning India, Churchill insists on Britain's mission to educate, "civilize," police, and harmonize; he treats European Spain by a different standard than he does India, huge subcontinent though the latter be.[58]

The slavery which was long a staple enterprise of this enlightened empire he callously dismisses with typical western self-satisfaction: "The bulk [of the slaves] had become adapted to their state of life, which, though odious to Christian civilization, was physically less harsh than African barbarism";[59] the slave's market value, like the medieval serf's, protected him from excessive ill-usage. The strongest objection he can finally muster is that slavery caused stagnation of the economy—even as, when a young man, he at first decried poverty and squalor only on the practical grounds that it was bad for service recruiting.[60]

Churchill is annoyed with Gladstone for bringing "conscience" and "morality" into the political vocabulary because of the consequent challenge to his own premises, just as in *The Second World War* he evades the moral issue raised by the pacifists. Yet, despite his scorn for "conscience," he speaks of Bismarck's behavior toward Denmark "as an ominous precedent . . . set for what the Germans politely called *Realpolitik.*"[61] Conscience, it seems, after having been dismissed through the front door with Gladstone, has been allowed to enter through the back door and has been loosed on Bismarck. And Churchill speaks as though no other nation, surely not Britain, had ever before availed itself of *Realpolitik.*

Churchill's writing is never completely free of Victorian sentimentality. The intermingling of Britons and Saxons he describes in terms of "a maiden's cry for pity, the appeal of beauty in distress."[62] When he states that "from the ground freedom raises itself unconquerable,"[63] that England was tyrannized by irresistible forces only "for a while" because "the grand lesson of history" is that despotism lasts only among "servile races," he either generalizes wildly or begs the question. The story of King Arthur, which he ranks with the *Odyssey* and the Bible, "is all true, or it ought to be; and more and better besides,"[64] for Arthur is a prototypic Briton who guarded Christianity and the idea of order by slaughtering barbarians, setting decent folk an example, and promising fame to all fighters against tyranny. Churchill cannot resist retelling various romantic legends about Alfred's Robin Hood–like life of exile in the forests or Henry II's "Fair Rosa-

mond" and Eleanor, no matter the cavils of "tiresome investiga-
tors."[65] Perhaps because he thinks that only great individuals
matter, his version of the Wars of the Roses reads like a paraphrase
of Shakespeare's poorest chronicle plays. He describes the leaders,
war cries, and battles but says little of the deeper currents and
nothing on the manner in which the people responded to the
fighting royal houses. A crotchet of his is to relate details of the
deaths of prominent persons to an extent out of proportion to the
attention given their careers. These English worthies—the medieval
kings, Drake, Pym, Clive, Peel, and especially the relatively
unimportant General Moore—must be given a noble exit as an
exercise in Victorian imperial stoic posturing.

*   *   *   *

Critical reception of the *History* has been mixed. The thesis
implicit in the title is at the least arguable, and scholars have
argued. Written with the purpose of prophesying and cementing
Anglo–American ties, the work is mainly a history of Britain and
of the United States, not of the English-speaking peoples; the unity
breaks down in the last volume into the parallel histories of the two
nations because of their tenuous links in the nineteenth century.
Another complaint is that the work does not establish a common
heritage for Britain and America. It overlooks the influence on
America of not only the very Puritans whom Churchill gives short
shrift but also of French culture. He is wrong to base the American
Constitution exclusively on the English.

Churchill's discussion of America has received as much criticism
as his treatment of the Great Rebellion. His perennial interest in
wars rather than peoples results in too much material, however
good, on the Civil War and too little on the idiosyncratic growth of
the colonies in the seventeenth and eighteenth centuries and on the
grand epic of the conquest of the West in the nineteenth. Since the
latter was a folk movement, something welling up from below, not
led from above, it is beyond Churchill's grasp. Above all, asserts
Lewis, Churchill does not understand American civilization at all.
It is too polyglot to be Anglo-Saxon; except for the upper-class,
New England, anglophiliac milieu from which his mother came, it
is too European to be merely an extension of British civilization,
and it has grown even less British in this century. With his love of

continuity and tradition, furthermore, Churchill cannot see that America represents in one sense an important break in continuity; that its greatest tradition is precisely that of making its traditions anew, of creating a new man free of the European heritage; that its open democratic ambience differs basically from the British aristocratic one. The entire English-speaking mystique, Lewis concludes, is smugly based on an Atlantic-centered, West-oriented outlook which sees one locale and age as the apex of the human experience.[66]

Historians have found the work further compromised by three limitations of Churchill's sensibility: his apparent love of war; his ruling-class orientation; his obsolete scholarship. Churchill's joy in great soldiers and spectacular campaigns engenders his scorn for peacemaking politicians like Fox and Gladstone. In a work less about peoples than wars, the French Revolution interests Churchill only as preparing the way for Napoleon, and the great error he discovers in the American Revolution is the ineptness of the British generals. Though he distinguishes between wars of national purpose and the adventurism of Henry V and though he sometimes sees the imbecility of bloodshed, he ascribes the rupture of peace to fate or chance—to a phenomenon beyond human control—and makes all English wars hinge on national honor. Writing in 1938–39, he sneers airily at peace and prosperity, and he is so fascinated by strategy that he often overlooks the purpose of a fight. He identifies the arts of civilization with the arts of war and lets success justify all—a vision triply repulsive, Lewis remarks, in that it distorts the past, elevates war making into a supreme value, and glorifies nationalism in a vastly changed world which renders it obsolete and dangerous.

Though his interest in war is complemented by a love of politics, vast areas of experience are excluded, scholars lament, by Churchill's restricted definition of history as "past politics." He concentrates on government and political institutions, on power expressed in diplomacy and in war making, at the expense of the study of economic forces, social change, and intellectual currents. He has nothing to say on what made the English-speaking peoples truly great in technology, science, philosophy, and the arts; many giants of thought are not even named. All these are levels of the historical process Churchill hardly understands. Simply not interested in anything but war and politics, he writes a narrative of certain events, not the evolution of a civilization, and the work cannot be a textbook of English history.[67]

Plumb and Lewis explore the consequent superficiality—noticeable in all his books but egregious here. The motives for conflict are those which the historical actors felt to be the causes of their actions. Churchill avails himself of neither modern psychology nor Namier's sociology of politics, and the *History* is curiously pre-Marxist and pre-Freudian. Himself a sort of last Plutarchian hero, he judges others by the Plutarchian criteria of honor, renown, dignity, and clemency. In the face of the findings of the modern disciplines produced by the liberal rationalism he dislikes, Churchill, imbued with the conservative sense that much remains a mystery, disposes of causality and motivation with imprecise, old-fashioned words like "race," "destiny," "character," "fate." Seeing all problems pragmatically, like a cabinet minister deciding on a course of action, he ignores the theories which, consciously or unconsciously, shape a man's response. Hence the French Revolution appears here cut off from its important roots in eighteenth-century philosophy. Believing that individuals act on practical assumptions, he cannot imagine that Descartes, Newton, and Marx have shaped men's minds more thoroughly than did Cromwell or Wellington. He studies the conflicts of men rather than of historical forces of which men are perhaps only the instruments. He understands Cromwell but not revolutionary republicanism. He sees the revolutionary as an individual rebel against fate and slights ideas as only a political weapon. Disliking theories and ideologies, he dismisses persons with convictions as bigots wedded to abstractions. Because the individual instead of a class or ideological faction seems to him central to the historical process, Churchill is oblivious to the likelihood that the individual can operate only within social currents, that his talents must be relevant to the needs of his age.[68]

This blindness springs not only from his devotion to politics and war but also from the limitations of the class whose values he expresses. For Churchill is interested in the men who govern, not the governed. He cannot see that the men at the top may be merely in the toils of what wells up from below rather than the shapers of events. He withholds, Plumb notes, his imagination and warmth from the laboring masses; he dwells on the glory of British arms while passing over the horrors of war, especially as experienced by the little man forced into soldiering by poverty and injustice. He can see the courage of the ordinary Englishman as soldier at Agincourt but not as the founder of a trade union. Though he waxes eloquent on British liberty, he seems unaware of the intricate class structure and the residues of feudalism in modern Britain. This is, concludes Plumb, a "Gentleman's history," with men and policies seen through the eyes of generals and statesmen. And even in terms of his own outlook, Churchill assumes that men holding prominent positions, participating in important events, or brandishing dashing and noisy personalities are the makers of history, or that the bloodiest battles are the most important. He thinks that moral greatness is a function of historical fame. In the end, he loves action and fame for their own sake.[69]

As a traditionalist and a chronicler of the British ruling class, Lewis explains, Churchill accepts that class's premises of imperial expansion, the British "mission," secret diplomacy, the balance of power. He is blind to the real meaning of the Great Rebellion, of the rise of dissent, trade unionism, or rationalistic liberalism. A political revolutionary gets a better hearing than a social revolutionary. In his absorption in the sheer flow of history rather than its depth or structure, Churchill twists the evidence in order to impose a spurious continuity, so that the 1688 settlement, for instance, is blindly canonized, its break with legitimacy ignored. Churchill celebrates the European conquerors, Lewis continues, without realizing that they often destroyed the stability and continuity that conservatism supposedly cherishes. He believes in the myth that the period from 1689 to 1914, when his own class of Britons persuaded themselves that they were the natural rulers of the world, was the ideal epoch. He sees power and responsibility as a ruling-class trusteeship, not democratically based. Free of the idea of a master nation in its coarse form, Churchill is yet suffused with the idea of a master class and is contemptuous of any ideas challenging that assumption. For all the talk about "English-speaking peoples," Scotland, Ireland, the U.S., and the Dominions exist here only as facets or branches of England and, at that, of only one class in England.[70]

The third serious flaw is that intellectually Churchill is a displaced person in the very century in which he achieved such resounding success as a man of action. Plumb points out that in writing the *History,* Churchill magisterially ignored the whole of modern scholarship. The result is an archaic work, based on Victorian sources and sounding rather like a nineteenth-century Whig history in its romanticized, patrician view of English institutions, its old-fashioned patriotism, its organic, deterministic, teleological superstructure, its banal judgments on men and events, its simple-minded portrayal of heroes and villains, and its carrying to an extreme certain flaws found in all the author's other books. Lewis and Allen would place the work even further back: Churchill writes it in a twentieth-century idiom but with eighteenth-century structure and assumptions.[71]

Thus the *History,* in itself episodic, wrongheaded, and anachronistic, takes on meaning only insofar as it sheds light on the author's political career and actions. Though hopeless as history, it is remarkable simply because it is by Churchill. Avoiding rigorous intellectual analysis, he has produced not a work with a unifying principle, like Gibbon's or Toynbee's, but a chronicle whose climaxes consist of battles and grand gestures, a sort of literary romance, a piece of brilliant panoramic journalism by a successful politician who does not leave his political temper behind when he turns to historiography. The greatest man of action of his time reflects on the course of English history, and only as a "monument to a great Englishman's sense of the past," Plumb concludes, is the work "a brilliant success."[72]

*   *   *   *

That the material on Marlborough, avowedly a précis of the earlier book, appears in the very middle, suggests that the *History* has its special place in Churchill's evolution as a politician-historian and is not merely something written on commission. Having paid homage to his father with *Randolph Churchill* and given in *The World Crisis* and the *Commission* the record of his own activities in high place, Churchill turned in *Marlborough* back to the origins of family and national greatness and then decided to rove even further afield, to round out the story in either direction. After studying the age of Victoria and then the age of Anne, he would peruse the entire English past.

But the life of Marlborough seems to remain a central event, the preceding 1,650 years and the succeeding 200 years receiving equal treatment. And as, by the way of coda, the last chapter of the *History* returns to the matter of *Randolph Churchill,* the tale leads up to and tacitly culminates in that other central historical event, Churchill's own life. The narrative concludes with the deaths of Victoria and Salisbury, which nicely coincided with the start of the twentieth century and of the author's long career as a writer of major historical works (beginning with *Randolph Churchill*) and as a politician continuing the incomplete mission of his father. Work on the *History,* moreover, ended just as World War II broke out and its author entered upon the major phase of his political career and then upon the writing of the memoirs which told of that phase. Having stepped out of politics in mid-career willy-nilly and thus been able to take stock of his life and times, and having in his writing filled out the canvas of the past, he was ready in 1939 to embark on his destiny with full comprehension of it; it is as if some uncanny foresight made him set his intellectual house in order in preparation for the struggle he would lead and chronicle. In other words, the content of the *History* leads up to the career of its author, and the composition of the *History* leads up to the climax of that career. Then, two decades later, when its publication crowns his career, the book's deepest meaning for author and nation are at last apparent to everyone else as well. The work has unexpectedly become a protracted historical explanation of Britain's and Churchill's roles in World War II and even in the twentieth century. No other writer has had such an odd, personal, and symbiotic relationship to history.

At the conclusion of his long life, then, appears his only real chronicle-history book, the other major works being either war memoirs or biographies. This is also the only nonfiction work of his without a Churchill as protagonist; yet Churchills are among the dramatis personae, and even the narrator appears on the fringe. At the close of the tale, we enter the milieu of his early career, the world depicted in the *Commission* and the *Contemporaries,* with its Jameson raid and Boer War, with men like Asquith, Balfour, Rosebery. A single personal footnote describes how the Anglo–American tension over Venezuela affected the young cadet returning from Cuba, and his one reference to his own entry on the English scene, as the young man we have met in his early books, appears in the discussion of the battle of Omdurman, a unique triumph "described at the time by a young Hussar who took part in the battle."[73] This allusion, poignant and wistful for the writer, looks back some forty (and sixty) years to his first glories. Lastly, the preface to the final volume, dated February 10, 1957, and among Churchill's very last pieces of writing concludes with a reference to World War I, when he entered upon the world stage, at the beginning of the Thirty Years War with Germany that is at the heart of his career. Like the mystical serpent whose tail is in its mouth, the eighty-two-year-old man ends where he began.

Thus we have, as a result of the long postponement, a final work that is not a personal summing up—no need of that, for had he not documented his career all too well every step of the way?—but a national summing up. The individual career is incorporated into the larger cycle, which it fulfills and from which it gains, even as it gives to it, significance. The past has swallowed him live. H. C. Allen complains that the theme of Anglo-American unity does not become a reality until the twentieth century and that therefore the *History* is without a climax.[74] But surely the climax is not absent; it is to be found in the two sets of world war memoirs. Everything Churchill has done and written is to be seen as part of that past which he, after a lifetime of invoking, portrays now in its fullness. The whole of English history, in other words, is like an introduction or prelude to the career and books, the sword and pen, of Sir Winston Churchill.

Conclusion

Churchill, Conservatism, and War

The two fields of interest in Churchill's many books are, of course, politics and war, and an important question about either is raised by a close reading: Was Churchill—who has been called everything from "Radical of the reddest type" to "reactionary" and "fascist"—in the last analysis a conservative? Was he a lover of war? Several subsidiary questions are: Was he a thinker? A man with a soul? A "modern"? A great writer? The answers are, briefly, that he was a moderate conservative who was ambivalent about war; who mixed in varying degrees altruistic impulses with monumental smugness, archaic ideas with adventurous ones; and who was an eloquent writer rather than a great thinker, in the sense that one speaks of someone as a versifier rather than a poet or of a playwright as having a theatrical rather than a literary talent. Each question, however, requires scrutiny.

Any approach to Churchill's political philosophy must consider six aspects: party affiliation, domestic policy, foreign policy, political processes, cultural heritage, philosophical tendencies. Party affiliation proves to be of little help in solving the riddle. Starting out with vaguely liberal proclivities, Churchill was by turns a Conservative, Liberal, coalitionist, Independent, Constitutionalist, Conservative, Conservative in exile, coalitionist, Conservative. He was in the political wilderness not once but four times—in 1904, 1915–17, 1922–24, 1931–39—and his career often seemed finished. Shaw was right in describing him as a man of deeds and individuality rather than of party politics.

In domestic policy, Churchill established himself early as a progressive and may be said to have adhered to such a position despite subsequent growing conservatism. But he did not envision, even in his radical days, any basic alterations in the structure of society; he wanted to preserve, not transform, it. He thought, for instance, in terms of increasing pension benefits, not the redistribution of wealth. Knowing, like Franklin Roosevelt after him, that in order to survive in its present form, capitalist society must attend to the worst abuses and grievances in its midst and that the ruling class must restrain itself a little, he was conservative in the wider sense: he changed in order to neutralize change; he yielded just enough to the oppressed and exploited to forestall revolution, steal the thunder of the socialists, and leave the basic oligarchic institutions untouched.

In foreign policy matters, Churchill grew deeply conservative on the question of empire but was by turns shrilly dogmatic and urbanely pragmatic on communism. If we see a simple shift from the early liberal views on South Africa and Ireland to a growing recalcitrance on India in 1930 and on the European empires in Asia in the 1940s (or an unchanging attitude which treated white European stock by a different standard than it did nonwhite, non-European peoples), Churchill's responses to Communist Russia are more complex. In 1919 and the early 1920s, he was a stern advocate of strangling bolshevism in the cradle; in the late 1930s, he urged a Western alliance with the Bolshevik monolith which, in the late 1940s, he again saw as the major threat to civilization; then, in the 1950s, he softened again and sought reconciliation and peaceful coexistence. He would of course say that all this springs not from vacillation or confusion but from flexibility of response in the face of constantly changing circumstances. And it must be granted of his turnabout in the 1930s that it reveals his greatness. A typical Tory like Chamberlain either could not see the emergent problem clearly or could not bring himself to take such a drastic step, whereas Churchill, the active, indeed for a while obsessive, anti-Communist was quicker to alter his course than the conventional, passive anti-Communist. What sets Churchill apart here from the run of conservative men was his sense of history, which instructed him in the need for a grand alliance, for a ring around a continental despotism; his military intuition of Hitler's fear of repeating the kaiser's two-front war; his political intuition that the old Comintern threat from the left had abruptly been replaced by a direct military threat from the right; his pragmatism, flexibility, and imagination which enabled him at a crucial point to go beyond dogmatic, ritualistic anticommunism (whereas, as he said in the 1950s, little men are tied to their texts) and to recur to his

1911 idea of an alliance with Russia, as if nothing had changed in the latter nation; his confidence and eloquence, which would carry the nation with him in such a dramatic political-diplomatic shift.

On questions of political processes, he was consistently conservative. He disliked women's and, later, universal adult suffrage; he considered periods of electioneering the most unfortunate phase of a democracy. During the dislocations of the 1930s, his reverence for a politically impotent constitutional monarch turned into a somewhat bookish admiration for strong leaders with Fascist inclinations. He believed that a society rent by civil strife can "only be reconstituted upon a military framework." Men discerned in him the stuff of tyrants, and did he not charmingly describe the essence of his political daydream when he said, "All I wanted was compliance with my wishes after a reasonable discussion"?

On questions of culture and social institutions, his nostalgia for allegedly chivalric, romantic periods of history, his ignorance of modern letters, his love of continuity and tradition—perfectly expressed in his explanation of why he had the Commons building reconstructed in its apparently inefficient and unaccommodating shape—mark him as a reactionary. He uses archaic words like "wicked" and "folly" in place of the modern disinterested ones like "totalitarian" and "historical forces"; he sees himself in moral terms, as simply a patriot, rather than in intellectual or sociological ones, as a representative of a particular culture, class, ideology, and a guardian of the status quo. And his philosophic reverence for paradox, sentiment, intuition, custom, ceremony, and the smudged, illogical nature, as he saw it, of British life, when combined with a suspicion of design, idealism, progress, philosophical systems, abstractions, and utopias, betrays a deeply conservative temperament.

In sum, then, his almost mystical vision of British destiny, his sense (partly expressed by his periodic acceptance of wars) of society established and maintained by means of judicious force and occasional bloodshed, his patrician concept of freedom and dignity, his reformist interludes, his acceptance of monarchy, aristocratic rule, and private property add up to an intellectual mélange of Burkean Romanticism, Disraelian-Randolphian Tory Democracy, and Machiavellian pragmatism. That Churchill in his later years fought Socialists and the left with the same vigor and zeal he used against the Lords and the Tories in his radical days suggests that he consistently and flexibly occupied a large central area of the political spectrum. Of his political philosophy one may say what Liddell Hart said of his military thinking: "His traditionalist impulses were always in conflict with his progressive instincts."[1]

*　　*　　*　　*

Conservatives are often accused, rightly or wrongly, of being unduly attached to war as an instrument of foreign policy, and indeed throughout his career many people considered Churchill a military jingo, a man who fancied himself a Napoleon or a Marlborough sending military forces here or there (even during strikes) and who seemed eager to commence hostilities at various times with the Boers, Germans, Russians, Turks, Irish, Chinese, Greeks, Indians. His military interests aided his career no little, for he found his earliest fulfillment on the battlefield, his initial fame in war-connected journalism, adventurism, and book writing, and his culminating glory as a war leader. He saw it as an inescapable and not always depressing fact that history was filled with wars, that, as Hardy said, "War makes rattling good history." The burdens of leadership in World War II seemed actually to rejuvenate him (at least at first, during the lean, heroic years) and bring out greatness of soul. Characteristic is the distinction he drew in one of the speeches between the "curse of war and the darker curse of tyranny" or the sentence in the *History* describing one of the peaceful interludes in the eighteenth century: "All that was keen and adventurous in the English character writhed under this sordid sleepy government." And since war has been a central experience of twentieth-century civilization, Churchill has naturally been a major figure in the history of this period. Though he was much criticized as an amateur general, perhaps Gallipoli, the war plane, the tank, the tank landing craft, and the artificial harbor constitute as large a contribution to the art of war (and to the victory of the democracies) as any individual, military or civilian, has made in history.

Churchill's writing began as a complement of his soldiering and never really departed from it. All of his books, except *Randolph Churchill,* are about combat, and he is often at his best on this subject, seemingly the only serious and respectable one. When he half jokingly said he would not write "this part of history" (the Parliament of 1951), we realize that he needed the stimulus of war before he could write at length, and we know why he had little to say in print about his life in the relatively quiescent 1900s, 1920s, and 1950s. "Arms and the man" is his recurring theme—the husbanding of resources for war, the application of advancing technology to it, the uses of strategy and power. He deploys military imagery throughout his writings and amply depicts in *Marlborough* and elsewhere the peculiar joys of campaigning, dawn surprise attacks, masterly victories. He saw his career as the climax of the grand tradition of world wars in which Britain was (in 1588, 1704, 1805, 1914, 1940) at or near the summit of a sometimes reluctant and quarreling grand alliance fighting for European freedom against a military tyranny. In the world wars of the early 1700s and 1800s, France was the enemy; in those of the twentieth century, Germany. Two of these world wars are sketched in the *History,* and the other three are treated by Churchill in great detail, with focus on the man, Marlborough or Winston Churchill, who singlehandedly, we are to believe, carried the alliance through the storms. That is the basic fable and perhaps the major theme of his writings.

Though modern thinkers stress the centrality of social and economic forces and though many say that wars are fruitless, Churchill is not among them. To him, great battles—if only they are won forcefully and peace is made with magnanimity and firmness—are watersheds of history. But the two conditions are rarely fulfilled together, so wars unfortunately come and go, and since Britain, after being roused to her noblest pitch by war, yearns for peace on less than perfect terms, Churchill is often gloomy about the ending of wars.

To be sure, he was not a warmonger. Though he was exhilarated by crisis and eager to play a Napoleonic role, he never urged an aggressive policy for its own sake. Though war was his lifelong vocation and avocation, he often tried valiantly to prevent its outbreak; in his last days of power, he eagerly wanted to round off his career by flying to Moscow to end the Cold War and be known as a man of peace. But his manner of seeking peace was based on his pessimistic and paradoxical reading of human nature. Insisting that appeasement is self-defeating, he is the most eloquent and persistent spokesman in modern history for the "hard line" as a diplomacy which would be neither evil nor bloodthirsty but compassionate. Whether the idea that if you wish peace you must prepare for war is the ethos of the caveman, an Orwellian logic that in fact leads to war, or is the height of wisdom in an absurd universe is endlessly disputable. What is clear is that Churchill advocated this philosophy when it was most apposite. His other, perhaps less defensible applications of it, history will forgive him on account of that climax.

He envisions war not in terms of the flying limbs and surrealist logic in which the modern literary imagination apprehends it, but as a noble, glorious struggle between good and evil, democracy and despotism, liberty-loving altruistic Britain and intolerant Mohammedans, Catholics, or atheists. When in 1944, he spoke to de Gaulle of the joy of being a young Frenchman "with good weapons in his hands and France to avenge," he would never have acknowledged, as would anyone with a smattering of modern psychology, any trace of bloodlust in such a zeal for defense of country. Yet war threatened to become an end of its own in Churchill's *Weltanschauung*. He ignored the Nietzschean warning that in fighting a monster one may become a monster. Unready to give peace or pacifism a chance, he ran the danger that his prophecies were self-fulfilling, that his toughness merely toughened the other side and so helped precipitate crises. His correctness on Hitler should not blind us to the strong possibility that he was wrong on other issues, such as India or Russia. He does not, concludes Lewis, see the moral limitations of his war policy, and there may be substance to the recurring suspicion among leftists that, in Higgins's words, "Churchill deplored not the immorality of war, per se, but merely its impersonality in modern times."[2]

The Man and the Hour

Some claim that Churchill's political career was unfulfilled, but surely his leading the free world in a terrible hour by helping forge an Anglo–American unity and a grand alliance against Hitler proved to be a grand climax. It was also a most unlikely climax in a life with an unpromising start. In 1946–47, he wrote a surprising short story about a visitation by the ghost of his father. In the ensuing colloquy between father and son, Churchill reveals to Randolph all of the momentous, unbelievable, bloody things that have occurred in the world since the latter's death. Randolph is so impressed with his son's knowledge of events that he wonders aloud if the latter would not have made a name for himself had he gone into politics; before anything can be said, however, he disappears. This moving fantasy on the relations of a forty-six-year-old father and his seventy-two-year-old son expresses—besides his horror at the modern history through which he has lived in high places—Churchill's regret that the father whom he admired and who thought little of him was never to know of the son's long career which ultimately redeemed the father's abrupt political demise and the son's familial and public reputation.[3]

For, as Cowles notes, that career is a tissue of paradoxes; and the greatest of all the paradoxes is that the very things which rendered Churchill a political failure in the 1930s made him indispensable in 1940. Some of his greatest weaknesses were transmuted by the elixir of global crisis into his greatest strengths. His fervid patriotism, his melodramatic approach to events, his archaic thinking, his theatrical, romantic mode of expression, his Joan of Arc stance, his pugnacity, his passion for obtaining power and leadership, his downright obstinacy, above all his conservative faith in tradition, empire, the British mission and his zeal for war making—these traits were often irrelevant, boring, or obnoxious, but in 1940 nothing else seemed to the point, and he was the only man for the challenge. The eccentric who began his career by seeking wars and who quaintly wrote in 1899 of defending London to the bitter end; the defiant imperialist and belligerent optimist who said of Egypt in 1909, "We shall hold on to [it]. We shall continue to hold it whatever happens"; the reactionary who in the 1930s and the early 1940s would not preside over the dissolution of the empire was an anachronism who became the necessary hero of Dunkirk and the blitz, saving much more than the empire though not the empire itself. The curiously nonpartisan politician, un-happy with all parties and always seeking coalitions, could best unite the nation. His brilliance, dynamism, and candor became bearable only at this juncture; his often disruptive demonic element gave a peculiar authenticity to his words of indomitability. Rather as a religious faith, however "false," may support one in a crisis, so did his archaic intellectual vocabulary provide an eloquence and a myth to conjure with—even as he himself retained in the *History,* over the objections of his scholarly advisers, the story of Alfred and the cakes, a parable of British resistance to invasion, on the grounds that legends play an important part in the life of a nation.[4] The simple, iron vision which made him as out of place in the complex postwar years as he had been before the war gave him a power in 1940 which was absent in more modern men like Lloyd George and Halifax, gentler men like Baldwin and Chamberlain, and iconoclastic left-wing intellectuals like Bevan and Cripps.

How lucky, said Attlee, was Churchill to be given the task for which he was ideally suited in the most dangerous, dramatic moment of his nation's history. Had Churchill, as a man unable to come to terms with modern social forces on such issues as the General Strike or India, been prime minister in the 1920s, the result might have been a catastrophe for him and for Britain. In 1940, however, his very unwillingness to compromise with the modern world kept him from the error of bargaining with Hitler, and the reactionary and warmongering qualities which had earlier blighted his career now helped save civilization. Discretion would have forestalled disappointments in his career yet it would also have deprived him of glory. Britain needed not a balanced, prudent, reasonable man who perceived the apparent hopelessness of the situation or who thought he could reason with Hitler, but a visionary, an impulsive, impatient, self-willed dynamo who, at the admitted price of committing many blunders, ignored counsels, fears, warnings and saw his country safely through on the main question of survival. Thus the *enfant terrible* turned out eventually to be a late bloomer, and the postponement of his glory during a quarter of a century proved the most disguised blessing of all, making possible a rare harmony of interests.

He became then the inspiring hero he had dreamed of being, thanks to the very fantasy life that had made him often seem hopelessly out of touch with the times. In a perilous moment, this familiar, somewhat dated and disreputable politician, this old warhorse ever seeking power and distinction, suddenly arose to evoke, with a peculiar mixture of ornate and colloquial English, the ghosts in the history textbooks: Henry V, Drake, Marlborough, Chatham, Wellington. This most astonishing of modern men, James and Taylor conclude, incorporated his nation's resolve in the last great moment·in British history. He gave the empire a "final blaze of glory" by not realizing that its grand days were gone and by making others believe they were not. Churchill was wrong: for once at least, dreams were better than facts.[5]

Churchill was born at just the right time to play a prominent role in both wars. Implying in *The World Crisis* that he would have been the best leader in World War I, he was, amazingly, given power in a second war in which to prove his assertion. On the one hand, his political career seemed finished in the 1930s, and in 1940 he was among the oldest of the eminent politicians. On the other hand, he was the only choice possible, because of his prophecies in the 1930s; his being untainted by the compromises and failures of those years; his rich knowledge of British history and parliamentary ways; his uniquely vast experience in nearly every branch of government; his abiding interest in and experience of war making —whether through direct participation, reporting, strategic planning, administration of the services, or chronicling of and commenting on battles—especially at the juncture of the military and the political; his healthy distrust of military experts. Also crucial were his eloquence, honed by decades of Commons oratory and debate, historical writings, and preoccupation with words; his belief in himself, in history as shaped by heroic individuals and great events, and in Britain as developed by great periods of endeavor; his participation in World War I in high places, as a prelude to the highest place in this concluding phase of the "Thirty Years War"; his maturing by means of the recent study of Marlborough's leadership of the Grand Alliance; his personal courage and indomitability on behalf of lost causes. It was proper, moreover, that the forger of the new Grand Alliance should be a descendant of the Churchill who established the first one two hundred years earlier and that the wartime coming together of Britain and America should be greatly facilitated by one who was himself half American and a historian-prophet of English-speaking civilization. The wartime Anglo-American "alliance" was probably inevitable, but only Churchill, because of his lineage, his vision, his personal contacts and charm, his eloquence, and his sense of the superiority of Anglo–Saxon culture, could endow it with an almost metaphysical significance.

Power came late in his life, but not too late. After forty-five years of preparation and twenty-five of postponement, the man and the hour met. Had not MacCallum Scott in 1905 and Harold Nicolson in 1931 daringly predicted that when Britain was forlorn, Churchill would lead her? Did not Amery observe that Churchill already showed crisis leadership in 1915, and did not Birkenhead suggest that if Gallipoli had succeeded, Churchill would have been regarded as the statesman whose genius won the war? And did not what Liddell Hart (and, earlier, Esher) wished in the 1930s had been true in World War I—Churchill as commander-in-chief surrounded by a trained military staff to keep him within bounds—in fact come to pass in World War II? Did he not long feel himself uniquely equipped to be a war leader? His destiny merged with his nation's, his finest hour with hers. He reached his flowering as orator even as his political career reached its summit, which in turn marked the climax of the flow around him of events of the first half of the century. Everything indeed seemed now a mere prelude to this storybook climax.[6]

And yet, had he died in 1939, at the age of sixty-five, he would have been regarded as an antiquary of political ideas, a brilliant failure, a talented, maverick politician who, after being close to the prime minister in 1914 and 1924, seemed incapable, because of a lack of consistency, judgment, and authority, of becoming a leader and who ended his career without party, power, or influence. In 1940, moreover, Britain was led by a man whose greatest accomplishment had in a sense been in literature, whose political success was due to speeches and paperwork, who was intoxicated by phrases, and who for a while fought Hitler with little more than brave words. John Connell finds it apropos that the leader of a sane, liberal civilization built on the spoken and written word should have been a professional writer, while Rowse believes that Britain produced a leader equally able to write and make history because politics and literature are the two chief English expressions in the arts of life. According to Aneurin Bevan, the secret of British endurance was partly her being led by an artist; a man of words, not deeds; a poet, not an orator; a man addressing history, not his contemporary audience; a man who was unable to face the facts and who made his people think of the Spanish Armada rather than of Dunkirk. Churchill is therefore a symbol of what inspired words can do when a devoted nation backs them.[7]

Being a historian indeed helped Churchill's statesmanship. His knowledge of the past enabled him to prophesy the future, buoyed him up during the years of waiting, became a mainstay in adversity and a means of leadership. In the darkest hours, he made Britons see the situation in a historical perspective. As one of the few among politicians and military men to appreciate the relevance of history, he pointed out in 1917, when everyone thought that the Russian Revolution and the American entry would spur Germany into peacemaking, that nothing in the Napoleonic Wars, the American Civil War, or the Boer War could give one such a hope, for men will often fight on without good prospects. In World War II, remembering the ultimate triumph of encircling alliances, he was not unnerved by the fall of France or the German penetration of Russia. And, fresh from his study in the *History* of the protracted and ferocious American Civil War, he knew, as Hitler and many others did not, of the American fighting prowess and will to win.

Forging a style redolent of the past, he imbued everyone with his faith that Britain could not lose. As the embodiment of British tradition, he made use of a people's strong sense of history and, with his vision of their heroic destiny, made the cause of the war seem to be worldwide liberty as well as British survival. But the very cast of mind which rendered Churchill great in crisis also limited his vision as a writer.[8]

The Writer and Thinker

Precisely how are his writings crippled? Not surely by the fact that his many works, particularly the major ones, are held together by a network of themes. Thus the idea of the unexpected twists of fortune is first seen at work in a petty war in the *Malakand,* then in politics in *Randolph Churchill,* then in global strategy in *The World Crisis.* It merges in the *History* with the "disguised blessings" (or "private vices, public benefits") motif, in the *Contemporaries* with the paradoxes of personality, and, in all his works, with the theme of sympathetic identification with generals and leaders. It sits uneasily with the optimistic belief which Churchill, as a man of action, often held, that the individual shapes history, a view expressed ambiguously in the early works and *The World Crisis*, forcefully in *Marlborough, The Second World War*, and the *History*. The questioning of progress begins with the first work, mushrooms in *The World Crisis*, recurs often in the subsequent books, and, in the form of an elegy for a vanished, glittering Victorian world, is the main theme of the *Commission* and the *Contemporaries*. The principle of Either/Or in *The World Crisis* is seen at work again in Hitler's method of taking up issues and taking on nations "one at a time." It is the political-diplomatic application of another Churchillian preoccupation, the military principle of concentrating one's resources on the decisive theater (which is in turn related to Churchill's personal habit of concentrating at work on one or two subjects of consuming interest to the exclusion of all else). This theme, or its corollary of "Too Little, Too Late," melds with the sense of the violence necessary in civilization (a motif notably clear in the *History*) to form the antiappeasement theme of all his works, signally the speeches of the 1930s and 1950s.

The theme of "Either/Or" is turned upside down to become its logical antithesis, "Both/And," in the form of the "harmony of interests" theme in the *Marlborough*. Traced in the career of one man (and anticipated in *Randolph Churchill*), it is universalized and applied on a large scale in the *History*, in conjunction with the emphasis on the "disguised blessings." Both themes, emerging in the form of the ideas of "personal diplomacy" and of the necessity of dealing pragmatically with tainted men, are given a personal application in *The Second World War*. The "personal diplomacy" theme also derives from the "adventure of life" motif in the first phase and is related to Churchill's lifelong dislike of idealists and purists, his respect for the seeking and exercising of power "worthily" as "among the noblest of human occupations."

The "harmony of interests" is in many ways the central motif of the entire corpus of writings. It is the natural expression of a professional writer compulsively explaining his own actions. It springs from a rage for order, a fear of randomness and of psychic waste, a need to constantly review one's life and place the discrete data of experience in a hierarchy or pattern. It conjoins a heroic or altruistic plane of experience to a worldly common-sense pragmatism in the tales of his heroes, Randolph and Marlborough, his nation, and his own checkered career. It is as if without the garb of this theory, the subjects of his narratives would be revealed as nakedly selfish or, more embarrassing for Churchill, nakedly idealistic. Ultimately, of course, it delineates a moral *via media* that is eminently urbane.

The works themselves no less than their themes have interesting interrelationships. *Randolph Churchill* and *Marlborough* are expressions of Churchill's filial and familial piety, biographies in which he adumbrates his own future by writing of the family past; *Marlborough* and the world war memoirs are apologias written during periods of quasi retirement; *Marlborough* and the *History* are studies of remote periods, of varied personalities, and of the development of English liberty, the earlier work studying a crucial period through the microscope and the later work examining the entire evolution; *Marlborough* and *The Second World War* are about leadership in global wars. *Marlborough* is clearly, then, a central work. Coming at a major crisis in his life and serving as a means of resurgence, it is the focus of Churchill's interests, while *The Second World War* is a climax of many of his themes as well as of his political career. If the other major works are about the disjunction of power and vision—Randolph and Winston himself (in *The World Crisis*) have the vision but not the power—*Marlborough* exhibits a Churchill who has both and *The Second World War* a Winston Churchill who has both. The latter work tells of the time when power was held by a man of foresight and action who also happened to be, as Marlborough was not, a memoirist and commentator. If *The World Crisis* is a long cry of "what might have been!" and *Marlborough* a celebration of "what was" (in the far past), *The Second World War* sees a rectification of the world of *The World Crisis* (and, tenuously, of *Randolph Churchill*) by means of the spirit of *Marlborough*.

For the argument of *The Second World War,* and Churchill's not unmerited claim to fame, is that a greater concord was achieved in World War II than in World War I simply because Churchill was at the helm. World War II produced greater concord between

Britain and the United States (by virtue of a Churchill–Roosevelt intimacy based solidly on Churchill's personal diplomacy, the lessons learned in *Marlborough,* and the English-speaking vision of the *History*); between Labor and Conservative (because Churchill seemed to fulfill his dreams of a coalition government, of being prime minister, of taking politics out of war, indeed—in the light of the harm wreaked by parties in *Randolph Churchill* and *Marlborough*—of taking partisanship out of politics); between the civilian "Frocks" and the military "Brass Hats" (because Churchill was also defense minister and claims to have "influenced" the chiefs of staff, in line with his lifelong principle that in war political and military considerations are inseparable); and, within the military field, between "Westerners" and "Easterners" (for this time everyone in Britain was an Easterner and Churchill finally had his grand design of *The World Crisis* fulfilled and the Gallipoli disaster redeemed to his satisfaction by successful Mediterranean operations, low casualty rates, and Allied use of sea supremacy to turn the flank of the western front into the soft belly of the enemy's weak ally). Churchill's grand theme, then, is that these harmonies were not just more fully achieved than in World War I but unique in history and that his varied war experiences—and the studies that went into the writing of his books, especially *Marlborough*—were responsible for the fulfillment of these major preoccupations of his career. *The Second World War* is thus Churchill's *Summa Theologica.*

*   *   *   *

The major works are also interrelated in other ways. The *Commission* and the *History* (as well as the *Malakand, The River War,* and *Savrola*) are comedies in the largest sense of the word, for, though the pictures of modern life in the one and of the bloodletting of history in the other are grim, the tale of the narrator and of British destiny ends happily. *Randolph Churchill, The World Crisis,* and *The Second World War* are in their different ways tragedies, even if *The World Crisis* does not qualify for the strict classical sense of that term. And *Marlborough* is a tragedy-epic with a Euripidean reversal at the conclusion.

For all his intermittent optimism, the happy endings of most of his books, and the many blessings of his career, Churchill's writings, willy-nilly, add up to a tragic vision. They tell of five British wars in which he participated; his country triumphed in all five—the last two fought on a huge scale and won with great glory and finality—and yet this intensely proud, patriotic man had to watch Britain plummet from her zenith as an imperial and world power in 1895 to, a half-century later, a condition of near-powerlessness. With the empire crumbling and the economy in the throes of an incipient socialism he had always decried, Britain was now a satellite of an ex-colony of her own.

On a philosophical plane, tragedy prevails as well. Churchill often portrays man as continually seeking a better world through science and never attaining it. The only redeeming qualities he can find in man's march to self-destruction, notes J. C. Cairns, are the beauties of the warrior spirit and of human endurance. But these are elusive in conditions of modern welfare. Knowing that history offers no certainties, disliking further democratization, beholding science destroying many of his romantic values, resisting change and yet doomed to pursue the application of science to war making for the sake of survival, Churchill tries to impose his antique views on a hateful, recalcitrant twentieth century. He peers into a disastrous future and hopes for a better age without really believing in it.

The writings also delineate a personal tragedy, of which Churchill was not fully aware. If an appraisal of one's achievements takes account, as Churchill himself often insisted it should, of the changing perspectives of history, some of his most renowned feats have, with the passage of time, proved flimsy: The South African settlement turned out to contain the seeds of racism and repression; Irish home rule did not in the long run free Britain of the Irish question; the post–World War I arrangements in the Middle East engendered the post–World War II international tinderbox; the dreamed-of English-speaking union has proved a will-o'-the-wisp; above all, the warnings and actions of 1944 and the Fulton speech of 1946, even if at first they had a salubrious effect in the Western camp, started, as Churchill himself came partly to realize, the machinery of an obsessive Cold War mentality which led in America to the awesome tragedies of McCarthyism and Vietnam.[9] These triumphs proved, then, to be short-term achievements, but it might be argued, as Churchill wrote on behalf of Disraeli's foreign policy, that a stability achieved even for only one or two generations is the best that a statesman can hope for, that hardly anyone has done better.

Approached in chronological order, the works reveal another tragic pattern, not unlike that of *King Lear.* The swings of the pendulum in Churchill's political career—he was, by turns, a jingo, a radical, a reactionary, and finally a moderate—are paralleled by the swings of a pendulum in his spiritual life. The books of the first phase radiate innocent optimism about Britain, empire, progress, modern life, and himself. In the second phase, the story of Randolph's tragic fall and the discovery of misery and poverty in England's midst cast a grim light on affairs, but not grim enough to impair the optimism. The perception of evil in the body politic is balanced by a sense of meliorism and activism; the father may have fallen, but his fall was noble and not in vain; the son, with a budget of remedies, will finish the tale happily.

The experiences of the third phase, however, are traumatic, and the writings of the third and fourth phases reflect terrible disillusionment. Taken together wtih the nadir of Churchill's own political career, they bespeak the death of all hope, for self, nation, or race. Churchill's political climax has somehow eluded him; his current warnings are not heeded; the world seems to be regressing rather than progressing. But the intellectual challenge of *Marlborough* points the way to the recovery that good fortune will make possible in the fifth phase. The disappearing climax is finally seized, the dream realized. Yet in its wake trails unresolved matter, and, having looked into the heart of evil (although he never reaches the nihilistic depths of Lear in spiritual mid-career), Churchill can never return to simple optimism. The writings of the sixth phase offer no easy cheer; but neither are they without a certain mellowing, an abiding hope. The journey was worth making, perhaps.

*   *   *   *

There are other, less important patterns. For *The River War,* *Randolph Churchill,* and *Marlborough* Churchill claims definitiveness of treatment, while he concedes *The World Crisis, The Second World War,* and the *History* to be only contributions to history, one man's version. Consciously or not, Churchill also oscillated between his two major interests: the frontier war books, *The World Crisis,* and *The Second World War* (phases 1, 3, 5) being devoted mainly to the military art, while in *Randolph Churchill, Marlborough,* and the *History* (phases 2, 4, 6) military matters are displaced or complemented by politics or diplomacy.

The works of the first three phases betray a limited purview. The frontier war books focus solely on colonial wars and military matters, as studied by a low-echelon officer and freshman correspondent. The writings of the early 1900s concentrate mainly on domestic politics, as seen through the sensibilities of an unsuccessful reform politician of the past and his callow present-day counterpart. *The World Crisis* is concerned with the problem of waging a European war—a disorganized war narrated in a disorganized fashion from a series of miscellaneous vantage points by a narrator who has had his political ups and downs. In the last three phases, by contrast, we behold a wide world as seen from the summit. Domestic politics (albeit admittedly nebulous), European war making, and, for the first time, foreign affairs and diplomacy are observed by successful leaders, Churchills past and present, and related by an experienced narrator gazing calmly at history from the Olympian vantage point of relative success and old age.

Commager, by contrast, finds three periods in Churchill's writing career. He sees the early books as advertisements for the author's talent as war correspondent, the middle-period works as monuments to the Churchill family, and the late works as tributes to Churchill's own genius as strategist and statesman. Plumb divides the works, so to speak, diagonally rather than horizontally. He finds the more numerous quasi-autobiographical works on contemporary events—tales of youthful adventures, world war memoirs, assessments of contemporaries—much more interesting than the formal, professional histories composed as "acts of piety." Though the latter attempt to vindicate Churchill's heroes—Randolph and Marlborough—they actually throw more light on his own character as a statesman than on the subjects. Though they are the works with the greatest claim to scholarliness and definitiveness, they are, Plumb believes, the lesser part of his output, for Churchill remains only a gifted amateur historian writing tendentious books.

Scholars comment that Churchill, lacking Gibbon's detachment, selects those parts of the past in which he participated, discerns relevance, or finds congenial men who could have been his colleagues. He enjoys delineating two idealized, supposedly golden ages: the Victorian, which he knew as a child and much of which he carried with him throughout his life, and the age of Anne, which in middle age he reconstructed as a labor of love. Worshiping a past shaped by aristocrats and parliamentary giants rather than by universal suffrage, he distorts history. Unable to foresee Britain's future clearly, he substitutes fantasy for analysis. Churchill the historian, says Hurwitz, is the essential Churchill; in politics he had to bow to democratic tendencies, but in his writings, his values shine without the modifications of compromise. Only political ambition and battle scenes stimulate his imagination and literary gifts. His world, already limited by choice and by tame philosophy to great events, persons, and issues, often seems finally coterminous with Blenheim Palace. It is inhabited by only Marlborough, Randolph, himself, a few subsidiary souls, and sometimes by Churchill alone, in proximity to high place. *The World Crisis* contains a vivid description of the joy of the Armistice and continues into the postwar world in which Churchill held various prominent offices; *The Second World War,* by contrast, ends abruptly, describing neither celebration nor aftermath because this time he held no government post in the immediate postwar years.

It is curious, moreover, to see, when we read Churchill on his father or Marlborough, or on men like Lloyd George, Clemenceau, and Chatham, many parallels with his own career. He wrote almost exclusively about matters close to his interests and about men by whose image he shaped himself. Since his subject is not really history so much as himself in history, his ego is on display both when he participates in events and when he chronicles that participation. His writings had a private, mystical importance. His own actions were a crucial part of his imaginative life, and his published portraits of himself in turn encouraged him to pursue a life style many found melodramatic and factitious. Since he treated events as less important than his response to them, these books give us not his actions in themselves but his reveries; his sense of his own active self intermingles with ruminations on Savrola, Randolph, Marlborough, Napoleon, Lloyd George,

Clemenceau, and Chatham, all of whom are interchangeable figments of his imagination. His historical scholarship proves to be a covert delving within—rather as Montaigne's rambling thoughts on the ancients are at bottom not ventures in archaeology but perambulations in the backyard of his own mind.

His need to justify himself often causes him to present as his own certain ideas he had appropriated from others or to slight what others did in helping him to his successes. But this stems from his egocentricity; his memoirs lack impartiality, not honesty. His ubiquitous and inflated ego charms us while we read and we accept the premise that he mattered. When we finish, however, we realize that, in his confusion of "his own action and advocacy" with history, we have been given only data which, Hurwitz remarks, prove to the narrator's satisfaction that he (or his alter ego) played his self-appointed role as statesman wisely. Yet, what remains valuable in all of his books is not only the siren song of his exculpatory narrative or commentary but also the rich source material and documents, however tendentiously selected. This is perhaps as it should be, for in most of his works Churchill discounted the role of the narrator vis-à-vis the original documents in authentically recapturing the past—though he proceeded to use all his literary resources as narrator to interpret the documents.[10]

What Guedella discerns in the *Contemporaries,* H. G. Wells in *The World Crisis,* and Graubard in the *History* applies to all of Churchill's writings. They are so many mirrors from which the author smiles at us; they depict a child's world with one hero and many villains; they betray a simplistic vision of good and evil, of character and motive. Plumb observes that like Gibbon and Macaulay, Churchill wrote for lovers of literature rather than professional historians. Though his books have what literature must have—personal views of life, a sense of human endurance—his simple, pungent judgments, his basic passions, his childlike unawareness, his self-centered ebullience are too much in evidence. Naïvely understanding history to be mainly "past politics" and battles, he believed that a knowledge of contemporary politics could open the door even of the remote past. The same verities apply in any period, the same political characters appear onstage. Lacking an analytic or critical mind, the training of a professional historian, and an interest in the history of ideas, Churchill portrays actions pictorially (the how) instead of examining the forces behind the actions (the why).

His narrative mastery, clarity of exposition, and ways with aphorisms are shared by few historians, but his undeniable intelligence and humor result in only lightweight reflectiveness. His stamina produces long books; his verve, imagination, craftsmanship, and polished phrases create a glittering surface; but the philosophy, psychology, and sociology of politics and war remain untouched. He writes only of what interests him: in Hurwitz's words, "dynasties, cabinets, generals—and Churchills." He writes persuasive defenses of self, father, ancestor. He was, according to Lewis, a kind of court memorialist, concerned with the famous and prominent men who, he believed, made everything turn. He presents life, according to Berlin, as a great Renaissance pageant, and he, the most public of public personalities, writes as an epic poet, revealing no moral ambiguities, no private selves. His range is enormous but narrow; he inhabits a world of ambition, power, and success, and, thanks to his own rich experience, he clarifies crisis leadership. He celebrates the glorious few—the Churchills—who played without complaint the role history assigned them, but he ignores the relation of the common man to the national experience.

Churchill's mind was sometimes so obtuse that no idea could violate it. To one colleague he seemed a "magnificent animal" without any spiritual side. Enslaved by words and phrases, especially his own, he had brilliant insights yet was frequently unable to follow an argument put forward by someone else. He found in history what he sought, the values he himself treasured. His books lack a speculative underpinning, except for some unanalyzed axioms about conduct and purpose. In place of a considered philosophy, he often proffers a mixture of pragmatism and romanticism, of undeveloped ideas and a few diluted Christian moral notions, all intermingled with political ambitions. His simple law of history is that a people flouting the heroic virtues would decay and a people respecting them would prosper. He celebrates in anglicized form the old Roman values of law, empire, order, fortitude, *pietas,* magnanimity in victory. Presenting a past distorted by Whig mythologizing, he tries to justify the ways of Britain—her genius and her right to be affluent and imperial. Like

Plutarch setting the reader examples of noble action or like an eighteenth-century writer regarding history as moral scripture and as counselor to statesmen, he offers a cautionary tale and applauds the virtues of outstanding individuals.

* * * *

Does Churchill grow at all? Scholars like Berlin, de Mendelssohn, and James note that notwithstanding his many political changes—from jingoist (1890s), to isolationist and radical (1900s), to interventionist and nationalist (1910s), to advocate of retrenchment (1920s), to interventionist and reactionary (1930s), to advocate of détente and moderation (1950s)—his basic vision, as expressed in his earliest writings, did not in the main change and that the consistency he prided himself on was but a sign of his intellectual limitations. His social welfarism seemed radical in the 1900s and conservative in the 1950s. Such emphasis on rigidity, however, overlooks subtle maturing processes. Churchill began by preaching venerable doctrines—isolationism, retrenchment, imperialism, strict economy, free trade, no increase of income taxes—which he had to discard or modify one by one in the twentieth century. The young Churchill was also, as Hyam puts it, "not easily deterred by apparent limitations to government actions,"[11] whereas in later years he preferred that government do nothing or little; the young Churchill liked words such as "logical," "symmetrical," while the older man preferred to talk about "smudged" lines in nature and "greys." The Tory of the 1920s and 1930s was decidedly different from the radical of the 1900s and the conciliator of the 1950s. Churchill likewise exhibits in his writings if not growth of wisdom at least growth in scope of interests, from soldiering and imperialism to parliamentary politics and domestic reform to modern European war making to European diplomacy.

If some deny that he ever matured, Churchill's ambiguity on the question of war, his frequent changes of party, and his many zigzags on issues like trade unions, naval expenditure, Germany, Turkey, the Lords, and the suffragettes have even led others to wonder whether he was not a hollow man, a politician to whom talk about tradition, national honor, and principles were mere ploys. Time and again, Churchill the political animal does reveal a peculiar moral blindness. When describing how rumors of peace in 1709 caused troops of the opposing sides to embrace, for instance, he is interested in this moving visionary moment solely as another example of Marlborough's craft, for allied officers used the opportunity to sketch the enemy's defenses. Churchill's reverent references to Napoleon are indicative of a pragmatic, war-loving, amoral side which sometimes overcomes even his patriotism. That he could denounce Gandhi and Hitler with equal zeal and repugnance suggests serious moral deficiencies. Though the "if" or "what might have been" is a favorite device of his, he uses it in a constrictive, self-serving fashion. It is, for instance, conceivable that if America had kept out of World War I, the contending nations would have reached a stalemate, and the chastened kaiser, remaining in power, would have dismissed his generals and turned an exhausted Germany toward peaceful reconstruction. Thus there might well have been no Hitler and no World War II. But Churchill, so sure of the righteousness of his cause, is oblivious to the possibility that the very finality of the Allied victory made the ensuing catastrophe inevitable. In other contexts, he would have savored this as potentially yet another of history's many ironic twists.

There are too many complacencies behind his English-speaking mystique, his parochial vision of a western-oriented world civilization. The vast slaughter of World War I disabused him of Victorian simplemindedness about a progress he had already begun to question, but Auschwitz and Hiroshima pushed him spiritually no further, caused no change in values or perspective. Not seeing the consequences of his own ideas, he inconsistently hopes for the march of progress by means of the very science which he continually turned to as an aid in warfare, which made wars more terrible, and, as he iterated, the modern world a nightmare. He does not look into the ultimate heart of darkness; when he speaks (early in his life) of the dark "abyss," he means bad working conditions, not the inner recesses of man. Tone-deaf to many moral nuances, he can detach himself to the point of looking at things under the aspect of history, but not of eternity.

Although he is an accomplished author, Churchill is also closed to contemporary literature and thought. He blandly accepts the received values: the established church, constitutional monarchy, a strong Parliament with limited suffrage and infrequent elections, the tradition and continuity of "English liberties," the empire, patriotism, martial prowess, the social order, and his own place in it. Though he moved from jingoist delight in Dr. Jameson's raid to respect for the Boers and to the realization that this event, a beginning of the twentieth-century turmoil, was a "fountain of ill," his mind remained curiously limited. Arriving in Cuba with secret sympathies for the rebels, the young gentleman-cadet received a shock of recognition: the Spaniards "felt about Cuba just as we felt about Ireland." He thus grew out of British parochialism into imperialist parochialism, but the latter shortsightedness he was never to be jolted out of. He remained certain of the British mission in India "to rule these primitive but agreeable races for their welfare and our own." Neither a methodical thinker nor a visionary, he could not dramatize, as do Conrad, Forster, and others, the horrific discovery on the frontiers of empire of the savage within the self and within the European imperialist venture. Neither is he a moralist for whom such a discovery would bring into question the modern faith in progress and technology. He never tried to find out what really lay behind the ringing slogans about British justice, order, and efficiency, or how the recipients felt about these ambiguous gifts. He learned nothing from modern literature's nagging doubts about heroism, patriotism, war, honor, civilization itself. Kipling being almost the only twentieth-century writer he seems even to have heard of, Churchill remained blithely unaware of his own blindness.

His recurring archaic belief in the power of the individual to alter history leads him into the simplistic idea that if only he, or Randolph or Marlborough, had had more enduring power, Britain "would have had more strength and happiness and Europe a surer progress." Perhaps, we may add, such a belief is necessary for a man of action; providing the momentum for Churchill's career and success in the high posts he came to hold, it dignified both the office and the man, whereas the opposite view of history comes easily to an observer and student of action like Tolstoy. Yet Churchill's sympathetic identification with others in high positions, his readiness to justify their actions and to show their plight as unavoidable, brings him perilously close to fatalism, to a sense that the individual is not in control of things; hence, he thinks the initiation of World War I to have been mainly outside man's control, and the "disguised blessing" theme in the *History* implies an unfolding destiny beyond the reach of man's conscious will.

*   *   *   *

Churchill's archaic vision finds its worthy expression in a style that has struck many as out of season. It seems, depending on the critic, overripe, oratorical, classical (à la Gibbon, Johnson, or Macaulay), romantic, antique. Some have found in it, as well as in his roles, the "noble Roman," a blend of Caesar and Cicero. Others have remarked on the curious mixture of mischievous humor with the breadth of outlook of a Pitt or Gibbon. Because of his inability to write a dull paragraph, because of the strong personality radiating from every word, he was often called (notably in his early years) the greatest living writer of English narrative prose. But some critics, like James and Guedella, decry the baroque overornateness, "the fatal lullaby of a majestic style" which, they believe, came to characterize his originally fresh writing; others, considering the early work too derivative and melodramatic, think that Churchill only gradually found his style. Plumb and Lewis speak of his eighteenth-century mannerisms, of the surface drama presented in a lavish prose with a rhetorical cast. Yet others, complaining of redundancy and windiness, find all his works to be vast orations, paeans, exhortations in which verbosity is meant to cover the absence of real thinking. The theatrical, the oratorical, and the romantic, they assert, often triumph over good sense, leaving us with bombast in place of style, a ponderousness meant to exploit the Churchill legend. Berlin's response to this charge is that the style is not fabricated for the sake of providing an artificial excitement or expressing, as some think, a childish romanticism and militant imperialism; it is rather a mirror of Churchill's naïve but genuine conservative, hierarchical vision. Churchill needed to find his bearings in the past as much as do Catholics and Marxists, and the style fuses the past to the present.[12]

The fairest judgment might perhaps be a tentative or relativistic one. Just as in considering Churchill's antiappeasement theme or his anticommunism, one may conclude either that Churchill is a prophet or that he is a deluded man indulging in self-fulfilling prophecies, depending on which philosophy one has about human nature and recent history; or just as the consistency, almost to the point of monotony, of Churchill's ideas, from his first work to his last, may be taken as evidence of his imperviousness to the stream of modern experience or of his integrity and stability; so whether one enjoys this orotund style is ultimately a matter of taste. To style one might apply what William James has said about religion: some like a sensuous, aesthetically oriented faith; others prefer an austere, chaste, ethereal one. The only certainty is that it is not a typical twentieth-century style. Churchill's reading was intense but very narrow. He was oblivious not only to twentieth-century literature, as many have complained, but, except for the all-important King James Bible, Shakespeare, Gibbon, and Burke, also to the literature of the centuries on the other side of the nineteenth. He betrays no awareness of Clarendon, to whom he is sometimes compared and from whom he could have learned much. No doubt Churchill thought the seventeenth-century style was not directly usable in the way Gibbon's or Macaulay's was and therefore did not bother with it.

Evaluations of Churchill's major works vary greatly. Guedella and Plumb regard *Randolph Churchill* as the best of the more ambitious works, while James prefers *The World Crisis,* but all three men, along with Somervell, find *A Roving Commission* to be the most satisfying and warm—perhaps because the least pretentious—of Churchill's books and hence deserving of a special niche. According to Ashley and Commager, *Marlborough* takes first place, though Rowse gives it joint honors with the *History,* and others single out *The Second World War.* Each of the major works, in short, is someone's favorite.[13]

The present writer, judging the books both as literature and history, finds *Marlborough* Churchill's magnum opus and *The Second World War* fascinating and unique. The *River War* and *Randolph Churchill* are in their different ways excellent, if limited in scope, while *The World Crisis* and the *History* are rather flawed books which remain always readable and at times illuminating. Among the less ambitious works, the *Commission* is a delightful little classic and one of his best things, *Great Contemporaries* a polished book filled with political wisdom, *Step by Step* enthralling, the *Malakand, My African Journey,* and *Thoughts and Adventures* constantly charming. Of the volumes of speeches, *Liberalism, While England Slept,* and *Blood, Sweat, and Tears* (and to a degree *The Unrelenting Struggle*) stand out as eloquent expressions of Churchill's three greatest periods as orator—zealous social reformer during the years from 1905 to 1910, prophet in the 1930s, indomitable war leader of a nation at bay from 1940 through 1942. Only the Boer War volumes and *Savrola* are failures, and even they have numerous interesting moments.

With respect to the entire output, reputable historians like Commager, Morison, Rowse, and Gilbert accept Churchill into their company, with certain qualifications, as a fine and sometimes great historian—or at least military historian—who wrote works that are among the most powerful of their kind in English. Other scholars, like Plumb, Hurwitz, and Howarth, find it difficult to consider him a historian at all. Still others, like Taylor, James, and Ashley, render a mixed judgment. Lewis, Muggeridge, and Hyam imply that he remained a journalist even in his most exhaustive and pretentious books, his virtues and vices being those of a journalist rather than a historian, while A. G. Gardiner sees his books rather as vast orations, his whole life as one long speech. Some would consider him a contributor to popular culture, were it not that his works are too self-centered, his style too lush for such a genre. If there are those who, regarding him as ultimately a man of action, dismiss his writings, others point to the long record of failures in action and find him to be essentially a contemplative man of words, sometimes thrust into the hurly-burly, and still others believe that his prophecies and his war leadership tower over all his achievements by sword and pen.[14]

*   *   *   *

That Churchill has ideas and that each of his major works has an informing theme this study has established. There remains the final question of whether these ideas are profound, whether the author is a thinker. Here Churchill fares less well. The various themes seem true as far as they go, but they do not go far enough.

They often remain hasty generalizations or hoary, questionable assertions presented as if Churchill had been the first person to discover them. (That boyish reaction, half-jokingly discussed in the *Commission*, of being annoyed to discover, through reading, that many of his own ideas had been anticipated by the Greeks, always remains with him.) They are not analyzed in depth, that is, not sufficiently knitted together with each other, with other ideas, with others' ideas. They do not cohere as part of an interpretation of life. The conservative, aristocratic sense of things which suffuses Churchill's works is not so much reflective philosophy as it is impulsive assertion of unexamined premises. His books, like his career, seem to lack an idea or vision other than simply the preservation and celebration of the past. His inability even to try to explain his 1945 defeat is symptomatic of the absence of an entire dimension, of almost a fear of treating data that his tacit first principles cannot digest.

It is enjoyable to watch the play of his mind, to listen to the limpid flow of his sentences, to behold the colorful cavalcade of history, but after the feast we are left desiring something more substantial. For Churchill the abstract idea remains close to its origin in experience, whereas a philosopher dismisses the context and concentrates on the logical ramifications of the idea. Churchill treasures events merely because they happened to him, and he has difficulty studying them without reference to himself.[15] If in the first books the ubiquitous, gregarious, inquisitive persona indulges in a certain authorial self-depreciation, in all the subsequent memoirs, he is scapegoat or hero, never bumbling clown, and we miss some of the irony with which he had regarded himself. The compulsiveness of the sentient ego's quest for experience and the blinders of a man harnessed to his own vanity limit the scope of his imagination and reason. His consequent unwillingness to think through moral and political questions is a limitation which he never fully overcomes.

Namier's designation of Metternich as a reasoner rather than a thinker fits Churchill perfectly; his mind can operate nimbly within an enclosed system, but it cannot break out, it cannot scrap received assumptions and start afresh. This limitation is perhaps as much a matter of philosophical choice as of individual intellectual handicap. The true conservative, remarks Clinton Rossiter, rarely engages in political speculation, preferring the "cake of custom" to the spinning of theories or the seeking of clear-cut principles; Churchill, perhaps the most famous twentieth-century conservative, refused in spite of all his literary skills to "reflect upon and write down the principles that animated his career."[16]

Churchill is an intellectual in the broad sense—he reads and writes, he lives and breathes words—but not in the narrow sense of assaying all experience anew by the light of the best that has been thought and said. (Few if any politicians or men of action, of course, have ever been that sort of intellectual.) That each work has a theme makes it something more than just a chronicle. That these themes interrelate up to a point makes the canon of his writings something more than just a miscellaneous collection. But the shallowness of the themes and the spottiness of their interrelation keeps Churchill from the first rank of writers. Despite the torrent of words and his numberless acts in high office, Churchill remains philosophically a mute, uncomprehending, passive witness of the turmoil; a chronicler, after all.

Yet, if these works fail on literary and historical grounds, they retain a cultural interest. They bear witness to one intelligent man's response to his age. They constitute an adorned and colored but valuable record of the only man to be intimately and consistently associated with major European political, diplomatic, and military developments from the 1890s to the 1950s. They provide, as do few documents and books, a fascinating twentieth-century case study, one sensibility's immediate, as well as retrospective, reaction, or lack of it, to all the tidal waves of modern history: the new liberalism, World War I, the depression, Auschwitz, Dresden, Hiroshima, the exploding technology, the vanishing past, the Cold War, even the space age. In one lifetime, one political-literary career, we can trace the most drastic change the human race has ever undergone, or ever will—from the last days of cavalry charges to the verge of possible atomic annihilation, from the nearly medieval glory of Omdurman to the futuristic odyssey of lunar rockets. In this sense, Churchill never really left his first phase; through the decades, the important decisions, the multivolumed books, he remained the eager participant-journalist, the correspondent on the front lines of history.

Of his writings, therefore, as of his statesmanship, it may finally be said, as he himself wrote of his teacher, colleague, and friend, Lloyd George:

> Strong currents of censure or at least disapproval are running against much of his life's work. Its merits will long be disputed; but no one will challenge its magnitude.

Appendix

Abbreviations Used in Notes

References to Churchill's works are cited using the following abbreviations:

C   *A Roving Commission: My Early Life* (New York: Charles Scribner's Sons, 1930)
EP   "New Epilogue," in *The Second World War,* abridged edition, ed. Denis Kelly (Boston: Houghton Mifflin Co., 1959)
ESP   *A History of the English-Speaking Peoples,* 4 vols. (1956–58; reprint New York: Bantam Books, 1963)
EU   *Europe Unite* (Boston: Houghton Mifflin Co., 1950)
G   *Great Contemporaries* (New York: G. P. Putnam's Sons, 1937)
H   *Ian Hamilton's March* (London: Longmans, Green and Co., 1900)
IB   *Blood, Sweat, and Tears (Into Battle)* (New York: G. P. Putnam's Sons, 1941)
IT   *In the Balance* (Boston: Houghton Mifflin Co., 1952)
L   *London to Ladysmith via Pretoria* (London: Longmans, Green and Co., 1900)
LS   *Liberalism and the Social Problem* (London: Hodder & Stoughton, 1909)
M   *The Story of the Malakand Field Force* (London: Longmans, Green and Co., 1898)
MAR   *Marlborough. His Life and Times,* 4 vols. (1933–38; reprint, 2 vols., London: George G. Harrap & Co., 1947)
O   *Onwards to Victory* (Boston: Little, Brown and Co., 1944)
R   *The River War,* 2 vols. (London: Longmans, Green and Co., 1899)
RC   *Lord Randolph Churchill,* 2 vols. (New York: Macmillan Co., 1906)
S   *Savrola* (1900; reprint New York: Random House, 1956)
SP   *The Sinews of Peace* (Boston: Houghton Mifflin Co., 1949)
ST   *Step by Step* (New York: G. P. Putnam's Sons, 1939)
STT   *Stemming the Tide* (Boston: Houghton Mifflin Co., 1954)
SWW   *The Second World War,* 6 vols. (Boston: Houghton Mifflin Co., 1948–53)
T   *Amid These Storms (Thoughts and Adventures)* (New York: Charles Scribner's Sons, 1932)
U   *The Unrelenting Struggle* (London: Cassell and Co., 1942)
UA   *The Unwritten Alliance* (London: Cassell and Co., 1961)
W   *While England Slept (Arms and the Covenant)* (New York: G. P. Putnam's Sons, 1938)
WC   *The World Crisis,* 6 vols. (New York: Charles Scribner's Sons, 1923–31)

Notes

Introduction

1. For some useful observations on Churchill's way with words, see Reed Whittemore, "Churchill as a Mythmaker," in *Language and Politics,* ed. T. P. Brockway (Boston: D. C. Heath and Co., 1965), p. 58; John Connell, *Winston Churchill,* Writers and Their Work, no. 80 (London: Longmans, Green and Co., 1956), pp. 7–9; *Churchill by His Contemporaries* (London: Hodder & Stoughton, 1965), p. 128; Peter de Mendelssohn, *The Age of Churchill* (New York: Alfred A. Knopf, 1961), pp. 72, 222.

2. Randolph Churchill, *Winston S. Churchill. Vol. I: Youth, 1874–1900* (Boston: Houghton Mifflin Co., 1966), pp. 367–69; Randolph Churchill, *Winston S. Churchill. Companion Volume I* (Boston: Houghton Mifflin Co., 1967), Part 2: 927; Randolph Churchill, *Winston S. Churchill. Companion Volume II* (Boston: Houghton Mifflin Co., 1969), Part 1: 454, 459; H. S. Commager, ed., *Marlborough* (New York: Charles Scribner's Sons, 1968), p. xxi; J. H. Plumb, "The Historian" in *Churchill Revised* (New York: Dial Press, 1969), p. 157; Martin Gilbert, *Churchill,* Great Lives Observed Series (Englewood Cliffs, N.J.: Prentice Hall, 1967), pp. 119, 166; D. C. Somervell, "Sir Winston Churchill," in *Nobel Prize Winners,* ed. E. J. Ludovici (London: Arco Publishing Co., 1956), p. 9; R. H. Davis, *Real Soldiers of Fortune* (New York: Collier, 1906), p. 111; Ronald Hyam, *Elgin and Churchill at the Colonial Office 1905–1908* (London: Macmillan and Co., 1968), p. 500; Shane Leslie, "Winston: A Sketch," *Review of Reviews* 67 (May 1923):477.

3. Commager, *Marlborough,* pp. xix–xx, xxxi; Connell, p. 26; Violet Bonham Carter, *Winston Churchill As I Knew Him* (London: Eyre & Spottiswoode, 1965), p. 225; de Mendelssohn, p. 103; A. L. Rowse, *The Churchills* (New York: Harper, 1958), p. 335; Preston Slosson, in *American Historical Review* 54 (1949):858; *TLS,* 30 April 1954, p. 273.

4. See Rowse in *Churchill By His Contemporaries,* ed. Charles Eade (London: Hutchinson & Co., 1953), p. 492; Connell, p. 22; Malcolm Muggerridge, in Eade, p. 349; Plumb, "The Historian," pp. 143–45; W. B. Hamilton, in *South Atlantic Quarterly* 50 (1951):401–2; Commager, pp. xx–xxi; J. M. Keynes, *Essays in Biography,* ed. G. Keynes (New York: Horizon, 1951), p. 61; *TLS,* 1 July 1949, p. 421.

Only a more recent example of this rare breed, de Gaulle, is regarded by some as a greater artist and statesman than Churchill; see, e.g., Vladimir Dedijer, in *TLS,* 30 May 1968, p. 556, and James Chace, in *New York Times Book Review,* 30 January 1972, p. 4. In a sensitive survey of de Gaulle's dual career, Stanley Hoffman (in *New York Review of Books,* 24 February 1972, pp. 23–30) lists many characteristics that we can readily find in Churchill as well.

5. Robert Rhodes James, *Churchill: A Study in Failure 1900–1939* (London: Weidenfeld and Nicolson, 1970), p. 316; Aneurin Bevan, in *Churchill by His Contemporaries,* p. 61; Commager, *Marlborough,* pp. xix, xxxii. Cf. Rowse, *The Churchills,* p. 361; Connell, p. 7; Stephen R. Graubard, *Burke, Disraeli, and Churchill* (Cambridge, Mass.: Harvard University Press, 1961), pp. 254–55.

6. Lord Moran, *Churchill* (Boston: Houghton Mifflin Co., 1966), pp. 501, 515, 547, 618, 699; Maurice Ashley, *Churchill As Historian* (New York: Charles Scribner's Sons, 1968), p. 104; James, *Study in Failure,* p. 6.

7. *London Daily Mail,* 4 January 1932, p. 10. See also Herbert Howarth, "Behind Churchill's Grand Style," *Commentary* 11 (1951):551; de Mendelssohn, p. xiv; A. L. Rowse, "Mr. Churchill and English History," in *The English Spirit* (New York: Macmillan Co., 1945), pp. 21–22.

8. James, *Study in Failure,* p. ix; F. W. Deakin, "Churchill the Historian," *Schweitzer Monatshefte* 49 (1969–70):3,18; Commager, *Marlborough,* p. xxiv; Rowse, in Eade, p. 507; de Mendelssohn, p. xi.

9. Commager, *Marlborough,* pp. xxi–xxii; Whittemore, pp. 57, 60.

10. Plumb, "The Historian," p. 137; Deakin, p. 1; *TLS,* 21 March 1958, p. 145; Randolph Churchill, *Companion Volume II,* Part 2:901; de Mendelssohn, p. 142; Hyam, pp. 491, 500–501; *Weekly Dispatch,* 29 June 1924, p. 8.

11. Brian Gardner, *Churchill In His Time* (London: Methuen & Co., 1968), p. 218.

Chapter 1

1. See Randolph Churchill, *Winston S. Churchill I:* 364, 422, 436, 497, 513; Randolph Churchill, *Companion Volume I,* Part 2: 620–21, 757, 779, 782, 804, 824. His only other completed works of fiction are three short stories: "Man Overboard" (1899), a sketch barely a thousand words long; "On the Flank of the Army" (1902), based on his Boer War experiences; and the moving, posthumously published, highly personal "Dream" (c. 1946–47).

2. R2:2. See appendix for list of abbreviations used in notes. For Churchill as an outstanding example of a new breed of journalists, see Colin Coote, in Eade, pp. 175–77, and de Mendelssohn, pp. 104, 157.

3. See Deakin, p. 3; Randolph Churchill, *Companion Volume I,* Part 2: 914, 971, 1017–18, 1043–44, 1082–90, 1101.

4. R1:1.

5. R1:312.

6. In "The Ethics of the Frontier Policy," *United Services Magazine* 17 (August 1898):510.

7. Cf. also the later Churchill's skeptical remark on medical experts: "the fashionable fallacies of the Royal physicians" (*Collier's,* 15 May 1937, p. 12). Young Churchill's first published letters at school, in the *Harrovian*—several of which were long, well argued, and signed "TRUTH"—complained of shortcomings at the school and made proposals for improvement; one of them even had to be censored for going beyond the bounds of "fair criticism." See Randolph Churchill, *Companion Volume I,* Part 1:308–19; Part 2:1169; Anthony Storr, "The Man," in *Churchill Revised* (New York: Dial Press, 1969), p. 259.

8. Churchill's working hypothesis appears to have been (and remained throughout his life) that strategy and tactics were but matters of common sense and that any imaginative civilian could solve problems in them and let the soldier translate the solution into military terms. (Hence his classic memorandum of 13 August 1911 on war strategy.) He always thought it great to command armies and greater to command the men who command armies. See Randolph Churchill, *Companion Volume I,* Part 2:1006; *Companion Volume II,* Part 2:893; A. MacCallum Scott, *Winston Spencer Churchill* (London: Methuen & Co., 1905), p. 81. For more on Churchill's perceptive analysis of Britain's strategic weaknesses, see de Mendelssohn, pp. 110–12, 161, 626. Here begins as well his lifelong interest in troop morale as it is affected by honors and awards: See Randolph Churchill, *Companion Volume II,* Part 3:1557, 1563, and Peter Gretton, *Winston Churchill and the Royal Navy* (New York: Coward-McCann, 1968), p. 196.

9. *Daily Graphic,* 24 December 1895, p. 4; ibid., 13 January 1896, p. 4; *Saturday Review* (London), 15 February 1896, p. 165. Cf. G. Ohlinger, in *Michigan Quarterly Review* 5 (1966):75–79; de Mendelssohn, p. 94.

10. Cf. his "British Cavalry," in his mother's *Anglo–Saxon Review* 8 (1901):240–47; and his "The British Officer," in *Pall Mall* (January 1901):66–75; de Mendelssohn, pp. 141–47.

11. Churchill was vindicated in his criticisms, but not alone in making them; see Scott, pp. 68, 141, 143, and de Mendelssohn, p. 210. He was not, however, transparent in his dealings: see Randolph Churchill, *Winston S. Churchill I:* 269, 368; Randolph Churchill, *Companion Volume I,* Part 2: 908–10. Cf. James, *Study in Failure,* p. 6*n*; Somervell, p. 8; de Mendelssohn, pp. 144–46.

12. L 339.

13. M 268.

14. M 281.

15. S 74.

16. Bryan Magee, "Churchill's Novel," *Encounter* 25 (October 1965):46–49.

17. M 72, 172.

18. R 2:73.

19. *Daily Graphic,* 24 December 1895, p. 4; foreword to D. S. Daniell, *Fourth Hussar* (Aldershot: Gale and Polden, 1959). Aneurin Bevan in 1942 accused Churchill of thinking of World War II "in medieval terms" and talking of it "as if it were a tourney" (quoted in Gardner, p. 190).

20. See Randolph Churchill, *Winston S. Churchill I:* 249, 336–48; Owen Edwards quoted in D. A. N. Jones, *New York Review of Books,* 23 May 1968, p. 35; Gilbert, p. 93; Samuel J. Hurwitz, "Winston S. Churchill," in *Some Modern Historians of Britain,* ed. H. Ausubel et al. (New York: Dryden, 1951), p. 306; Isaiah Berlin, *Mr. Churchill in 1940* (London: John Murray, 1949), p. 39. For his relishing of fame and success (through "notability" or "notoriety") and his shameless praise- and medal-hunting, see Randolph Churchill, *Companion Volume I,* Part 2: 783, 804, 839, 854–56, 914, 933, 1158, 1190–91; Part 3: 1984; de Mendelssohn, p. 163.

21. For his sense of theater, see Randolph Churchill, *Winston S. Churchill I:* 336, 346–50, 497; Randolph Churchill, *Companion Volume I,* Part 1: 386; Part 2: 805; *Companion Volume II,* Part 1: 53; Scott, p. 109; de Mendelssohn, pp. 380, 588; Gilbert, pp. 86, 95; Magee, p. 51; James, *Study in Failure,* pp. 18–19, 34; Berlin, p. 39; Moran, pp. 185, 659–60, 766; Ashley, *Churchill as Historian,* p. 112.

22. For remarks like "uncanny luck" and "I shall do something in the world," see Randolph Churchill, *Companion Volume I,* Part 1: 603; Part 2: 805, 813–14; Scott, p. 247. Cf. "I believe I am watched over. Think of the perils I have escaped," quoted in Lord Riddell, *More Pages from My Diary* (London: Country Life, 1934), p. 197. See also Hyam, p. 357; Virginia Cowles, *Churchill* (New York: Harper, 1953), pp. 154, 285; de Mendelssohn, p. 162; Martin Gilbert, *Winston S. Churchill,* Vol. 3 (Boston: Houghton Mifflin Co., 1971), pp. 594, 610. For a psychological explanation, see Storr, p. 250.

23. H 17.

24. M 55, 158.

25. H 57–58.

26. L 188–89.

27. L 462.

28. M 253.

29. M 246–47.

30. R 2:351.

31. L 291.

32. On his changing values, see Randolph Churchill, *Winston S. Churchill I:* 248–52, 279, 288–90, 306, 328–92, 427, 494, 523–27; Randolph Churchill, *Companion Volume I,* Part 1: 559, 580–87; Part 2: 702, 720–33, 828, 858, 861, 961–63, 974, 984, 1129, 1177–78; *Companion Volume II,* Part 1: 42; Part 2: 912; Part 3: 1884; James, *Study in Failure,* p. 34; B. H. Liddell

Hart, "The Military Strategist," in *Churchill Revised,* p. 175; de Mendelssohn, p. 159; Cowles, pp. 4–5; Gilbert, *Winston S. Churchill,* pp. 608, 617, 738.

33. This "liberal" attitude seems to have been virtually innate; see Randolph Churchill, *Winston S. Churchill I:* 223–25, 270; Randolph Churchill, *Companion Volume I,* Part 2: 1083–84; *Companion Volume II,* Part 1: 559, 567.

34. R 1:103.

35. *Daily Graphic,* 13 December 1895, p. 4; ibid., 17 December 1895, p. 5; ibid., 13 January 1896, p. 4; *Saturday Review* (London), 15 February 1896, p. 165; ibid., 29 August 1896, p. 213. Churchill's first composition extant, an essay on ancient Palestine written when he was thirteen years old, evinces characteristic interest in patriots and rebels; see Randolph Churchill, *Companion Volume I,* Part 1: 164.

36. For comments on how Churchill's novel is a prophecy of modern political currents and crises, see J. Paço d'Arcos, *Churchill,* trans. F. R. Holliday and P. S. Pernes (London: Caravel, 1957), p. 19; de Mendelssohn, p. 120; Commager, *Marlborough,* p. xxiii; Compton Mackenzie, in Eade, p. 69.

37. *Saturday Review* (London), 15 February 1896, pp. 165 ff. Cf. Moran, p. 138.

38. L 21.

39. L 24.

40. S 206.

41. L 158.

42. Randolph Churchill, *Companion Volume I,* Part 2: 810.

43. L 453.

44. Yet Churchill inconsistently criticized founders of religions (including Jesus) for upsetting the status quo with turmoil and bloodshed. See Randolph Churchill, *Companion Volume I,* Part 2: 712.

45. S 81.

46. R 1:412. For the marked change from his militant jingoism of 1897, see Randolph Churchill, *Winston S. Churchill I:* 435, 505; Randolph Churchill, *Companion Volume I,* Part 2: 938, 1162–69; *Companion Volume II,* Part 1: 521, 530, 564; Scott, pp. 69–75.

47. L 434.

48. H 68.

49. L 220.

50. L 481.

51. R 2:143.

52. M 157.

53. L 163–64.

54. R 2:162.

55. R 1:126.

56. R 1:177.

57. M 230.

58. R 1:152.

59. M 36, 10.

60. R 2:164.

61. R 2:322.

62. R 1:119.

63. Scott, p. 35. Churchill acknowledged in a 1901 interview (Ohlinger, pp. 75–79) that as civilized nations grow more powerful they become ruthless. Cf. James Morris, *Pax Britannica* (London: Harcourt Brace, 1968), p. 418; Hyam, pp. 225–28, 251, 494, 527, 539.

64. R 2:225.

65. R 2:247.

66. R 1:34;2:162.

67. R 2:44.
68. R 1:169.
69. R 2:398.
70. See Hyam, pp. 195–96, 202, 369.
71. L 137. Churchill's short story, "On the Flank of the Army" (1902), the main theme of which is the mutual courtesy and respect between Boer guerilla and British officer, shows further awakening. See also H. L. Stewart, *Sir Winston Churchill as Writer and Speaker* (London: Sidgwick and Jackson, 1954), pp. 3, 6; Scott, pp. 32–33.
72. L 132.
73. Jones, p. 34.
74. See Randolph Churchill, *Companion Volume I,* Part 2: 774, 836–39; *Companion Volume II,* Part 1: xxvii; de Mendelssohn, p. 148. Cf. Hoffman (pp. 27, 29) on de Gaulle.
75. R 2:143.
76. M 103*n*, 232.
77. R 1:169.
78. R 2:389.
79. R 2:393.
80. R 2:396.
81. See for example Magee, p. 49, and R. R. James, "The Politician," in *Churchill Revised* (New York: Dial Press, 1969), p. 124.
82. But its affinities are with the literary midgets of the period; for the influence of Anthony Hope's popular 1894 Ruritanian romance, *The Prisoner of Zenda* and, in the state ball scene, of Seton Merriman's works, not to speak of more eminent writers like Lytton, Macaulay, Disraeli, Meredith, see Mackenzie, in Eade, pp. 74–80; Somervell, p. 3; Commager, *Marlborough,* p. xxiii; Scott, p. 87; Connell, p. 16; *The Bookman* (July 1908):135.
83. Mackenzie, in Eade, p. 80; Magee, pp. 45, 48–51; de Mendelssohn, pp. 114, 118–28; Commager, *Marlborough,* pp. xxiii–xxiv. Cf. Randolph Churchill, *Companion Volume I,* Part 2: 779, 800–815, 884, 889, 907, 912, 915, 922–38, 960–64; Scott, p. 241; Storr, pp. 245–46, 265; James, *Study in Failure,* p. 6; Rowse, *The Churchills,* p. 260; Ashley, *Churchill as Historian,* p. 51.
84. Cf. A. G. Gardiner, quoted in Gilbert, *Churchill,* p. 95.
85. See Randolph Churchill, *Companion Volume I,* Part 2:827, 834; Randolph Churchill, *Winston S. Churchill I:* 367; G. W. Price and Colin Coote, in Eade, pp. 50, 178–82; Philip Guedella, *Mr. Churchill* (New York: Reynal & Hitchcock, 1942), pp. 51–53; Ashley, *Churchill as Historian,* p. 39; Rowse, *The Churchills,* p. 259; Plumb, "The Historian," pp. 156–57; de Mendelssohn, p. 109.
86. For high praise of the book as greater than the *Malakand,* see Paço d'Arcos, p. 13; Rowse, *The Churchills,* pp. 262–63; Gilbert, *Churchill,* p. 98; James, *Study in Failure,* pp. 6, 27; Somervell, p. 7; de Mendelssohn, pp. 141–47; Guedella, pp. 69, 109; Davis, p. 107; but see Plumb, "The Historian," p. 158; Cyril Falls, "Sir Winston Churchill in War," in *Illustrated London News Eightieth Year Tribute to Winston Churchill,* ed. Bruce Ingram (London: 1954), p 17; Liddell Hart, "The Military Strategist," p. 175.
87. Cf. L. G. Brock in *The Bookman* (December 1900):87; *American Historical Review* 12 (1906):303; Scott, p. 55; Falls, "Sir Winston in War," pp. 15, 17; *The Bookman* (July 1908):136; James, *Study in Failure,* p. 6; de Mendelssohn, p. 192; Rowse, *The Churchills,* p. 266; Somervell, p. 8; Plumb, "The Historian," p. 159.
88. See de Mendelssohn, pp. xii, 108, 141, 196–97; Commager, *Marlborough,* p. xxi; Scott, pp. 24–25; Hurwitz, p. 311; Falls, "Sir Winston in War," p. 17; Randolph Churchill, *Winston S. Churchill I:* 514, 528; Gilbert, *Winston S. Churchill,* p. 646. As Deakin (p. 6) puts it, Churchill had learned to transform into literature his vision of empire tempered by his military experience; he had created his own university and graduated from it; he had established his lifelong values. This was the function of his writing.

Chapter 2

1. RC1:ix. On the timeliness of the book, see Randolph Churchill, *Companion Volume I,* Part 2: 744, 927, 1004; *Companion Volume II,* Part 1: 427–36, 453–65, 491–93; Rowse, *The Churchills,* pp. 249, 282; Deakin, pp. 4–5; Connell, p. 18; Cowles, pp. 109–10; Commager, *Marlborough,* p. xxii; Somervell, p. 9.

2. RC1:108.

3. RC2:280.

4. But see R. R. James, *Lord Randolph Churchill* (New York: A. S. Barnes, 1960), p. 373; L. S. Amery, *My Political Life,* 3 vols. (London: Hutchinson & Co., 1953–55) 1:393; Rowse, *The Churchills,* pp. 250, 278; Cowles, p. 96.

5. RC2:247.

6. RC1:301.

7. RC1:270. For Churchill's recurring awe at the twists and turns of history, see for example (on the decade 1914–24) *The Weekly Dispatch,* 21 September 1924, p. 8, or (on Lloyd George and Ramsay MacDonald from 1918 to 1932) *The Daily Mail,* 1 November 1932, p. 12.

8. RC2:296.

9. RC1:x.

10. RC1:294–95.

11. RC2:190.

12. RC2:264.

13. See for example de Mendelssohn, p. 47; James, *Randolph,* pp. 121, 128, 140, 213, 269, 320, 347, 372–73; Rowse, *The Churchills,* pp. 224, 230, 249.

14. RC2:442.

15. Guedella, p. 108; cf. G. S. Street in the *Quarterly Review* (1907):249: Randolph crushed mediocrity (Northcote) only to be crushed in turn by mediocrity (Salisbury). But see James, *Randolph,* p. 155.

16. For Churchill's recreating his father's different and much less stable character in his own image, see de Mendelssohn, pp. 301–3, and Commager, *Marlborough,* p. xxii. Cf. Scott, pp. 240, 254.

17. RC1:193.

18. RC1:84–86.

19. RC2:68.

20. RC1:74. See Randolph Churchill, *Winston S. Churchill I:* 24; James, *Randolph,* pp. 12, 203; James, *Study in Failure,* p. 17; Connell, p. 18.

21. RC1:302.

22. RC2:128–29.

23. For criticism of Churchill's naïve excuses for his father, see the anonymous piece in the *Edinburgh Review* 204 (July 1906):20,33; Cowles, p. 25; W. S. Blunt, *My Diaries 1888–1914* (New York: Alfred A. Knopf, 1921) 2:124; de Mendelssohn, p. 307; James, *Randolph,* p. 211; James, *Study in Failure,* pp. 11–12; Roy Jenkins, *Asquith* (New York: Chilmark, 1964), p. 274n; Storr, p. 257.

24. RC2:243.

25. Many interpretations have, of course, been offered. See R. C. K. Ensor, *England 1870–1914* (London: Oxford University Press, 1936), pp. 174–75; Dennis Bardens, *Churchill in Parliament* (New York: A. S. Barnes, 1967), p. 17; de Mendelssohn, pp. 68–69; James, *Randolph,* pp. 223, 303–11, 318; W. S. Hamer, *The British Army* (London: Oxford University Press, 1970), pp. 100–103; Rowse, *The Churchills,* pp. 219–21, 238–42; Viscount Esher, *Journals and Letters,* ed. M. V. Brett (London: Nicholson and Watson, 1934) 1:132–33; Ashley, *Churchill as Historian,* p. 61; Randolph Churchill, *Winston S. Churchill II:* 426.

26. RC2:515.

27. See James, *Randolph*, pp. 11–13; Plumb, "The Historian," pp. 146, 148; Sir Charles Petrie, "Sir Winston Churchill's Place in History," in Ingram, p. 57; Ashley, *Churchill as Historian*, pp. 61, 66, 68.

28. On the complementary careers of father and son—the one providing a vision, the other a fulfillment—see de Mendelsohn, pp. xi, 85, 138, 226, 304, 307, 352–55, 483, 572; Cowles, p. 121; Plumb, "The Historian," p. 139; Rowse, *The Churchills*, p. 281. That in a sense he never shook his father off is to be seen in the moving fantasy "The Dream" written c. 1946–47.

29. Cf. de Mendelssohn (p. 35), who believes that it was not so much a case of the debacle changing Randolph's character as of the character causing the debacle; his unbalanced temper proved fatal to him and handicapped his son. James (*Randolph*, pp. 53, 58) and Rowse (*The Churchills*, p. 202), on the other hand, agree with Churchill on the importance of this incident in shaping Randolph's hitherto apolitical character.

30. See, on this book, Hurwitz, p. 312; Ashley, *Churchill as Historian*, pp. 12, 55–56, 68; Plumb, "The Historian," pp. 145–47; de Mendelssohn, pp. 300–309; Rowse, *The Churchills*, p. 282; cf. Muggeridge, pp. 346–47; Deakin, p. 6; Connell, p. 20.

31. See Randolph Churchill, *Companion Volume I*, Part 2: 876; *Companion Volume II*, Part 2: 865, 937; Bardens, pp. 42–43; de Mendelssohn, p. 247; Cowles, pp. 74–84, 92.

32. Hyam, pp. 43, 58. But see Churchill's anxieties on this score in his review of Upton Sinclair's *The Jungle*, in *P.T.O.*, 16 June 1906, pp. 25–27.

33. LS 67.

Chapter 3

1. WC3:xi.

2. WC1:49.

3. WC1:422–24.

4. WC2:377.

5. WC2:391.

6. WC5:369.

7. WC2:58, 375.

8. WC2:449; 6:36.

9. WC1:57–58. The italics are Churchill's.

10. See Barbara Tuchman, *The Guns of August* (New York: Dell Books, 1962), p. 70; de Mendelssohn, pp. 626, 630; Randolph Churchill, *Winston S. Churchill II:* 510; Gilbert, *Winston S. Churchill*, p. 64. Cf. the universal contemporary praise for his 1912 War Staff memo: Randolph Churchill, *Companion Volume II*, Part 3: 1471–73.

11. WC2:30.

12. WC2:526. Amery, 2:80; Tuchman, pp. 70, 114, 136; James, *Study in Failure*, p. 87; Cowles, p. 215. Churchill's Somme computations are disputed by Colonel Sydenham in *The "World Crisis" by Winston Churchill: A Criticism* (London: Hutchinson & Co., 1927), ch. 2 and his inferences by C. R. Cruttwell, *A History of the Great War* (London: Oxford University Press, 1934), pp. 276–77, but even so devoted a "Westerner" as Colonel C. Repington in "Churchillian Strategy," *Blackwood's Magazine* 214 (December 1923):830–36 pays tribute, amid a slashing attack on his strategic views, to Churchill's achievements in office.

13. See Gilbert, *Churchill*, pp. 90, 102, 167; Riddell, *War Diary 1914–18* (London: Nicholson and Watson, 1933), p. 204; David Lloyd George, *War Memoirs* (Boston: Little, Brown, & Co., 1933–37) 1:333–44; Amery, 1:394; 2:59, 66, 80; A. J. Marder, *From the Dreadnought to Scapa Flow* (New York: Oxford University Press, 1961–70) 2:260–62; Rowse,

The Churchills, p. 313; Gretton, pp. 214–15; Liddell Hart, "The Military Strategist," pp. 189–93; Cyril Falls, "Sir Winston in War," p. 18; Cruttwell, pp. 144–46, 209; A. J. P. Taylor, "The Statesman," in *Churchill Revised* (New York: Dial Press, 1969), pp. 21–22; Taylor, *English History 1914–45* (New York: Oxford University Press, 1965), pp. 23, 25*n*, 48–49; James, *Study in Failure,* pp. 64–87; James, *Gallipoli* (New York: Macmillan Co., 1965), pp. 12, 25–41, 215, 249, 322, 332; John Terraine, *The Great War 1914–1918* (New York: Macmillan Co., 1965), pp. 142–46, 164–66; General S. L. A. Marshall, *The American Heritage History of World War I* (1964; reprint New York: Dell Books, 1966), pp. 143–48; Ashley, *Churchill as Historian,* pp. 87–88; Trumbull Higgins, *Winston Churchill and the Dardanelles* (New York: Macmillan Co., 1963), pp. 116, 148, 185–90, 210, 249; Fuller, quoted in Correlli Barnett, *Britain and Her Army 1509–1970* (London: Allen Lane, 1970), p. 386; cf. *TLS,* 8 November 1923, p. 739. Actually at first Lloyd George and Hankey turned eastward and Churchill opposed cheap victories in easy fields. See Gilbert, *Winston S. Churchill,* pp. 229–46, 324; for his later lapses see ibid. 311, 350.

14. WC2:69.

15. WC1:348.

16. See Amery, 2:125, 159; Lloyd George, *War Memoirs,* 2:80, 96–97; Terraine, p. 256; Marshall, pp. 236–37, 322; Taylor, "The Statesman," p. 17; James, *Study in Failure,* pp. 63, 80; James, *Gallipoli,* pp. 11, 56, 193; Gilbert, *Churchill,* p. 102; Falls, "Sir Winston in War," p. 18; Liddell Hart, "The Military Strategist," pp. 189, 195–98; Cruttwell, pp. 416, 547*n*; Gilbert, *Winston S. Churchill,* pp. 537*n*, 810. Cf. E. M. Earle, ed., *Makers of Modern Strategy* (Princeton: Princeton University Press, 1943), pp. 296, 431, 486–90, 499.

17. Churchill's hostility colors even his subsequent retelling of Shakespeare's *Julius Caesar:* Lepidus was a "stupid professional general" allowed into the triumvirate "presumably as a concession to military orthodoxy"! (*Six Stories from Shakespeare* [London: George Newnes, 1934], p. 57).

18. WC3:249. See Esher, 3:92; *Collier's,* 24 March 1917, pp. 7 ff; *London Magazine* (October 1916):127; ibid. (November 1916):235–44; ibid. (December 1916):395–404; ibid. (February 1917):653–60; *Sunday Pictorial,* 8 April 1917, p. 5. For the wish that Churchill, properly hedged with a trained military staff, had been in charge in World War I (as in fact he would be in World War II), see Esher, 4:290; Liddell Hart, in *The English Review* (December 1934):709. But for Lloyd George's equal or even superior understanding of the new "Wizard War" and of the military blindness, see Harvey de Weerd, in Earle, pp. 294–96.

19. WC5:479.

20. Esher, 4:121; Lloyd George, *War Memoirs* 6:347, 352; Attlee, in *Churchill by His Contemporaries,* p. 15; Keynes, pp. 54–61; Cowles, p. 215; Liddell Hart, "The Military Strategist," pp. 188–89; Randolph Churchill, *Winston S. Churchill II:* 189, 218; Moran, pp. 280, 655; Rowse, *The Churchills,* p. 322; Ashley, *Churchill as Historian,* pp. 98–100; Tuchman, pp. 137, 485; Gilbert, *Winston S. Churchill,* p. 817.

21. WC1:281.

22. WC6:131–32.

23. WC1:539.

24. WC2:283.

25. WC2:503.

26. WC4:48. Hence Churchill was ready in the prewar years—to Esher's shock and in contrast with his World War II policy—to abandon the Mediterranean, for if the gathered forces of the navy once won a big battle in the North Sea, all else would follow; otherwise, Britain might face defeat in the Mediterranean and uncertainty to the north. See Randolph Churchill, *Companion Volume II,* Part 2: 997, 1494; Part 3: 1549, 1578, 1593, 1615, 1779; Esher, 3:98, 101.

27. WC5:304. Churchill concedes here that "in ordinary domestic politics these sharp dichotomies are usually inapplicable," but when blood has been shed, "it ought to be one thing or the other" (WC5:304). The Irish case is a special one in which he unites the Either/Or with a Both–And. Success, he claims, came from pursuing simultaneously two "antagonistic" policies: "drastic processes" and handsome offers of self-government. Pursued halfheartedly, they would have been ruinous. See James, *Study in Failure,* pp. 46, 175, and Taylor, "The Statesman," pp. 17–19, for the Churchillian pattern of victory followed by generosity. See also, Amery, 1:443.

28. WC2:445.
29. WC2:338.
30. WC2:248.
31. WC2:534.
32. WC2:505.
33. WC4:100.
34. WC5:144.
35. WC5:294.
36. WC5:286.
37. WC5:285.
38. Marshall, p. 148.
39. WC3:195.
40. WC1:224.
41. WC5:379. Cf. Gilbert, *Winston S. Churchill,* pp. 91, 208. On the vexed question of whether Churchill's prewar anti-Turk zealotry alienated a potential ally, historians seem uncertain. See Tuchman, pp. 163–64, 185; Marshall, p. 116; James, *Gallipoli,* pp. 9, 11; David Walder, *The Chanak Affair* (London: Macmillan & Co., 1969), p. 25. The same controversy surrounds his postwar ultimatum to Turkey. See Harold Nicolson, quoted in Cowles, p. 239; Amery, 2:234; Walder, pp. 190–91, 215, 224–27, 287–88, 359.

42. WC1:361.
43. WC5:436, 449.
44. See the *Empire Review* (July 1923):698; *London Magazine* (March 1917):58; Marshall, p. 195; Tuchman, p. 223. But for a less well-known side of Churchill, see Gilbert, *Churchill,* p. 46n; Keynes, p. 63; Austen Chamberlain, quoted in *South Atlantic Quarterly* 51 (1952):226.

45. WC6:74.
46. WC1:20.
47. WC6:42.
48. WC5:483.
49. Rowse ("Mr. Churchill and English History," p. 15) draws the same contrast between *The World Crisis* and Lloyd George's memoirs and therefore finds the latter superior. See also Plumb, "The Historian," p. 160, and *TLS,* 3 March 1927, p. 135.

50. WC5:171.
51. WC5:263.
52. WC5:287.
53. WC5:61.
54. WC1:538.
55. And for the sake of a non-Communist Russia, Churchill was ready to sacrifice the small states at Russia's periphery. See *Sunday Pictorial,* 10 June 1917, p. 5; Blunt, 2:322, 336;H. H. Asquith, *Memories and Reflections 1852–1927* (Boston: Little, Brown, and Co., 1928) 2:82; Taylor, "The Statesman," p. 24; Dedijer, p. 555; Gilbert, *Winston S. Churchill,* pp. 202, 321, 332, 356. Many of Churchill's military and political ideas found their counterpart in the German camp, in the writings of Delbrück; see Gordon Craig, in Earle, pp. 276–78.

56. WC1:85. See James, *Gallipoli,* pp. 28–31, 197, 322; James, *Study in Failure,* pp. 119, 124–27; Cowles, pp. 169, 196, 234; Ashley, *Churchill as Historian,* p. 76.

57. See Lloyd George, *War Memoirs* 3:482–84; Lloyd George, *The Truth About the Peace Treaties* (London: Victor Gollancz, 1938) 1:324–25, 367; Lord Riddell, *Intimate Diary of the Peace Conference 1918–1923*(New York: Reynal and Hitchcock, 1934), pp. 15, 50, 222–24; Keynes, pp. 62–63; Plumb, "The Historian," p. 163; James, "The Politician," p. 91; James, *Study in Failure,* pp. 111, 124, 134; Graubard, p. 192; John M. Thompson, *Russia, Bolshevism and the Versailles Peace* (Princeton: Princeton University Press, 1966), pp. 139, 214–18, 397; Richard Ullman, *Britain and the Russian Civil War* (Princeton: Princeton University Press, 1968), pp. 90, 96, 128, 135, 140, 181–82, 212–21, 247, 287, 294–98, 301–4, 339.

58. Esher, 4:287; Cowles, p. 193; Tuchman, p. 519; Plumb, "The Historian," pp. 160–64; Muggeridge, p. 349; Hurwitz, pp. 313–16; *The "World Crisis": A Criticism,* passim.

59. Leslie, p. 477; Guedella, pp. 223–24, 237; Keynes, p. 61; Connell, p. 22; Plumb, "The Historian," p. 163; Hurwitz, pp. 313–16; Berlin, p. 8.

Chapter 4

1. C. P. Snow, *Variety of Men* (New York: Charles Scribner's Sons, 1966), pp. 163–64.

2. C Preface.

3. G 77–78.

4. C 67.

5. G ix. Cf. *The Evening Standard,* 9 May 1935, p. 23; *News of the World,* 18 September 1938, p. 12; de Mendelssohn, p. 230.

6. T 269.

7. T 279–80.

8. *Daily Telegraph,* 30 December 1929, p. 10; ibid., 27 January 1930, p. 10; *Saturday Evening Post,* 29 March 1930, p. 6; *Collier's,* 28 December 1935, p. 32; *News of the World,* 4 September 1938, p. 12. He concedes, however, that more books are now read than before, that the radio has brought the family back to the hearth, and that the film could make school texts come alive; and he eagerly awaits the coming of television.

9. *News of the World,* 13 January 1935, p. 5. Amery (2:510) believes that only Churchill's exuberance and vitality hide the fact that he was a Victorian out of place in the modern world, and Martin Greenberg, in "Winston Churchill, Tory Democrat," *Partisan Review* 18 (1951):194, remarks on the paradox that Churchill functioned so well in the twentieth century he was at odds with.

10. C 27.

11. Cf. Stewart, p. 51; C. E. M. Joad, "Churchill the Philosopher," in Eade, pp. 482–87. But Taylor (in "The Statesman," p. 28) points out that Churchill's romantic nationalism prevented him from sharing in the postwar disillusionment of the intellectuals.

12. G 187. Many of these observations were being made during the same years by José Ortega y Gasset (*The Revolt of the Masses,* etc.) and others.

13. G 117.

14. *Daily Mail,* 2 October 1931, p. 10; ibid., 26 May 1932, p. 12; *Collier's,* 25 February 1933, pp. 10–11; *Saturday Evening Post,* 29 March 1930, pp. 6 ff; *Collier's,* 27 August 1932, p. 10; 29 December 1934, pp. 24 ff; 16 February 1935, p. 29; 20 June 1936, p. 11; 22 August 1936, p. 27; cf. *The Listener* (November 1923):1217.

15. T 237.

16. T 232.

17. *The Listener,* 17 January 1934, pp. 86 ff.; *Collier's,* 16 February 1935, pp. 14, 19. Cf. Randolph Churchill, *Companion Volume I,* Part 2: 1002; Harold Nicolson, *Diaries and Letters,*

ed. Nigel Nicolson (New York: Atheneum Publishers, 1966–68) 1:61, 108; Cowles, p. 277; James, "The Politician," pp. 100–101, 114; James, *Study in Failure,* pp. 299–302, 305. Churchill's nostalgia for the "real political democracy" of 1900, James reminds us, is really a yearning for an oligarchic society with a restricted franchise and docile workers. Cf. also Churchill's desire to see the Sandhurst discipline (like daily inspection) introduced into the great universities in place of the prevailing "long hair, untidy clothes, and subversive opinions" (*News of the World,* 13 January 1935, p. 5).

18. C 330.

19. See his interesting apologia (in *Strand* [January 1936]:776–86), in which he identifies with great men hounded out, e.g., Clemenceau and Lloyd George.

20. *News of the World,* 24 March 1935, p. 5. In 1931, Amery (2:510) heard Churchill—set in his ways, unwilling to listen, cynical about politics—declare that, having attained everything he had wanted except the highest post (which there was no chance now of his reaching) and finding politics not what it had been, he thought of retiring. But in the *News of the World,* 13 January 1935, p. 5, Churchill later remarked prophetically that in politics one does not achieve one's peak until the years between sixty and eighty.

21. C 59.

22. T 19.

23. See also Mendelssohn, pp. 88, 101, 134; *TLS,* 23 October 1930, p. 851; Cowles, p. 278; James, *Study in Failure,* pp. 313–14; Somervell, pp. 3, 14; Plumb, "The Historian," p. 159; Guedella, p. 247; Muggeridge, pp. 347–51; Howarth, p. 557; Connell, p. 24.

24. *TLS,* 17 November 1932, p. 847.

25. G 21.

26. G 103.

27. G 12.

28. The sympathetic portrait of Parnell here seriously qualifies the hostile one in *Randolph Churchill.* At first Churchill saw only a ruthless troublemaker, but, more than thirty years later, the emphasis is on Parnell's integrity and zeal, his moderation, his dedication to a single goal until (as it did for Savrola!) "the world of love" opened to him and caused his egress from politics.

29. G 195.

30. G 218.

31. See also de Mendelssohn, p. 103. In the light of subsequent events, Churchill's sketches of Hitler and Roosevelt are of great interest; see *Collier's,* 29 June 1935, pp. 12 ff. The antibolshevism which predisposed him to Mussolini and Hitler also blinded him to Lenin and Trotsky as molders of a nation; see Hurwitz, p. 320, and Greenberg, p. 197n.

32. Hurwitz, p. 320; Rowse, "Sir Winston Churchill as an Historian," in *The English Spirit,* rev. ed. (New York: Funk & Wagnalls Co., 1966), p. 80; Plumb, "The Historian," pp. 139, 163–64; E. D. O'Brien, "Sir Winston Churchill—The Man," in Ingram, p. 42; Ashley, *Churchill as Historian,* pp. 224–29; Greenberg, pp. 196–97; de Mendelssohn, pp. 550–51, 591; Graubard, pp. 215–17; Somervell, p. 14; Guedella, p. 250; Stewart, pp. 47–60; *TLS,* 17 November 1932, p. 847; ibid., 9 October 1937, p. 725; Connell, pp. 24, 29; James, *Study in Failure,* pp. 307–10; Gordon K. Lewis, "Mr. Churchill as Historian," *The Historian* 20 (August 1958):401.

33. For the role of this book in Churchill's career, see Cowles, pp. 16, 285, 290; Richard Lodge, in *English Histroical Review* 49 (1934):715; Commager, *Marlborough,* pp. xxviii–xxix; Rowse, "Historian," pp. 80, 83; Ashley, *Churchill as Historian,* pp. 138, 143–44; Paço d'Arcos, p. 20; Plumb, "The Historian," p. 148; Somervell, p. 17; Stewart, p. 75; Deakin, pp. 11–13; James, *Study in Failure,* pp. 310–13; Scott, p. 254; Leslie, p. 477; Petrie, p. 58. Cf. Randolph Churchill, *Companion Volume I,* Part 2: 927–38; *Companion Volume II,* Part 2: 912, 980.

34. MAR2:888.

35. MAR1:40.
36. MAR1:896.
37. MAR1:570–71.
38. MAR1:43.
39. MAR2:996. See Graubard, p. 200; Plumb, "The Historian," p. 154; Violet Barbour, in *American Historical Review* 41 (1936):334.
40. MAR1:483.
41. MAR2:286. For criticisms of such oversimplifications, see Maurice Ashley, *Marlborough* (New York: Macmillan Co., 1939), pp. 88, 156, and Violet Barbour, in *American Historical Review* 44 (1939):887. But G. M. Trevelyan, in *England Under Queen Anne* (London: Longmans, Green and Co., 1931–34) 2:317, 395, also sees history turning on "straws," and Ivor Burton, in *The Captain-General* (London: Constable and Co., 1968), p. 77, also sees Blenheim as the turning point of the war.
42. MAR2:492. For Churchill's cavalier handling of Marlborough's flaws, see Moran, p. 830; Stewart, p. 76; Commager, *Marlborough*, p. xxx; Ashley, *Churchill as Historian*, p. 156; Ashley, *Marlborough*, pp. 108, 116–17, 139; Petrie, p. 57.
43. MAR1:493.
44. MAR1:905.
45. Trevelyan (1:180, 182, 391; 2:48, 105, 305; 3:xi, 40–41, 133–34, 200) agrees with this judgment of Marlborough the soldier.
46. MAR1:580.
47. MAR1:954–55.
48. MAR2:373.
49. Ashley, *Churchill as Historian*, pp. 148–49, 153. Though Liddell Hart, in the *English Review* (1934):703–4, concedes to Marlborough the broad continental vision that the "Westerners" lacked, Trevelyan (2:159; 3:78,82) believes that Marlborough's persisting in a costly, useless Spanish campaign he did not even understand was a major flaw in his strategy. Cf. Gretton, p. 246; Burton, pp. 97, 193, 197.
50. See Barnett, *Britain and Her Army*, pp. 128–29, 145–46, 152–54, 160–61; Trevelyan, 1:183, 224–31, 386; 2:52–56, 361, 368; 3:20; Ashley, *Marlborough*, pp. 115, 123, 131; Liddell Hart, in *English Review*, pp. 702–9; Burton, pp. 34–38, 61, 81–82, 158, 192–94, 197–99.
51. MAR1:741.
52. MAR1:489.
53. MAR2:228.
54. MAR2:275. Trevelyan (1:143–48, 182–84; 2:288, 292; 3:190–92) agrees with Churchill only up to a point.
55. MAR2:758.
56. MAR2:141.
57. *TLS*, 3 September 1938, p. 563; Barbour, in *American Historical Review* 43 (1938):377, and in *AHR* 44 (1939):887; Barnett, *Britain and Her Army*, p. 161; Graubard, p. 203; Rowse, "Historian," p. 83; Ashley, *Marlborough*, pp. 13, 45, 68, 79, 141; Ashley, *Churchill as Historian*, pp. 148, 153; Liddell Hart, in *English Review*, pp. 704–5; Trevelyan 2:vii, 130–31, 367n, 397, 401–9; 3:viii, 27–28, 134, 209, 230; Burton, pp. 3, 190, 192–96.
58. MAR2:754. But see Trevelyan 1:178–83; 2:398; 3:19, 26, 130.
59. MAR2:126.
60. MAR2:533.
61. MAR1:620.
62. MAR1:283.
63. MAR2:504.
64. MAR1:889.
65. MAR1:615.

66. MAR2:154.
67. MAR1:919.
68. MAR2:154.
69. Plumb, "The Historian," p. 152; Trevelyan 1:179–80; 2:viii, 134–35, 397; 3:192, 271; Ashley, *Marlborough*, pp. 13, 25, 28–29, 60, 78, 88, 103, 106–11, 127, 139, 143; Burton, p. 197.
70. The harmony of interests idea is applicable to Churchill himself. On the Sidney Street incident, Churchill makes a confession which does not accompany the narration of similar forays in wartime: "Convictions of duty were supported by a strong sense of curiosity which perhaps it would have been well to keep in check" (T 68). He applies it also to Britain, but Plumb ("The Historian," p. 152) finds Churchill's simplistic ideas—France as a tyrant, England as freedom loving, Parliament as a watchdog of liberty—to be part of the Whig claptrap that mars this work and will pervade the *History* even more. Cf. James, *Study in Failure*, p. 312.
71. Hurwitz, pp. 317–19; Plumb, "The Historian," pp. 149–52; James, *Study in Failure*, pp. 309–13; Guedella, p. 250; Taylor, *English History*, p. 356; Lodge, in *English Historical Review* 49 (1934):716–19; in *EHR* 50 (1935):340; Muggeridge, pp. 347–48.
72. Stewart, pp. 64–74; Cowles, p. 290; Commager, *Marlborough*, p. xxxiii; Somervell, pp. 17–18; Barbour, in *American Historical Review* 41 (1936):332–34; in *AHR* 43 (1938):376–77; in *AHR* 44 (1939):886–87; Liddell Hart, in *English Review*, pp. 708–9; Guedella, p. 248; Somervell, p. 16; de Mendelssohn, p. 300. James (*Study in Failure*, pp. 307–9, 313), speaking of the substantial body of work Churchill produced in the 1930s and of its greater technical sophistication, yet finds a decline in quality; the style becomes rhetorical as his studies in Marlborough enhance his romanticized version of English history.
73. Commager, *Marlborough*, pp. xx, xxix–xxxi; de Mendelssohn, p. 13; *TLS,* 3 September 1938, p. 563; Rowse, "Historian," pp. 79, 82–83; *The Churchills*, p. 348; Ashley, *Churchill as Historian*, pp. 156–57; Connell, p. 25; Trevelyan, 3:xi–xiii.
74. MAR1:435.
75. If many parallels existed between Churchill and his father, there were also, historians have noted, a good many between Churchill and his ancestor (though hardly as many as Churchill probably liked to think), and these became evident only during World War II, when Churchill entered upon his Marlborough-like tasks. The number and extent of these parallels may be a matter of dispute, but one major difference everyone agrees on: Churchill lacked the quality which was central to Marlborough's successes—patience. To this one may add that Churchill also lacked, according to Alanbrooke, the ability to grasp the interrelation of all the war theaters—the very ability he celebrated in his writings on generals, above all in *Marlborough*. See Arthur Bryant, *The Turn of the Tide* (Garden City, N.Y.: Doubleday & Co., 1957), p. 500.
76. T 287.
77. Some of these points were made by Amery 2:511; Connell, p. 26; Stewart, p. 69; Ashley, *Churchill as Historian*, p. 147; Plumb, "The Historian," p. 151; Rowse, in Eade, p. 500; Rowse, "Historian," p. 81; Rowse, *The Churchills*, p. 401; Cowles, pp. 285, 292, 325; de Mendelssohn, p. 28; Salter, in Gilbert, *Churchill*, p. 125; Gilbert, *Winston S. Churchill*, p. 603; Graubard, pp. 199–200, 207; James, *Study in Failure*, p. 313; Commager, *Marlborough*, pp. xxiii, xxviii, xxxi–xxxii; Deakin, p. 11. For a dissenting view, see James (*Study in Failure*, p. 349), who asserts that Churchill underwent no such political or personal development in the 1930s.
78. Stewart (p. 46) speaks of *Step by Step* as Churchill's best journalism—vivid, succinct, satiric, rich in startling similarities.
79. ST 150.
80. See R. H. Powers, in *Journal of Modern History* 26 (1954):179–82; James, *Study in Failure*, pp. 124–25, 134, 165–68, 221–22, 230–39, 253–68, 278–80, 319–30; Taylor, *English*

History, pp. 369–89, 410–25, 435, 445, 560; Taylor, *The Origins of the Second World War,* 2d ed. (New York: Fawcett Publications, 1961), pp. 76, 116–17, 129, 174, 284–86; Graubard, p. 213; Cowles, p. 300; Liddell Hart, "The Military Strategist," pp. 198–203, 207; Barnett, *Britain and Her Army,* pp. 411, 415.

81. ST 48.

82. ST 232.

83. IB 440.

84. Lady Astor, Lord Riddell, Beaverbrook, and Hore Belisha sensed, at various junctures, the potential tyrant in Churchill; see Riddell, *Intimate Diary,* pp. 117–18; James, *Study in Failure,* p. 297; R. J. Minney, *The Private Papers of Hore-Belisha* (London: Wm. Collins Sons & Co., 1960), p. 115. Some have believed (including, to judge from his words, Churchill himself) that if he had been prime minister during the general strike of 1926, blood would have run in the streets; see Gilbert, *Churchill,* p. 110. The *TLS,* 1 July 1949, p. 422, noted the portrait Churchill drew of himself as a benevolent despot in a democracy. Yet Churchill realized (*Collier's,* 3 September 1938, p. 26) that dictators are inefficient and self-destructive, and in any case he was not alone in being taken in by them, for there was the notorious case of Lloyd George and Hitler, as well as that of Austen Chamberlain and Ramsay MacDonald vis-à-vis Mussolini. See Taylor, *Origins,* pp. 59–60; Bardens, pp. 192, 244.

85. ST 169.

86. W 166.

87. ST 76.

88. W 186.

89. W 263.

90. ST 286.

91. ST 305.

92. W 73.

93. *News of the World,* 13 June 1937, p. 12; cf. ibid., 13 January 1935, p. 5, and 24 March 1935, p. 5.

94. See Amery 2:80, 511; 3:376, 399; Falls, "Sir Winston Churchill," p. 22; Taylor, *English History,* p. 472. For the view that Churchill was not a prophet, see James, "The Politician," p. 127.

Chapter 5

1. For an analysis of the origin and development of each of Churchills's famous phrases of 1938–42, see my "Churchill the Phrase Forger," *Quarterly Journal of Speech* 58 (April 1972):161–74. By far the most graphic eyewitness descriptions of the delivery, the accompanying gestures, and the great impact of these speeches are to be found in the second volume of the diaries of a fellow MP, Harold Nicolson.

2. Chester Wilmot, in *The Struggle for Europe* (New York: Harper, 1952), p. 148, relates the fact that in 1941–42 Britain outproduced Germany in war materiel to Churchill's asking for "blood, sweat, and tears" at the same time that Hitler cemented his popularity by assuring his people of early victory and prosperity. See also Cowles (p. 311) and Nicolson (*Diaries* 2:37, 125) on the Churchill–Chamberlain contrast. Cf. Liddell Hart, *"The Military Strategist,"* p. 209.

3. Quoted in Gilbert, *Churchill,* p. 162. Comparison is often made to Elizabeth's speech at Tilbury in 1588 (see Gardner, p. 57*n*). For stylistic considerations, see Ivor Brown, in Eade, p. 456; Connell, p. 11; Gilbert, *Churchill,* pp. 65, 169; Hyam, p. 152; Gardner, pp. 104, 118, 149, 179, 256, 297; Berlin, pp. 26–30, 38; Connell, p. 12; Gretton, p. 261; Taylor,

English History, pp. 488–89; Taylor, *"The Statesman,"* pp. 41, 45; L. S. Amery, in *Winston Spencer Churchill,* ed. Sir James Marchant (London: Cassell and Co., 1954), p. 68; Bardens, pp. 224, 238–45, 259; W. P. Hall, in *Journal of Modern History* 21 (1949):358; G. M. Thomson, *Vote of Censure* (New York: Stein and Day, 1968), pp. 206, 221; Nicolson, *Diaries* 2:97; James, *"The Politician,"* pp. 121–22; Moran, pp. 14, 47, 749, 773; T. O. Lloyd, *From Empire to Welfare State* (London: Oxford University Press, 1970), p. 251.

4. U 276.

5. See Petrie, p. 62; Plumb, "The Historian," p. 137; Berlin, pp. 28–30; Whittemore, p. 62; Nicolson, *Diaries* 2:121; Churchill's foreword to the speeches of Pitt, ed. R. Coupland (London: Oxford University Press, 1940). But see Plumb, "The Historian," pp. 164–65.

6. O 82.

7. IB 305.

8. SWW1:iv. The *TLS,* 30 April 1954, p. 27, also speaks of the uniqueness of this *Iliad* written by Agamemnon, but Lloyd George made rather similar and not unjustified claims to uniqueness in his *War Memoirs* (1:vi; 5:vi); cf. Cowles, p. 362.

9. See Moran, pp. 649, 802; Whittemore, p. 60, Plumb, "The Historian," pp. 145, 164; Ashley, *Churchill as Historian,* pp. 159, 168; *Action This Day,* ed. J. Wheeler-Bennett (London: Macmillan and Co., 1968), p. 37.

10. See Liddell Hart, "Churchill in War," *Encounter* 26 (April 1966):21; Liddell Hart, "The Military Strategist," p. 219; Nicolson, *Diaries* 2:409–10; O'Brien, p. 44; Wheeler-Bennett, p. 20; Somervell, p. 20; Gretton, p. 285; Attlee, in *Churchill by His Contemporaries,* pp. 17–18; Plumb, "The Historian," p. 164; Whittemore, pp. 58–59; Howarth, p. 556; Preston Slosson, in *American Historical Review* 54 (1949):860; 56 (1950):533; 57 (1951):653; 59 (1953):596.

11. SWW1:667.

12. SWW1:181.

13. SWW1:201–2.

14. SWW4:549–50.

15. SWW3:671.

16. That the opposition could muster the same number of votes against him as against Pitt in a similar dark period in 1799 seemed more proof of a benign "interference," a "guiding hand." Others were willing to carry this kind of thinking further: Amery (1:394) regards even Churchill's 1915 fall as a good thing in the long run, and Lloyd George (quoted in Riddell, *War Diary,* p. 94) seems even to have predicted as much at that time. Cf. the young Churchill on C. J. Fox as an "agent of high purposes" (Randolph Churchill, *Companion Volume II,* Part 1: 460). For the rather eerie record of how from an early age Churchill (and others) was sure of his high destiny, see Randolph Churchill, *Winston S. Churchill I:* 271, 338–41, 373, 422, 445, 467, 494–96; Ian Hamilton, quoted in Higgins, *Dardenelles,* p. 205; Nicolson, "Portrait of Winston Churchill," p. 100; Bardens, p. 214; Cowles, pp. 83, 316–18; Somervell, p. 20; Amery 3: 372–75, 399–400. See also n. 22 of Chapter 1, above.

17. SWW4:90.

18. SWW2:369.

19. See *Illustrated Sunday Herald,* 9 November 1919, p. 5. On Churchill, Wavell, and Auchinleck, see Higgins, *Winston Churchill and the Second Front* (New York: Oxford University Press, 1957), p. 50; Bryant, *Turn,* pp. 137, 199, 271–72, 308, 357, 388, 411–12; Bryant, *Triumph in the West* (Garden City, N.Y.: Doubleday & Co., 1959), p. 226; Taylor, *English History,* pp. 523–28, 541, 557; Wheeler-Bennett, p. 62; Moran, pp. 114, 721, 765; Plumb, "The Historian," p. 166; Barnett, *Britain and Her Army,* pp. 443, 451–52; Barnett, *The Desert Generals* (New York: Viking Press, 1961), pp. 67–74, 153–67, 174, 209, 215, 223–30; Thomson, pp. 216–17; Ashley, *Churchill as Historian,* pp. 174, 185–88, 198, 202. Moran thinks

it a comment on Churchill that he was unable to work with three highly intelligent soldiers, Wavell, Dill, Auchinleck. Nor would one know from *The Second World War* that Churchill was reluctant to have Montgomery command the Eighth Army or, later, receive a prize.

20. On the bomber offensive, see Liddell Hart, "Churchill in War," p. 18; Liddell Hart, "The Military Strategist," p. 209; Taylor, *English History*, pp. 390–92, 515–20, 541, 552, 558, 571, 592; Taylor, "The Statesman," p. 49; Moran, p. 82; Wheeler-Bennett, pp. 86, 221, 282; Gardner, pp. 87, 95, 168, 198, 219–21, 236; James, *Study in Failure*, pp. 235–40; Bryant, *Turn*, pp. 169, 311, 485; Higgins, *Second Front*, pp. 31, 49, 190–91; Higgins, *Dardanelles*, p. 254; Thomson, p. 206; Gretton, pp. 292–97; Ashley, *Churchill as Historian*, pp. 196–97; Nicolson, *Diaries* 2: 121–22, 171, 225; 3:52. Cf. Gilbert, *Winston S. Churchill*, p. 91. For the scope of this "disastrous flop," see R. Clairborne, *New York Times Book Review*, 26 December 1971, pp. 2–3. Should there be any remaining doubts as to the impotence of bomber offensives, the Vietnam War has disposed of these.

21. For some of his archaic views, see *Collier's*, 30 July 1938, p. 102, and 7 October 1939, p. 12; *Empire Review* (July 1923):691–98; Randolph Churchill, *Companion Volume II*, Part 3: 1912; Blunt 2:400; Amery 2:201; Wheeler-Bennett, pp. 100, 276. Some of Churchill's inferences from the Spanish Civil War may be found in ST 218.

On the general question of Churchill's views on weaponry, see Liddell Hart, "Churchill in War," pp. 15–16; Liddell Hart, "The Military Strategist," pp. 198, 200, 203–6; James, *Study in Failure*, pp. 235–40, 253; Thomson, p. 173; Ian Jacob, in *Churchill By His Contemporaries*, p. 66; Gretton, pp. 248, 271, 298; Moran, p. 37; Hamilton, p. 404; Bryant, *Turn*, p. 219; Taylor, *English History*, p. 231; Taylor, "The Statesman," p. 40; Wheeler-Bennett, pp. 200–203; Gardner, pp. 113, 116, 132, 138. Taylor, however, finds Churchill's crippling of the air force in the 1920s to be a long-range blessing, in that by waiting the longest, Britain obtained the most advanced fighter planes in 1940–42.

22. For the theory that the strategy of Marlborough and of Chatham vindicated Churchill on Gallipoli and led to the "soft underbelly" strategy, see *The "World Crisis": A Criticism*, pp. 84 ff; Gretton, p. 246; Thomson, p. 131. See also Randolph Churchill, *Companion Volume II*, Part 2: 997, 1494; Part 3: 1513, 1549, 1578, 1593, 1779–80; Esher 3: 98, 101.

23. Historians (Barnett, *Desert*, pp. 225, 255–56, 274; Bryant, *Triumph*, p. 48; Taylor, "The Statesman," p. 55) believe that the famous battle of El Alamein was a political ploy.

24. This discussion of the second front is based on Gardner, pp. 222*n*, 227; Cowles, p. 341; Higgins, *Second Front*, pp. vii–viii, 30, 51, 62–66, 85–93, 125–27, 135, 151–66, 180–214; Higgins, *Soft Underbelly* (New York: Macmillan Co., 1968), pp. 34, 124, 131, 215–22; Ashley, *Churchill as Historian*, p. 195; Wilmot, pp. 64, 130, 452, 543; Thomson, pp. 49, 74, 89–90, 165, 219, 233–34; Barnett, *Britain and Her Army*, pp. 425–26, 439; Liddell Hart, "Churchill in War," pp. 19–21; Liddell Hart, "The Military Strategist," pp. 214–18; Taylor, "The Statesman," pp. 48–52; Taylor, *English History*, pp. 460, 515, 520–22, 556–63, 573–78, 638; Bryant, *Turn*, pp. 288, 344*n*, 432, 451–58, 507, 520–28, 553, 560, 573, 595; Bryant, *Triumph*, pp. 34, 129, 150; Rowse, in Eade, p. 496; Michael Howard, *The Mediterranean Strategy in the Second World War* (New York: Frederick A. Praeger, 1968), pp. 31, 34, 46, 56–57, 69–70; Robert E. Sherwood, *Roosevelt and Hopkins* (New York: Harper, 1950), pp. 239, 591, 765–88; Moran, pp. 49, 187. Cf. Earl of Birkenhead, *Halifax* (London: Hamish Hamilton, 1965), p. 459; Gilbert, *Winston S. Churchill*, pp. 274, 296, 324.

25. SWW1:260.

26. SWW1:314.

27. SWW3:545.

28. Cf. Liddell Hart, "Churchill in War," p. 18; Higgins, *Second Front*, pp. 20–21; Taylor, *Origins*, pp. 71, 238; Taylor, *English History*, p. 532*n*; Gardner, pp. 90, 272; Nicolson, *Diaries* 3:51–52.

29. SWW6:296.
30. SWW6:667.
31. To Hans Morgenthau, in *World Politics* 7 (January 1955):290–91, Churchill's strength lay precisely in his seeing that World War II was part of a political continuum. Cf. Denis Brogan, *Spectator,* 4 July 1958, p. 27.
32. On these ironies see Greenberg, p. 203; Randolph Churchill, *Companion Volume II,* Part 1: 86; Riddell, *War Diary,* p. 303; Falls, "Sir Winston in War," pp. 24–26; Petrie, pp. 64–66; Cowles, pp. 337–48; Liddell Hart, "The Military Strategist," pp. 219, 221, 225; Wilmot, pp. 122–23, 142; Taylor, *English History,* pp. 475, 529; Taylor, "The Statesman," p. 55; Thomson, pp. 234–35; O'Brien, p. 50; Charles de Gaulle, *Complete War Memoirs,* trans. J. Griffin and R. Howard (New York: Simon and Schuster, 1968), p. 233.
33. Attlee, in *Churchill by His Contemporaries,* p. 19; Taylor, "The Statesman," p. 42. Cf. Gilbert, *Winston S. Churchill,* pp. 284–85, 492.
34. The command structure, Churchill's relations with the military, and his strategic blinders are discussed in Cowles, pp. 307, 317–24; Petrie, p. 57; Gretton, pp. 160, 240–41, 266, 286; Jacob, in *Churchill by His Contemporaries,* p. 70; Barnett, *Britain and Her Army,* pp. 433, 442; Barnett, *Desert,* pp. 214, 222; Higgins, *Second Front,* pp. 38, 53, 192, 210; Taylor, *English History,* pp. 479–81, 541; Taylor, "The Statesman," pp. 41–43, 50; Wilmot, pp. 131, 633–46; Wheeler-Bennett, pp. 20, 27, 113–17, 150, 198–200, 259; Amery 2: 123; Amery in Marchant, p. 64; Falls, "Sir Winston in War," pp. 25–26; John Ehrman, "Lloyd George and Churchill as War Ministers," *Transactions of the Royal Historical Society,* 5th series, vol. 2. (London: 1961), pp. 109–10; de Mendelssohn, pp. 554–55; Hyam, pp. 495–96; Moran, pp. 259–61, 314, 745, 759, 767, 834; Hamilton, p. 405; Nicolson, *Diaries* 2: 74, 135, 153–61; Thomson, pp. 92, 111, 232–33; Esher 3: 212; 4: 120; Gardner, pp. 49, 75, 117, 128, 134, 150–51, 157, 180, 194, 215–16, 227, 302, 313; General Montgomery, in Gilbert, *Churchill,* p. 133; Bryant, *Turn,* pp. 9–15, 222–23, 239, 246n, 257, 274, 334–35, 360–73, 470, 500, 513, 540, 560, 583, 591; Bryant, *Triumph,* pp. 7, 22–23, 98–99, 105, 118–24, 204–8, 266, 356n; Liddell Hart, "Churchill in War," pp. 21–22; Liddell Hart, "The Military Strategist," pp. 202, 219–24; Ashley, *Churchill as Historian,* p. 172; Lloyd, p. 254. For an interesting example of Churchill's pulling in his horns, see Gretton, p. 263, but Bryant (*Turn,* pp. 274–75) suggests that Churchill's "senseless" desire to return to Norway did keep Hitler worried.
35. SWW2:100.
36. The last few paragraphs are based in part on Taylor, "The Statesman," pp. 36, 54, 59; Taylor, *English History,* pp. 482, 494, 526, 585; Nicolson, *Diaries* 2: 101, 244; Liddell Hart, "Churchill in War," pp. 16–19; Liddell Hart, "The Military Strategist," pp. 208–17; Moran, pp. 107n, 720, 834–36; Gardner, pp. xv, 48, 96, 137, 188, 191–92, 207, 221, 226, 236, 248, 291, 347; Gretton, pp. 84, 225–26, 263–66, 296, 301–2, 318; Falls, "Sir Winston in War," pp. 24–25; Thomson, pp. 65, 104–11, 221–35; Bryant, *Triumph,* p. 23; Wilmot, p. 65; Wheeler-Bennett, p. 149; Snow, p. 167; Rowse, *The Churchills,* 381; Bardens, p. 225. Aneurin Bevan (in *Churchill by His Contemporaries,* pp. 59, 63), by contrast, believes that Churchill expressed not what Britain felt but what he thought it should feel in such circumstances.
37. Nicolson, *Diaries* 2: 101, 176, 187; Thomson, pp. 98, 147–49, 187, 212–13, 222, 228–30.
38. *Sunday Pictorial,* 10 June 1917, p. 5; Nicolson *Diaries* 2: 99, 102, 130, 139, 143, 237n, 274, 281–82; Thomson, pp. 78–79; Greenberg, p. 203; Attlee, in *Churchill by His Contemporaries,* pp. 11, 27, 32; Taylor, "The Statesman," pp. 36, 41, 56–57; Taylor, *English History,* p. 567; Gardner, pp. 214, 221, 237, 243; James, "The Politician," pp. 123, 127; Lloyd, p. 257; Dedijer, p. 556. In World War I he also became evasive about war aims; see Gilbert, *Winston S. Churchill,* pp. 202, 321.
39. On the reasons for Churchill's defeat, see Thomson, pp. 79, 113, 150; Nicolson, *Diaries* 2: 103n, 114, 332, 346, 381, 473–75; 3: 33; O'Brien, p. 40; Gardner, pp. xiv, 86, 296,

310; James, "The Politician," pp. 123, 127; Taylor, "The Statesman," p. 22; Taylor, *English History,* pp. 467, 477, 598; Amery, 2: 299, 504; Berlin, p. 25; de Mendelssohn, p. 398; Winterton, "Sir Winston Churchill in Parliament," in Ingram, p. 9; Cowles, pp. 353–54; de Gaulle, pp. 899–900; Greenberg, p. 205; Lloyd, pp. 257, 266–67. Cf. Petrie, p. 60; Riddell, *Intimate Diary,* p. 15; *Weekly Dispatch,* 29 June 1924.

40. SWW5:624.

41. SWW5:142.

42. SWW6:123.

43. SWW2:333.

44. SWW6:395.

45. See Bryant, *Turn,* pp. 386–87; Bryant, *Triumph,* p. 335; Nicolson, *Diaries* 2:381; Wheeler-Bennett, p. 158; Moran, p. 185; Bardens, p. 68; Rowse, "Historian," p. 83; de Mendelssohn, pp. 107, 576; Asquith, 2:71; Gretton, p. 75; Randolph Churchill, *Winston S. Churchill II:* 688; Gilbert, *Winston S. Churchill,* p. 745.

46. SWW6:280.

47. SWW3:606, 608.

48. SWW4:663, 666, 703.

49. SWW6:270.

50. SWW5:628.

51. So would he in 1950 criticize Attlee for having allowed five years to pass without a visit to Washington and so had he urged Lloyd George to go to a newly belligerent U.S. in July 1917 to confer with Wilson (see Riddell, *War Diary,* p. 259), and a few months earlier he wrote that to have the chief Allied war leaders in continual consultation would be worth a million soldiers a year (see *London Magazine* [February 1917], pp. 653–60). For even earlier manifestations of his faith in personal diplomacy, see Randolph Churchill, *Companion Volume II,* Part 1: 626; Part 2: 754, 766, 839, 935. Neville Chamberlain, curiously enough, shared this faith: see Birkenhead, p. 365; cf. Nicolson, *Diaries* 3: 381.

52. As Taylor concedes, Churchill, having by 1942 finished his job of saving Britain, found a new role as a diplomat holding the Grand Alliance together—though sometimes Churchill complained that the alliance, with Russia at one end and America at the other, was too cumbersome a machine to run a war with. Even in the postwar years, Eisenhower had no objection to Churchill's making a "solitary pilgrimage" to Moscow. See Nicolson, *Diaries* 2: 422; Gardner, pp. 199, 213; Moran, pp. 611, 767; Taylor, *English History,* pp. 536, 557; Ehrman, pp. 112–13; Rowse, "English History," p. 5; Wheeler-Bennett, p. 204; Bryant, *Turn,* p. 410.

53. SWW4:702–4.

54. SWW4:816.

55. O:32.

56. SWW5:478.

57. SWW2:153.

58. SWW4:475.

59. This scene reveals another secret of his personal diplomacy: his use of homely illustrations. "I have often tried to set down the strategic truths I have comprehended in the form of simple anecdotes" (SWW4:312), especially to cross the language barriers. When not drawing crocodile bellies or moving matchsticks about on a table, Churchill writes numbers on a slip of paper to symbolize the "spheres of influence" to be carved out in postwar Eastern Europe.

60. But not everyone agrees that this visit was a success; see Thomson, p. 226.

61. Others, unfortified by either Churchill's philosophy or gregariousness, found the talk

and toasts boring, repetitious, and hypocritical; see Brooke's diaries in Bryant, *Triumph*, passim.

62. SWW4:459.

63. SWW4:496.

64. It is undeniable that he had met all the prominent politicians of the western world during the past half-century, that to influence Roosevelt he made himself into a new man, self-disciplined and taciturn, and that in place of a formal Anglo–American alliance, there was the unparalleled personal relationship of Roosevelt and Churchill. See Taylor, "The Statesman," pp. 20, 39, 56; Taylor, *English History*, pp. 537, 588; Hamilton, pp. 408–9; Birkenhead, p. 474; Moran, pp. 21, 67, 143, 204, 217, 221, 241, 244, 250, 292, 322, 370–71.

65. See Moran, pp. 71, 111, 229, 256, 294–96, 623, 632, 742; Birkenhead, pp. 534–35; Taylor, *English History*, pp. 557, 566, 585. For Churchill's affection or awe for the men he dealt with and his faith in his ability to influence them, see Gardner, p. 248, 260; Moran, p. 447; Taylor, *English History*, p. 588; Bryant, *Turn*, pp. 373–74, 382. Thomson (p. 234) is one of the few who believe him to have in fact imposed his will on nearly everyone, while Petrie (p. 64) singles out his influence on Roosevelt. Already in World War I one can see the advantages and the more numerous disadvantages of Churchill's personal diplomacy: See Gilbert, *Winston S. Churchill*, pp. 74, 90–92, 165–67, 187, 425.

66. SWW6:65.

67. SWW6:674, 603.

68. SWW4:489.

69. SWW6:511.

70. SWW6:237–38.

71. SWW3:581.

72. SWW4:640; 6:186.

73. SWW3:654.

74. SWW2:622.

75. SWW3:370.

76. SWW5:627.

77. SWW3:722.

78. SWW2:699.

79. SWW2:279, 345.

80. SWW6:19.

81. SWW3:432. The *TLS*, 3 August 1951, pp. 477–78, observes that SWW4 reads like a picaresque novel, the narrator being a triumphant leader who, with boyish zest and romanticism, realizes the daydreams found in all adventure books. Acquaintances at the time remarked that Churchill had not seemed so fit in the previous twenty years, that "being P.M. and a historic figure" rejuvenated him, that "his responsibility seems to have given him a new lease on life." See Nicolson, *Diaries* 2:103, 186; Cowles, p. 324.

82. SWW4:67.

83. SWW3:611.

84. SWW6:631.

85. For this question and for numerous deleted, distorted, or misunderstood facts, see James, *Study in Failure*, pp. 175, 188–89, 221–22, 268–69, 341; Taylor, "The Statesman," pp. 43–44; Taylor, *English History*, pp. 455, 472n, 474, 636; Moran, pp. 195–96, 293n, 346–47, 443; Bryant, *Triumph*, p. 124; Gardner, pp. 218, 225–27, 244, 258, 263, 270, 273, 287; Cowles, p. 332; Thomson, p. 90; Ashley, *Churchill as Historian*, pp. 171–77, 189–90, 207–8; Plumb, "The Historian," pp. 164–65; Stewart, p. 126; Hamilton, p. 403; Higgins, *Second Front*, p. 173; Connell, p. 36; Liddell Hart, "The Military Strategist," p. 206; Slosson, in *American*

Historical Review (1949): 859; Petrie, p. 62; Nicolson, *Diaries* 3: 163–64; Hall, p. 358; Amery, 3: 371.

86. Whittemore, pp. 63–67. Cf. Hamilton, in *South Atlantic Quarterly* 1 (1949):133; Thomson, pp. 117, 165; Liddell Hart, "The Military Strategist," p. 219; Gardner, p. xiii; Plumb, "The Historian," p. 166. Greenberg (p. 200) remarks on the outmoded eloquent style as matching the antique vision.

87. SWW6:288.

88. SWW5:382.

89. SWW3:695.

90. SWW4:220.

91. Muggeridge, pp. 348–51.

Chapter 6

1. For his qualities as leader of the opposition and as conservative prime minister, see *Churchill by His Contemporaries,* pp. 34, 62; R. H. S. Crossman, *The Charm of Politics* (London: Hamish Hamilton, 1958), pp. 18–19; Nicolson, *Diaries* 3: 79, 114; Winterton, pp. 9, 12; Cowles, pp. 359–60, 369–70; Bardens, p. 357; Moran, pp. 673–74; Gardner, p. 86; James "The Politician," pp. 122–27; Eade, pp. 385–87; Wheeler-Bennett, p. 37; Lloyd, pp. 335, 348.

2. SP 46.

3. EU 99.

4. Churchill's very first publication, and 1894 letter to a newspaper, attacked temperance ladies for trying to bring forth by laws and coercion what can only be done with education, moderation, and evolution. Cf. also his remark in 1908 that nature deals in greys and smudges lines, although at this early time he could also express a taste for symmetry, clairty, logic rather than "something fading into something else"; see Randolph Churchill, *Companion Volume I,* Part 1: 526–27; *Companion Volume II,* Part 2: 782, 969; de Mendelssohn, p. 229; Hyam, p. 341.

5. See de Mendelssohn, pp. 362–65, 398–99, 435; Stewart, p. 155; Bardens, pp. 315, 327; Winterton, p. 9; Cowles, pp. 357–63.

6. UA 111.

7. Moran's diary is filled with signs of yet another major change in Churchill's attitude to Soviet Russia. He holds on to office in old age because of his certitude that he alone can, in the teeth of rabid American anticommunism as well as the skepticism of State Department and Foreign Office, reconcile East and West by means of a "solitary pilgrimage" to Moscow, where his charm, personal diplomacy, and World War II fame would bestir the new rulers. Only then could he retire, having rounded out his career in war and peace with a final triumph as a peacemaker. The day even came in 1954 when he had to reply heatedly to an American suggestion that British policy towards Russia was one of appeasement. See Moran, pp. 436–674; Wheeler-Bennett, pp. 42, 126–33; Cowles, pp. 364–71; Petrie, p. 68; Bardens, p. 352.

8. EU 468.

9. IT 44.

10. EU 138.

11. UA 100.

12. UA 78.

13. *The Listener,* 21 November 1934, p. 841; *Collier's,* 29 June 1935, p. 49. And as early as 1947 (*Collier's,* 4 January, p. 11) he asserted that the atom bomb is a guarantee of peace, shocking though that may be to those born in the nineteenth century.

14. IT 251.

15. UA 141.

16. UA 230.

17. SP 122–23.

18. STT 135.

19. UA 327.

20. UA 329–30.

21. EP 1016.

22. For poignant information on the aging Churchill working with difficulty in 1955–57 on the last major goal of his life, revising and publishing the *History,* see Deakin, p. 14; Ashley, *Churchill as Historian,* p. 212; Rowse, "Historian," p. 83; Moran, pp. 488, 618, 691–711, 727.

23. That a Teutonic people like the British, with its English language and King James Bible, was specially chosen was a motif of the New England historians; see David Levin, *History as Romantic Art* (1959; reprint New York: Harcourt Brace, 1963), pp. 79–82. Cf. de Gaulle on France (Hoffman, p. 27).

24. ESP 2:294.

25. See David Harris, in *American Historical Review* 64 (1968):71–72; Commager, preface to abridged edition of the *History* (New York: Dodd, Mead, & Co., 1965), pp. v–vi; Deakin, p. 14; Connell, pp. 38–39.

26. This analysis approximates that of Stubbs. See *William Stubbs on The English Constitution,* ed. N. F. Cantor (New York: Crowell, 1966), p. 201.

27. Gordon K. Lewis, "Mr. Churchill as Historian," *The Historian* 20 (August 1958):395, 410, 413. For an excellent synopsis of the "Whig myth" which, as a creed of Churchill's, aided his wartime statesmanship, inspired his oratory, and crippled his historical writings, see Plumb, "The Historian," pp. 133–37, 152–55; cf. Rowse, "Historian," pp. 86–87; Ashley, *Churchill as Historian,* p. 216.

28. Lewis, pp. 397–99, 402–3; cf. Cantor, introduction to *Stubbs,* p. 5.

29. ESP1:xvi.

30. ESP1:275.

31. ESP1:181.

32. ESP1:231.

33. ESP1:178.

34. ESP2:217.

35. ESP2:250.

36. See Wallace Notestein, in *American Historical Review* 62 (1956):94; Stubbs in Cantor, pp. 198–99, 216–31; cf. Hurwitz, pp. 306–7.

37. ESP1:xvii.

38. ESP3:103.

39. Lewis (pp. 393–95) comments on this oscillation in Churchill's thinking between Accident and Purpose. He also criticizes Churchill for regarding liberty as a conscious achievement of the British ruling class rather than as an accidental by-product, but Churchill in fact usually presents it as a by-product, a result to which all factions in all quarrels unconsciously contribute, not as anyone's conscious achievement.

40. ESP1:49.

41. ESP1:57.

42. For an extensive analysis (independent of Churchill's writings) of this paradoxical and painful principle, see my "Violence and Progress," *Centennial Review* 14 (Summer 1970):241–66.

43. ESP4:24.

44. ESP1:270.

45. ESP2:225.

46. ESP2:243.

47. ESP4:ix.

48. As Harris (p. 71) says, Churchill's allegiance to a quasi-Macaulayan sense of progress leaves him with no explanation for how the twentieth century crept in.

49. ESP3:231.

50. ESP1:156.

51. ESP2:207.

52. ESP2:151.

53. This species of determinism is common in nineteenth-century historiography; see for example Stubbs in Cantor, pp. 220, 228; Levin, p. 31. Cf. Hoffman (p. 30) on de Gaulle.

54. ESP1:76; 4:132.

55. Cowles, p. 108; *TLS,* 27 April 1956, p. 246; de Mendelssohn, p. x; cf. Rowse, "Historian," pp. 86–91; Plumb, "The Historian," p. 154; Lewis, p. 412.

56. See Lewis, pp. 392, 405–6.

57. ESP2:78–79.

58. ESP3:259. Contrast his sapient remark in 1906 that any intelligent community would rather govern itself ill than be well governed by someone else and that Britain has not an understanding of the Boers' problem; see Randolph Churchill, *Companion Volume II,* Part 1: 559, 567.

59. ESP4:116.

60. Randolph Churchill, *Companion Volume II,* Part 1:111.

61. ESP4:209.

62. ESP1:46.

63. ESP1:224.

64. ESP1:44.

65. Lewis, p. 409; *TLS,* 27 April 1956, p. 245; Deakin, p. 14; James, *Study in Failure,* p. 309. Cf. Stubbs in Cantor, pp. 232–33; Levin, pp. 188–89.

66. See Lewis, pp. 395, 403–5; Ashley, *Churchill as Historian,* pp. 210, 219–23; Rowse, "Historian," pp. 85, 88–90; H. C. Allen, in *English Historical Review* 74 (1959):307–8.

67. See Lewis, pp. 392–96, 407, 412–13; Richard Pares, in *English Historical Reivew* 73 (1958):498–99; Rowse, "Historian," pp. 85–91; Allen, p. 308; Plumb, "The Historian," p. 154; Ashley, *Churchill as Historian,* p. 211.

68. This paragraph is a paraphrase of Lewis, pp. 395–99, 410–11; John Cairns, "Clio and the Queen's First Minister," *South Atlantic Quarterly* 52 (1953):515; Hamilton, p. 401; *TLS,* 30 November 1956, p. 705; Noel Annan, in *New York Review,* (10 July 1969), pp. 30–31.

69. Rowse, "Historian," p. 86; Plumb, "The Historian," pp. 154–55; Pares, p. 497; Lewis, pp. 392–93, 410; *TLS,* 18 October 1957, p. 619; Harris, p. 71.

70. Lewis, pp. 392, 395–97, 406, 413.

71. Plumb, "The Historian," pp. 152–53; Lewis, pp. 390–91, 396–97, 408; Allen, p. 309; James, *Study in Failure,* p. 312; Graubard, p. 245; Ashley, *Churchill as Historian,* p. 215; Cantor, p. 11; Notestein, p. 94.

72. Allen, p. 310; Plumb, "The Historian," p. 153; Lewis, pp. 396–97, 401; Ashley, *Churchill as Historian,* p. 220; Notestein, pp. 93–95; Lewis, pp. 396–97.

73. ESP4:286.

74. Allen, p. 308. According to Moran (p. 744), however, the work stops with the Victorians because Churchill thought the twentieth century too dreary to write about. Cf., incidentally, Shakespeare's cycle of chronicle plays, which, after covering a span of 130 years, ends with *Henry VIII,* celebrating the birth of the queen under whom the playwright began his career.

Conclusion

1. Liddell Hart in "The Military Strategist," p. 202.

2. Lewis, p. 412; Higgins, *Second Front,* pp. 136, 195; Gilbert, *Winston S. Churchill,* p. 816.

3. *Sunday Telegraph,* 30 January 1966, pp. 4–5; Cowles, p. 3; Winterton, in *Churchill By His Contemporaries,* pp. 44–45. The idea for this fantasy grew out of Churchill's recurring nonfictional preoccupation with the hypothetical; cf., for example, "If We Could Look Into the Future!" in *Weekly Dispatch,* 21 September 1924, p. 8, and the challenging "If Lee Had Not Won the Battle of Gettysburg," in *Scribner's Magazine* 88 (December 1930):587–97.

4. James, *Study in Failure,* p. 309; Deakin, p. 14.

5. On the idea that some of Churchill's chronic weaknesses proved to be his strengths in 1940, see Liddell Hart, "Churchill in War," p. 16; Storr, pp. 250, 271–74; Snow, p. 168; de Mendelssohn, p. 14; Gilbert, *Churchill,* p. 65. Plumb, "The Historian," p. 133; Rowse, *The Churchills,* p. 378; Jones, pp. 34, 37; Crossman, pp. 17–18; Attlee, in *Churchill by His Contemporaries,* pp. 11–12; Harry W. Porter, "Churchill and the Empire," *South Atlantic Quarterly* 51 (1952):230; Moran, pp. 10, 348, 745–46, 760, 766, 773, 827–32; Graubard, p. 245; Taylor, "The Statesman," p. 58; James, *Study in Failure,* p. 349; James, "The Politician," pp. 120–22, 128; Greenberg, p. 204; *London Times,* 28 July 1964, editorial; Hurwitz, pp. 306–7.

6. On the man and the hour, see Moran, pp. 113, 826–27; Stewart, p. 145; Petrie, p. 62; Marder, 1:404; Wheeler-Bennett, pp. 12, 24, 38–40, 155; Gilbert, *Churchill,* p. 125; Gilbert, *Winston S. Churchill,* p. 823; Plumb, "The Historian," pp. 137–38, 165; James, *Study in Failure,* p. 316; James, "The Politician," p. 122; Gardner, pp. 39, 95; Rowse, *The Churchills,* pp. 400–401; Rowse, in Eade, pp. 506–7; Rowse, "Mr. Churchill and English History," pp. 1, 19; Berlin, p. 26; Connell, p. 11; Scott, p. 82; Nicolson, *Diaries* 2:142; Nicolson, "Portrait of Winston Churchill," p. 98; Nicolson in Gilbert, *Churchill,* p. 125; Bardens, pp. 112, 214; Liddell Hart, in *English Review* (December 1934):708; Lewis, p. 402; Somervell, pp. 1, 13, 20; Taylor, *English History,* pp. 4*n,* 475; Higgins, *Second Front,* p. vii; Cowles, p. 229, 257; Esher, 4:121; Amery, 2:80; 3:372; Snow, pp. 155, 163; Howarth, p. 554; Lucy Masterman, in *History Today* 14 (1964):744; *London Times,* 28 July 1964, editorial; Attleee, in *Churchill by His Contemporaries,* p. 35; de Mendelssohn, pp. 84, 555; Hyam, p. 357.

7. Gardner, pp. xvi, 194, 206; Gilbert, *Winston S. Churchill,* p. 362; Nicolson, *Diaries* 3: 112; Connell, p. 12; de Mendelssohn, p. 364; Rowse, *The Churchills,* p. 361; Bevan, in *Churchill By His Contemporaries,* pp. 60–63.

8. For the role of family tradition and history in Churchill's career, see Allen, p. 307; *Collier's,* 20 May 1917; Rowse, "Historian," p. 92; Commager, *Marlborough,* pp. xix, xxxii; Lewis, p. 388; Plumb, "The Historian," pp. 138, 141–42, 155–56, 166–69; de Mendelssohn, pp. 102, 208; Hurwitz, pp. 315, 321–22; Hamilton, pp. 400–401; Cairns, pp. 511–12; Moran, pp. 320, 462; Gilbert, p. 173; Attlee in *Churchill by His Contemporaries,* pp. 20–22; Samuel Eliot Morison, in *Saturday Review* 36 (31 October 1953):23.

9. Hyam, p. 191; de Mendelssohn, p. 346; Taylor, *Origins,* p. 292; Cairns, pp. 512–14. So did his social reforms lead to a bureaucracy he detested; the tank which helped the Allies win in 1918 nearly destroyed them in 1940; his war leadership led to Britain's displacement by the U.S. and Russia, and to the substitution of Soviet totalitarianism in Eastern Europe for Nazi totalitarianism.

10. The three phases Commager discerns in the writing career nearly parallel the three (of fifteen, twenty-five, and fifteen years) James finds in the political career. In the first fifteen years, Churchill established himself as a rising and successful if controversial politician, and then the very traits which made him rise led to the quarter-century of limited achievement and frequent failure; this was capped by the fifteen years in which he was *the* towering personage in British politics. See Commager, *Marlborough,* pp. xxv–xxviii;

James, *Study in Failure,* p. 345; Plumb, "The Historian," pp. 135–37, 145, 156–60; Ashley, *Churchill as Historian,* pp. 12–16, 228–31; Cowles, p. 16; Lewis, pp. 390, 408–9; Barbour, p. 887; Deakin, pp. 1, 8, 11, 14, 18–19; Moran, p. 819; Morison, p. 22; Crutwell, p. 547*n*; Hurwitz, pp. 314–15, 322–24.

11. Moran, p. 830; Guedella, p. 251; Commager, *Marlborough,* p. xxv; Plumb, "Churchill the Historian," *Spectator,* 1 July 1966, p. 10; Berlin, p. 16; James, *Study in Failure,* pp. 312, 345–46; de Mendelssohn, pp. 398–99; Hyam, p. 58; Storr, p. 259; Cowles, pp. 74–84, 92.

12. Snow, p. 170; Commager, *History,* p. vi; Commager, *Marlborough,* pp. xxv–xxviii; Rowse, "Historian," pp. 82–83, 91; Nicolson, in Gilbert, *Churchill,* p. 124; James, *Study in Failure,* pp. 25–28, 310, 313; Berlin, pp. 8–13; Greenberg, p. 200; Bevan, p. 60; Cowles, p. 74; Graubard, p. 15; Lewis, p. 407; O'Brien, pp. 30, 56; Hyam, p. 497; Plumb, "The Historian," pp. 144, 160; Ashley, *Churchill as Historian,* pp. 175, 207; Coote, in Eade, p. 180; Howarth, pp. 550, 555–57; Paço d'Arcos, p. 22; Connell, p. 10; de Mendelssohn, p. 104; Storr, pp. 265–68. Cf., on Prescott, Levin, p. 178.

13. Guedella, pp. 107, 247; Plumb, "The Historian," p. 145; James, *Study in Failure,* pp. 185, 309, 313; Somervell, p. 3; Ashley, *Churchill as Historian,* p. 157; Commager, *Marlborough,* pp. xx, xxxi; Rowse, "Historian," p. 79. De Mendelssohn (p. 300) awards joint honors to the *Randolph* and the *Marlborough.*

14. Commager, *Marlborough,* p. xxii; Commager, *History,* p. vi; Graubard, p. 245; James, *Study in Failure,* pp. 279, 312; Moran, pp. 198, 324; Lewis, pp. 393, 399, 402; Gilbert, *Churchill,* p. 28; Muggeridge, pp. 347–49; Pares, pp. 498–99; Plumb, "The Historian," pp. 152, 155; Cowles, pp. 4, 108, 275; Cairns, p. 507; Rowse, "Historian, " pp. 82, 85; Storr, p. 265; Berlin, pp. 12–13, 21, 24–25, 28; Brown and Birkett, in Eade, pp. 8, 331, 341, 458; Petrie, p. 62.

15. For Churchill's favoring in his writing the concrete, pictorial, dramatic, egocentric, current at the expense of the speculative, theoretical, timeless, see de Mendelssohn, pp. 101, 591, and Lewis, p. 408. For the idea that his egocentricity and his consequent lack of interest in people and weak grasp of psychology would have handicapped his work as a reporter or novelist, see Coote, in Eade, p. 182, and Storr, p. 265.

16. Clinton P. Rossiter, "Conservatism," *Encyclopedia of the Social Sciences* (New York: Macmillan Co., 1968) 3: 293. A literary rather than ideological interpretation would consider Churchill to be in the line of the nineteenth-century "literary" historians, who stressed the importance of experience (soldiers on front lines, they said, in tones familiar to a reader of Churchill, know more of war than do comfortable statesmen). They cleaved to romantic literary conventions and methods, and, setting themselves against the theological argument or metaphysical speculation of the "philosophical" historians, wanted to write an interesting narrative on a "grand theme"—like the origins of a nation or the progress and invincibility of liberty (again familiar ideas!)—containing heroic characters who embody the personality of a people; see Levin, pp. 9–11, 38, 45, 49, 229–30.

Bibliography

The definitive listing of Churchill's writings, as well as of books on Churchill, is Frederick Woods's massive *Bibliography of the Works of Sir Winston Churchill,* 2d ed. (Toronto: University of Toronto Press, 1969). An annotated list of books and articles on the subject of this study is my "Bibliography of Material on Churchill's Writings," in the December 1973 *Papers of the Bibliographical Society of America.* The following is simply a list of all books and articles (exclusive of those by Churchill) referred to more than once in text and footnotes of this book. Those preceded by an asterisk were found to be signally helpful towards an understanding and evaluation of Churchill's writings.

Allen, H. C. Review of *A History of the English-Speaking Peoples. English Historical Review* 74 (1959):305–11.

Amery, L. S. *My Political Life.* 3 vols. London: Hutchinson & Co., 1953–55.

Annan, Noel. *New York Review of Books,* 10 July 1969, pp. 27–31.

Ashley, Maurice. *Marlborough.* New York: Macmillan Co., 1939.

*———. *Churchill As Historian.* New York: Charles Scribner's Sons, 1968.

Asquith, H. H. *Memories and Reflections 1852–1927.* 2 vols. Boston: Little, Brown, and Co., 1928.

Barnett, Correlli. *The Desert Generals.* New York: Viking Press, 1961.

———. *Britain and Her Army 1509–1970.* London: Allen Lane, 1970.

Barbour, Violet. Review of *Marlborough. American Historical Review* 41 (1936):332–34; 43 (1938):376–77; 44 (1939):886–87.

Bardens, Dennis. *Churchill in Parliament.* New York: A. S. Barnes, 1967.

Beaverbrook, Lord. *Politicians and the War, 1914–16.* Garden City, N.Y.: Doubleday & Co., 1928.

———. *Men and Power, 1917–18.* London: Hutchinson & Co., 1956.

*Berlin, Isaiah. *Mr. Churchill in 1940.* London: John Murray, 1949.

Birkenhead, Earl of. *Halifax.* London: Hamish Hamilton, 1965.

Blunt, W. S. *My Diaries 1888–1914.* 2 vols. New York: Alfred A. Knopf, 1921.

Bryant, Arthur. *The Turn of the Tide.* Garden City, N.Y.: Doubleday & Co., 1957.

———. *Triumph in the West.* Garden City, N.Y.: Doubleday & Co., 1959.

Burton, Ivor. *The Captain-General.* London: Constable and Co., 1968.

*Cairns, John. "Clio and the Queen's First Minister." *South Atlantic Quarterly* 52 (1953):505–20.

Cantor, N. F., ed. *William Stubbs on the English Constitution.* New York: Crowell, 1966.

Carter, Violet Bonham. *Churchill As I Knew Him.* London: Eyre & Spottiswoode, 1965.

Churchill, Randolph. *Winston S. Churchill. Volume I: Youth, 1874–1900.* Boston: Houghton Mifflin Co., 1966.

*———. *Winston S. Churchill. Companion Volume I, Parts 1 and 2.* Boston: Houghton Mifflin Co., 1967.

———. *Winston S. Churchill. Volume II: Young Statesman, 1901–1914.* Boston: Houghton Mifflin Co., 1967.

*———. *Winston S. Churchill. Companion Volume II, Parts 1, 2, 3.* Boston: Houghton Mifflin Co., 1969.

Churchill by His Contemporaries. London: Hodder & Stoughton, 1965.

*Churchill Revised. New York: Dial Press, 1969.

*Commager, Henry Steele. Preface to *Marlborough.* New York: Charles Scribner's Sons, 1968.

———. Preface to *A History of the English-Speaking Peoples.* New York: Dodd, Mead & Co., 1965.

Connell, John. *Winston Churchill.* Writers and Their Work, no. 80. London: Longmans, Green and Co., 1956.

Cowles, Virginia. *Churchill.* New York: Harper, 1953.

Crossman, R. H. S. *The Charm of Politics.* London: Hamish Hamilton, 1958.

Cruttwell, C. R. M. F. *A History of the Great War.* London: Oxford University Press, 1934.

Davis, R. H. *Real Soldiers of Fortune.* New York: Collier, 1906.

Deakin, F. W. "Churchill the Historian." *Schweitzer Monatshefte* (1969–70).

Dedijer, Vladimir. *TLS,* 30 May 1968, p. 555–56.

Eade, Charles, ed. *Churchill By His Contemporaries.* London: Hutchinson & Co., 1953.

Earle, E. M., ed. *Makers of Modern Strategy.* Princeton: Princeton University Press, 1943.

Ehrman, John. "Lloyd George and Churchill as War Ministers." In *Transactions of the Royal Historical Society.* 5th ser., Vol. 2. London: 1961.

Esher, Reginald Viscount. *Journals and Letters,* ed. M. V. Brett. 4 vols. London: Ivor Nicholson and Watson, 1934–38.

Falls, Cyril. *The Great War 1914–18.* New York: Capricorn Books, 1959.

———. "Sir Winston Churchill in War." In *Illustrated London News Eightieth Year Tribute to Winston Churchill,* edited by Bruce Ingram. Pp. 15–27. (London: 1954).

*Gardner, Brian. *Churchill In His Time.* London: Methuen & Co., 1968.

Garvin, J. L. "Mr. Churchill and the War of Empires." *The Empire Review* 37 (May 1923):423–41.

de Gaulle, Charles. *Complete War Memoirs.* Translated by J. Griffin and R. Howard. New York: Simon and Schuster, 1968.

*Gilbert, Martin, ed. *Churchill.* Great Lives Observed Series. Englewood Cliffs, N.J.: Prentice-Hall, 1967.

———. *Winston S. Churchill. Volume III: 1914–16.* Boston: Houghton Mifflin Co., 1971.

Graubard, Stephen R. *Burke, Disraeli, and Churchill.* Cambridge, Mass.: Harvard University Press, 1961.

Greenberg, Martin. "Winston Churchill, Tory Democrat." *Partisan Review* 18 (1951):193–205.

Gretton, Vice Admiral Sir Peter. *Winston Churchill and the Royal Navy.* New York: Coward-McCann, 1968.

Guedella, Phillip. *Mr. Churchill.* New York: Reynal and Hitchcock, 1942.

Hall, W. P. Review of *The Second World War. Journal of Modern History* 21 (1949):357–59.

Hamilton, W. B. Review of *The Second World War. South Atlantic Quarterly* 48(1949):133; 50(1951):399–411.

Harris, D. Review of *A History of the English-Speaking Peoples. American Historical Review* 64 (1958):71–72.

Higgins, Trumbull. *Winston Churchill and the Second Front.* New York: Oxford University Press, 1957.

———. *Winston Churchill and the Dardanelles.* New York: Macmillan Co., 1963.

———. *Soft Underbelly.* New York: Macmillan Co., 1968.

Hoffman, Stanley. "De Gaulle Redux." *New York Review of Books,* 24 February 1972, pp. 23–30.

*Howarth, Herbert. "Behind Churchill's Grand Style." *Commentary* 11 (1951):549–57.

*Hurwitz, Samuel J. "Winston S. Churchill." In *Some Modern Historians of Britain,* edited by H. Ausubel *et al.,* pp. 306–24. New York: Dryden Press, 1951.

Hyam, Ronald. *Elgin and Churchill at the Colonial Office 1905–1908.* London: Macmillan and Co., 1968.

Ingram, Bruce, ed. *Illustrated London News Eightieth Year Tribute to Winston Churchill.* London, 1954.

James, Robert Rhodes. *Lord Randolph Churchill.* New York: A. S. Barnes & Co., 1960.

————. *Gallipoli.* New York: Macmillan Co., 1965.

*————. "The Politician." In *Churchill Revised,* pp. 63–132. New York: Dial Press, 1969.

*————. *Churchill: A Study in Failure 1900–1939.* London: Weidenfeld and Nicolson, 1970.

Jenkins, Roy. *Asquith.* New York: Chilmark, 1964.

Joad, C. E. M. "Churchill the Philosopher." In *Churchill by His Contemporaries,* edited by Charles Eade, pp. 475–89. London: Hutchinson & Co., 1953.

Jones, D. A. N. *New York Review of Books,* 23 May 1968, pp. 33–37.

*Keynes, John Maynard. *Essays in Biography.* Edited by Geoffrey Keynes, pp. 53–67. New York: Horizon Press, 1951.

Leslie, Shane. "Winston: A Sketch." *Review of Reviews* 67 (May 1923):470–77.

Levin, David. *History As Romantic Art.* 1959. Reprint. New York: Harcourt, Brace, 1963.

*Lewis, Gordon K. "Mr. Churchill As Historian." *The Historian* 20 (August 1958):387–414.

Liddell Hart, B. H. Review of *Marlborough. English Review* (December 1934):702–9.

————. "Churchill in War." *Encounter* 26 (April 1966):14–22.

*————. "The Military Strategist." In *Churchill Revised,* pp. 173–228. New York: Dial Press, 1969.

Lloyd, T. O. *From Empire to Welfare State.* London: Oxford University Press, 1970.

Lloyd George, David. *War Memoirs.* 6 vols. Boston: Little, Brown and Co., 1933–37.

————. *The Truth about the Peace Treaties.* 2 vols. London: Victor Gollancz, 1938.

Lodge, Richard. Review of *Marlborough. English Historical Review* 49 (1934):715; 50 (1935):338–41.

*Magee, Bryan. "Churchill's Novel." *Encounter* 25 (October 1965):45–51.

Marchant, Sir James, ed. *Winston Spencer Churchill.* London: Cassell and Co., 1954.

Marder, A. J. *From the Dreadnought to Scapa Flow.* 5 vols. New York: Oxford University Press, 1961–70.

Marshall, Gen. S. L. A. *The American Heritage History of World War I.* New York: Dell Books, 1964.

Masterman, Lucy. *C. G. F. Masterman.* London: Frank Cass, 1968.

————. *History Today* 14 (1964):744–46, 823–27.

*de Mendelssohn, Peter. *The Age of Churchill: Heritage and Adventure 1874–1911.* New York: Alfred A. Knopf, 1961.

Miller, J. D. B. *Sir Winston Churchill and the Commonwealth of Nations.* Queensland, Australia: University of Queensland Press, 1967.

Minney, R. J. *The Private Papers of Hore–Belisha.* London: William Collins, Sons & Co., 1960.

Moran, Lord. *Churchill.* Boston: Houghton Mifflin Co., 1966.

Morgenthau, Hans. Review of *The Second World War. World Politics* 7 (January 1955):284–91.

Morison, Samuel Eliot. "Sir Winston Churchill: Nobel Prize Winner." *Saturday Review* 36 (31 October 1953):22–23.

*Muggeridge, Malcolm. "Churchill the Biographer and Historian." In *Churchill by His Contemporaries,* edited by Charles Eade, pp. 343–53. London: Hutchinson & Co., 1953.

Nicolson, Harold. "A Portrait of Winston Churchill." *Life* 15 March 1948, pp. 95–106.

————. *Diaries and Letters,* ed. Nigel Nicolson. 3 vols. New York: Atheneum Publishers, 1966–68.

*Notestein, Wallace. Review of *A History of the English-Speaking Peoples. American Historical Review* 62 (1956):93–95.

O'Brien, E. D. "Sir Winston Churchill—The Man." In *Illustrated London News Eightieth Year Tribute to Winston Churchill,* edited by Bruce Ingram, pp. 28–57. London, 1954.

Ohlinger, Gustav. "A Midnight Interview with Churchill." *Michigan Quarterly Review* 5 (1966):75–79.

Paço d'Arcos, J. *Churchill.* Translated by F. R. Holliday and P. S.Pernes. London: Caravel, 1957.

Pares, Richard. Review of *A History of the English-Speaking Peoples. English Historical Review* 73 (1958):496–99.

Petrie, Sir Charles. "Sir Winston Churchill's Place in History." In *Illustrated London News Eightieth Year Tribute to Winston Churchill,* edited by Bruce Ingram, pp. 57–68. London, 1954.

Plumb, J. H. "Churchill the Historian." *Spectator* 216 (24 June 1966):782–83; 217 (1 July 1966):10–11.

*————. "The Historian." In *Churchill Revised,* pp. 131–69. New York: Dial Press, 1969.

Porter, Harry W. "Churchill and the Empire." *South Atlantic Quarterly* 51 (1952):222–34.

Repington, C. "Churchillian Strategy." *Blackwood's* 214 (1923):830–36.

Review of *A History of the English-Speaking Peoples. TLS,* 27 April and 30 November 1956, pp. 245–46, 705–6.

Riddell, Lord. *War Diary 1914–18.* London: Nicholson and Watson, 1933.

————. *More Pages From My Diary.* London: Country Life, 1934.

————. *Intimate Diary of the Peace Conference 1918–23.* New York: Reynal and Hitchcock, 1934.

Rowse, A. L. "Mr. Churchill and English History." In *The English Spirit,* pp. 1–21. New York: Macmillan Co., 1945.

————. *The Churchills.* New York: Harper, 1958.

————. "Churchill Considered Historically." *Encounter* 26 (January 1966):45–50.

*————. "Sir Winston Churchill As An Historian." In *The English Spirit.* Rev. ed., pp. 78–92. New York: Funk and Wagnalls Co., 1966.

Scott, A. MacCallum. *Winston Spencer Churchill.* London: Methuen & Co., 1905.

Sherwood, Robert E. *Roosevelt and Hopkins.* New York: Harper, 1950.

Slosson, Preston. Review of *The Second World War. American Historical Review* 54 (1949):858–60.

Snow, C. P. *Variety of Men.* New York: Charles Scribner's Sons, 1966.

Somervell, D. C. "Sir Winston Churchill." In *Nobel Prize Winners,* edited by E. J. Ludovici, pp. 1–20. London: Arco Publishing Co., 1956.

Stewart, H. L. *Sir Winston Churchill As Writer and Speaker.* London: Sidgwick and Jackson, 1954.

Storr, Anthony. "The Man." In *Churchill Revised.* New York: Dial Press, 1969.

Taylor, A. J. P. *The Origins of the Second World War.* 2d ed. New York: Fawcett Publications, 1961.

*————. *English History 1914–1945.* New York: Oxford University Press, 1965.

*————. "The Statesman." In *Churchill Revised.* New York: Dial Press, 1969.

Terraine, John.*The Great War 1914–1918.* New York: Macmillan Co., 1965.

Thompson, John M. *Russia, Bolshevism and the Versailles Peace.* Princeton University Press, 1966.

Thomson, George Malcolm. *Vote of Censure.* New York: Stein & Day, 1968.

Trevelyan, G. M. *England Under Queen Anne.* 3 vols. London: Longmans, Green and Co., 1931–34.

Tuchman, Barbara. *The Guns of August.* New York: Dell Books, 1962.

Ullman, Richard. *Britain and the Russian Civil War.* Princeton: Princeton University Press, 1968.

Walder, David. *The Chanak Affair.* London: Macmillan & Co., 1969.

Weidhorn, Manfred. "Churchill the Phrase Forger." *Quarterly Journal of Speech* 58 (April 1972):161–74.

Wheeler-Bennett, J. ed. *Action This Day.* London: Macmillan & Co., 1968.

*Whittemore, Reed. "Churchill As A Mythmaker." In *Language and Politics,* ed. T. P. Brockway, pp. 56–68. Boston: D. C. Heath and Co., 1965. (Originally in *Yale Review* 44 [Winter 1954–55].)

Wilmot, Chester. *The Struggle for Europe.* New York: Harper, 1952.

Winterton, Earl. "Sir Winston Churchill in Parliament." In *Illustrated London News Eightieth Year Tribute to Winston Churchill,* edited by Bruce Ingram, pp. 3–14. London: 1954.

The "World Crisis" by Winston Churchill: A Criticism. London: Hutchinson & Co., 1927.

Index

Africa: Churchill in, 17, 22, 23, 64; in World War II, 167. *See also* Algiers; East Africa; Egypt; North Africa; South Africa; Sudan; Tripoli
Alexander, Harold, 145, 146
Alfonso XIII (king of Spain), 7, 103
Alfred the Great (king of England), 188, 202, 218
Algiers, 161
Allen, H. C., 207, 209
American Civil War, 191, 203, 221
American Revolution, 186, 190, 204
Amery, L. S., 135, 145, 220
Anabasis (Xenophon), 44
Angevin Empire, 190
Anne (queen of England), 111, 114, 121, 123, 208, 228
Antony and Cleopatra (Shakespeare), 170
Antwerp, capture of (1703), 116
Antwerp defense (1914), 12, 85
Aquinas, Saint Thomas. *See* Thomas Aquinas, Saint
Aristotle, 80
Armenia, 85
Armies of the Night, The (Mailer), 16
Arms and the Covenant (While England Slept) (Churchill), 13, 131, 236
Arthur (legendary king of England), 202
Ashley, Maurice, 60, 117, 172, 235, 236
Asquith, Herbert Henry, 4, 71, 74, 80, 91, 99, 103, 108, 208
Ataturk, Kemal, 133
Attlee, Clement R., 78, 139, 218
Auchinleck, Sir Claude John Eyre, 145, 146, 159
Austria, 72–73, 79, 87, 89, 90, 91, 131

Badoglio, Pietro, 28, 167
Baldwin, Stanley, 12, 103, 144, 218
Balfour, Arthur James, 6, 62, 71, 99, 108, 182, 208
Barbour, Violet, 119
Barnett, Correlli, 151
Battle of Britain, 146, 153
Beatty, David, 70
Becket, Thomas à. *See* Thomas à Becket, Saint

Belgium, 70, 135, 173; in World War I, 79, 170; in World War II, 77, 166
Berlin, Congress of, 189
Berlin, Isaiah, 92, 230, 231, 234
Berlin airlift, 182
Bevan, Aneurin, 3, 180, 218, 220
Beveridge Plan, 157, 158
Bevin, Ernest, 155
Bible, 202, 235. *See also* church; religion
Birkenhead, first earl of, 220
Bismarck, Otto von, 65, 166, 202
Black and Tans, 85
Blenheim, victory at, 113, 115, 118
Blenheim Palace, 121, 126, 228
Blood, Sweat, and Tears (Into Battle) (Churchill), 13, 236
Blunt, Wilfrid Scawen, 90–91
Boadicean rebellions, 195–96
Boer War, 18, 19–20, 29, 32, 37–38, 43, 54, 62, 72, 208, 221, 236
Boers, 11, 233
Bolingbroke, Henry St. John, Viscount, 113, 127
bolshevism, 104, 134, 153, 154. *See also* communism
Braudy, Leo, 10
Britain, *passim;* frontier wars, role in, 36–37; Indian policy, 27, 28; pre–World War II policy, 132–33; rise of, 186–209 *passim;* South African policy, 27–28; in World War I, 73, 77–86 *passim,* 90, 91; in World War II, 146–75 *passim,* 185. *See also individual leaders and monarchs*
Brooke, Alan Francis, 146
Bulgaria, 80, 150, 168
Burke, Edmund, 104, 189, 201, 235
Burma, 59
Burton, Ivor, 117
Butt, Isaac, 49–50, 54
Byron, George Gordon Noel, Lord, 196

Caesar, Gaius Julius, 3, 134, 234
Cairns, J. C., 225
Cairo, Egypt, 23
Calvinism, 197
Canute II (king of England), 188
Carlyle, Thomas, 2, 126, 201